'I would like to recommend strongly *New Models of Human Resource Management in China and India*. The book highlights the enormous changes in global economic power and influence and the major lessons for international human resource management stemming from these developments. This comparative work is especially valuable for highlighting patterns of continuity and change in these two countries and for drawing out the fundamentally important implications for theory.'

Michael Poole, Professor of HRM, Cardiff Business School, Cardiff University, UK.

Editor of the *International Journal of Human Resource Management*.

Co-author of *International Human Resource Management*, London: Routledge.

'With the re-emergence of China and India – the world's two most populous nations – in the global economy, it is imperative that researchers and practitioners have an accurate understanding of human resource management in both countries. This book provides a comprehensive analysis of the similarities and differences between these two countries and presents a new model of human resource management that can explain more adequately the dynamics and challenges associated with these two emerging giants. It is a must read for all who seek further insights on managing and doing business in China and India.'

Rosalie L. Tung, Ming and Stella Wong Professor of International Business at Simon Fraser University, BC, Canada.

Author of *Learning from World Class Companies*, London: Thomson Learning.

'*New Models of Human Resource Management in China and India* is a must-read book for everyone interested in knowing as much as possible about the latest developments and thinking about human resource management in China and India. Based upon the in-depth expertise of all the authors in China and India, all the chapters are filled with extremely valuable information and insights and the latest references and websites for further investigation. The book is concise and to the point. It is perfect for a course focusing on human resource management in China and India or as a supplemental book in a more general human resource management course.'

Randall S. Schuler, Distinguished Professor, International Human Resource Management, Rutgers University, New Brunswick, NJ, USA.

Co-author of *International Human Resource Management*, London: Routledge.

'This book provides an excellent basis for a new understanding of emerging human resource management in the two largest countries in the world. A central issue highlighted is the inability of Western HRM models to incorporate the diversity of HRM systems and practices in multiple organizational types in both countries and the need for more scholarships on variants of indigenous models of HRM.'

Sarosh Kurivalla, Professor of Industrial Relations, Asian Studies and Public Affairs, Cornell University, Ithaca, NY, USA.

Co-author of *From Iron Rice Bowl to Informalization: Markets, Workers and the State in a Changing China*, Ithaca and London: Cornell University Press.

'Since the global attention has shifted to China and India, this is the finest book I have read on how the management of the people resource has been contributing to the mystery of the emerging "Asian Century". Being some of the leading global thinkers on the subject, the authors have demonstrated amazing clarity and panache in identifying and discussing comparative HRM issues in the two countries. The book provides a powerful framework of the evolving HRM models in China and India, with rich combinations of strategic and operational insights. Corporates working in and dealing with these countries, and scholars studying and researching Comparative HRM issues in Asia, will benefit immensely by reading this long awaited book.'

Debi S. Saini, Professor and Chairperson – HRM Area, Management Development Institute, Gurgaon, India.

Author of *Social Security Law in India*, The Hague: Kluwer Law International.

'This book has made a timely and cutting-edge contribution to the field of human resource management (HRM). It provides fresh insights into a wide range of topics in HRM in the two largest emerging economies, China and India. Given the arrival of the Asian century, and the rapidly increasing impact of China and India on global economic development, the dynamic HRM architectures and models detailed in this book are critical and valuable. This is because the book has captured the essence of changes as well as future development trends of HRM in these two countries and their multinationals – highly recommended for researchers, practitioners and students interested in the field of HRM in the two resurgent powers.'

Dr Cherrie Jiuhua Zhu, Professor of Human Resource Management and Chinese Studies, Monash University, Melbourne, Australia.

New Models of Human Resource Management in China and India

This book presents a comprehensive analysis of the similarities and differences of contemporary human resource management systems, processes and practices in the two increasingly important economic great powers in Asia. It covers the full range of human resource management activities, including recruitment, retention, performance management, remuneration and career development, as well as discussing changing industrial relations systems, and setting the subject in its historical, social and cultural contexts. It examines newly emerging strategies, and assesses the extent to which human resource management systems in the two countries are converging or diverging.

Alan R. Nankervis is Adjunct Professor of Human Resource Management at Curtin Business School, Western Australia.

Fang Lee Cooke is Professor of Human Resource Management and Chinese Studies at Monash University, Australia.

Samir R. Chatterjee is Professor at Curtin Business School, Western Australia.

Malcolm Warner is Professor and Fellow Emeritus at Wolfson College and Judge Business School, University of Cambridge, UK.

Routledge Studies in the Growth Economies of Asia

1 **The Changing Capital Markets of East Asia**
Edited by Ky Cao

2 **Financial Reform in China**
Edited by On Kit Tam

3 **Women and Industrialization in Asia**
Edited by Susan Horton

4 **Japan's Trade Policy**
Action or reaction?
Yumiko Mikanagi

5 **The Japanese Election System**
Three analytical perspectives
Junichiro Wada

6 **The Economics of the Latecomers**
Catching-up, technology transfer and institutions in Germany, Japan and South Korea
Jang-Sup Shin

7 **Industrialization in Malaysia**
Import substitution and infant industry performance
Rokiah Alavi

8 **Economic Development in Twentieth Century East Asia**
The international context
Edited by Aiko Ikeo

9 **The Politics of Economic Development in Indonesia**
Contending perspectives
Edited by Ian Chalmers and Vedi R. Hadiz

10 **Studies in the Economic History of the Pacific Rim**
Edited by Sally M. Miller, A. J. H. Latham and Dennis O. Flynn

11 **Workers and the State in New Order Indonesia**
Vedi R. Hadiz

12 **The Japanese Foreign Exchange Market**
Beate Reszat

13 **Exchange Rate Policies in Emerging Asian Countries**
Edited by Stefan Collignon, Jean Pisani-Ferry and Yung Chul Park

14 **Chinese Firms and Technology in the Reform Era**
Yizheng Shi

15 **Japanese Views on Economic Development**
Diverse paths to the market
Kenichi Ohno and Izumi Ohno

16 **Technological Capabilities and Export Success in Asia**
Edited by Dieter Ernst, Tom Ganiatsos and Lynn Mytelka

17 **Trade and Investment in China**
The European experience
Edited by Roger Strange, Jim Slater and Limin Wang

18 **Technology and Innovation in Japan**
Policy and management for the twenty-first century
Edited by Martin Hemmert and Christian Oberländer

19 **Trade Policy Issues in Asian Development**
Prema-chandra Athukorala

20 **Economic Integration in the Asia Pacific Region**
Ippei Yamazawa

21 **Japan's War Economy**
Edited by Erich Pauer

22 **Industrial Technology Development in Malaysia**
Industry and firm studies
Edited by Jomo K. S., Greg Felker and Rajah Rasiah

23 **Technology, Competitiveness and the State**
Malaysia's industrial technology policies
Edited by Jomo K. S. and Greg Felker

24 **Corporatism and Korean Capitalism**
Edited by Dennis L. McNamara

25 **Japanese Science**
Samuel Coleman

26 **Capital and Labour in Japan**
The functions of two factor markets
Toshiaki Tachibanaki and Atsuhiro Taki

27 **Asia Pacific Dynamism 1550–2000**
Edited by A. J. H. Latham and Heita Kawakatsu

28 **The Political Economy of Development and Environment in Korea**
Jae-Yong Chung and Richard J. Kirkby

29 **Japanese Economics and Economists since 1945**
Edited by Aiko Ikeo

30 **China's Entry into the World Trade Organisation**
Edited by Peter Drysdale and Ligang Song

31 **Hong Kong as an International Financial Centre**
Emergence and Development 1945–1965
Catherine R. Schenk

32 **Impediments to Trade in Services**
Measurement and policy implications
Edited by Christoper Findlay and Tony Warren

33 **The Japanese Industrial Economy**
Late development and cultural causation
Ian Inkster

34 **China and the Long March to Global Trade**
The accession of China to the World Trade Organization
Edited by Alan S. Alexandroff, Sylvia Ostry and Rafael Gomez

35 **Capitalist Development and Economism in East Asia**
The rise of Hong Kong, Singapore, Taiwan and South Korea
Kui-Wai Li

36 **Women and Work in Globalizing Asia**
Edited by Dong-Sook S. Gills and Nicola Piper

37 **Financial Markets and Policies in East Asia**
Gordon de Brouwer

38 **Developmentalism and Dependency in Southeast Asia**
The case of the automotive industry
Jason P. Abbott

39 **Law and Labour Market Regulation in East Asia**
Edited by Sean Cooney, Tim Lindsey, Richard Mitchell and Ying Zhu

40 **The Economy of the Philippines**
Elites, inequalities and economic restructuring
Peter Krinks

41 **China's Third Economic Transformation**
The rise of the private economy
Edited by Ross Garnaut and Ligang Song

42 **The Vietnamese Economy**
Awakening the dormant dragon
Edited by Binh Tran-Nam and Chi Do Pham

43 **Restructuring Korea Inc.**
Jang-Sup Shin and Ha-Joon Chang

44 **Development and Structural Change in Asia-Pacific**
Globalising miracles or end of a model?
Edited by Martin Andersson and Christer Gunnarsson

45 **State Collaboration and Development Strategies in China**
The case of the China–Singapore Suzhou Industrial Park (1992–2002)
Alexius Pereira

46 **Capital and Knowledge in Asia**
Changing power relations
Edited by Heidi Dahles and Otto van den Muijzenberg

47 **Southeast Asian Paper Tigers?**
From miracle to debacle and beyond
Edited by Jomo K. S.

48 **Manufacturing Competitiveness in Asia**
How internationally competitive national firms and industries developed in East Asia
Edited by Jomo K. S.

49 **The Korean Economy at the Crossroads**
Edited by Moon Joong Tcha and Chung-Sok Suh

50 **Ethnic Business**
Chinese capitalism in Southeast Asia
Edited by Jomo K. S. and Brian C. Folk

51 **Exchange Rate Regimes in East Asia**
Edited by Gordon de Brouwer and Masahiro Kawai

52 **Financial Governance in East Asia**
Policy dialogue, surveillance and cooperation
Edited by Gordon de Brouwer and Yunjong Wang

53 **Designing Financial Systems in East Asia and Japan**
Edited by Joseph P. H. Fan, Masaharu Hanazaki and Juro Teranishi

54 **State Competence and Economic Growth in Japan**
Yoshiro Miwa

55 **Understanding Japanese Saving**
Does population aging matter?
Robert Dekle

56 **The Rise and Fall of the East Asian Growth System, 1951–2000**
International competitiveness and rapid economic growth
Xiaoming Huang

57 **Service Industries and Asia-Pacific Cities**
New development trajectories
Edited by P. W. Daniels, K. C. Ho and T. A. Hutton

58 **Unemployment in Asia**
Edited by John Benson and Ying Zhu

59 **Risk Management and Innovation in Japan, Britain and the USA**
Edited by Ruth Taplin

60 **Japan's Development Aid to China**
The long-running foreign policy of engagement
Tsukasa Takamine

6

6

6.

64

65

66

Dilip K. Das

67 Innovation and Business Partnering in Japan, Europe and the United States
Edited by Ruth Taplin

68 Asian Informal Workers
Global risks local protection
Santosh Mehrotra and Mario Biggeri

69 The Rise of the Corporate Economy in Southeast Asia
Rajeswary Ampalavanar Brown

70 The Singapore Economy
An econometric perspective
Tilak Abeyshinge and Keen Meng Choy

71 A Basket Currency for Asia
Edited by Takatoshi Ito

72 Private Enterprises and China's Economic Development
Edited by Shuanglin Lin and Xiaodong Zhu

73 The Korean Developmental State
From dirigisme to neo-liberalism
Iain Pirie

…rating Japan's Economic …h
…ing Japan's growth controversy
…by F. Gerard Adams, Lawrence …, Yuzo Kumasaka and … Shinozaki

… Emergent Political Economy
…m in the dragon's lair
…y Christopher A. McNally

…tical Economy of the SARS …c
…ct on human resources in …
…M. Lee and Malcolm Warner

…nerging Financial …
…unds model
…re

78 Outsourcing and Human Resource Management
An international survey
Edited by Ruth Taplin

79 Globalization, Labour Markets and Inequality in India
Dipak Mazumdar and Sandip Sarkar

80 Globalization and the Indian Economy
Roadmap to a convertible rupee
Satyendra S. Nayak

81 Economic Cooperation between Singapore and India
An alliance in the making
Faizal Yahya

82 The United States and the Malaysian Economy
Shakila Yacob

83 Banking Reform in Southeast Asia
The region's decisive decade
Malcolm Cook

84 Trade Unions in Asia
An economic and sociological analysis
Edited by John Benson and Ying Zhu

85 Trade Liberalisation and Regional Disparity in Pakistan
Muhammad Shoaib Butt and Jayatilleke S. Bandara

86 Financial Development and Economic Growth in Malaysia
James Ang

87 Intellectual Property and the New Japanese Global Economy
Ruth Taplin

88 Laggards and Leaders in Labour Market Reform
Comparing Japan and Australia
Edited by Jenny Corbett, Anne Daly, Hisakazu Matsushige and Dehne Taylor

89 Institutions for Economic Reform in Asia
Edited by Philippa Dee

90 Southeast Asia's Credit Revolution
From moneylenders to microfinance
Aditya Goenka and David Henley

91 Economic Reform and Employment Relations in Vietnam
Ngan Thuy Collins

92 The Future of Asian Trade and Growth
Economic development with the emergence of China
Linda Yueh

93 Business Practices in Southeast Asia
An interdisciplinary analysis of Theravada Buddhist countries
Scott A. Hipsher

94 Responsible Development
Vulnerable democracies, hunger and inequality
Omar Noman

95 The Everyday Impact of Economic Reform in China
Management change, enterprise performance and daily life
Ying Zhu, Michael Webber and John Benson

96 The Rise of Asia
Trade and investment in global perspective
Prema-Chandra Athukorala

97 Intellectual Property, Innovation and Management in Emerging Economies
Edited by Ruth Taplin and Alojzy Z. Nowak

98 Special Economic Zones in Asian Market Economies
Edited by Connie Carter and Andrew Harding

99 The Migration of Indian Human Capital
The ebb and flow of Indian professionals in Southeast Asia
Faizal bin Yahya and Arunajeet Kaur

100 Economic Development and Inequality in China
The case of Guangdong
Hong Yu

101 The Japanese Pharmaceutical Industry
Its evolution and current challenges
Maki Umemura

102 The Dynamics of Asian Labour Markets
Balancing control and flexibility
Edited by John Benson and Ying Zhu

103 Pakistan – The Political Economy of Growth, Stagnation and the State, 1951–2009
Matthew McCartney

104 Korean Women Managers and Corporate Culture
Challenging tradition, choosing empowerment, creating change
Jean R. Renshaw

105 Trade Liberalisation and Poverty in South Asia
Edited by Prema-Chandra Athukorala, Jayatilleke S. Bandara and Saman Kelegama

106 Pro-poor Growth and Liberalization in Developing Economies
The case of Nepal
Sanjaya Acharya

107 China and the Global Economy in the 21st Century
Edited by John Saee

108 State Structure and Economic Development in Southeast Asia
The political economy of Thailand and the Philippines
Antoinette R. Raquiza

109 An Economic History of Indonesia
1800–2010
Jan Luiten van Zanden and Daan Marks

110 Taxation in ASEAN and China
Local institutions, regionalism, global systems and economic development
Edited by Nolan Cormac Sharkey

111 Macroeconomic and Monetary Policy Issues in Indonesia
Akhand Akhtar Hossain

112 Economic Reform Processes in South Asia
Toward policy efficiency
Philippa Dee

113 Manufacturing Enterprise in Asia
Size structure and economic growth
Dipak Mazumdar and Sandip Sarkar

114 Managers and Management in Vietnam
25 years of economic renovation (Doi moi)
Vincent Edwards and Anh Phan

115 New Models of Human Resource Management in China and India
Alan R. Nankervis, Fang Lee Cooke, Samir R. Chatterjee and Malcolm Warner

New Models of Human Resource Management in China and India

Alan R. Nankervis, Fang Lee Cooke, Samir R. Chatterjee and Malcolm Warner

Routledge
Taylor & Francis Group
LONDON AND NEW YORK

First published 2013
by Routledge
2 Park Square, Milton Park, Abingdon, Oxon OX14 4RN

Simultaneously published in the USA and Canada
by Routledge
711 Third Avenue, New York, NY 10017

Routledge is an imprint of the Taylor & Francis Group, an informa business

British Library Cataloguing in Publication Data
A catalogue record for this book is available from the British Library

Library of Congress Cataloging in Publication Data
New models of human resource management in China and India/
Alan R. Nankervis ... [et al.].
p. cm. – (Routledge studies in the growth economies of Asia; 115)
Includes bibliographical references and index.
1. Personnel management–China 2. Personnel management–India.
3. Human capital–China–Management.
4. Human capital–India–Management.
5. Manpower planning–China. 6. Manpower planning–India.
7. Industrial relations–China. 8. Industrial relations–India.
I. Nankervis, Alan R.
HF5549.2.C6N49 2013
658.3—dc23 2012010860

ISBN: 978-0-415-67527-7 (hbk)
ISBN: 978-0-203-10027-1 (ebk)

Typeset in Times New Roman
by Sunrise Setting Ltd, Torquay, UK

Contents

Figures and tables

Figures

Tables

Authors

This book is the result of the collegial efforts of all the authors, based upon their collective research and personal experience in China and India. However, individual authors assumed primary responsibility for the research and preparation of particular chapters, as listed below:

Chapter 1: Alan R. Nankervis
Chapter 2: Samir R. Chatterjee
Chapter 3: Fang Lee Cooke
Chapter 4: Fang Lee Cooke
Chapter 5: Alan R. Nankervis
Chapter 6: Alan R. Nankervis
Chapter 7: Malcolm Warner and Alan R. Nankervis
Chapter 8: Samir R. Chatterjee, Fang Lee Cooke, Alan R. Nankervis and Malcolm Warner

1 The Asian century

The shift of global economic power to China and India

Introduction

In recent years there has been rigorous discussion about the unexpected and relatively rapid emergence of China and India (or the so-called 'Asian century') as models of global economic growth, in counterpoint to the historical dominance of world markets by the United States and, to a lesser extent, Japan. Their comparative insulation and swift recovery from the ravages of the 2009 global financial crisis (GFC) have been evidenced as clear indicators of the strength of their contemporary economies (Anonymous 2010a; De Carlo 2010). As Yeates (2010: 3) explained,

> Asia (notably, China and India) … avoided many of the toxic debt products that wreaked havoc in other parts of the world … (and) Asian countries played a greater role in response to the recession than in past crises *because the G20 became the key forum for leaders, replacing the* G7 (our italics).

However, there were some effects of the GFC. In India, for example, the rupee was devalued; and in China foreign direct investment (FDI) declined by 20 per cent in early 2009, economic growth fell to around 6 per cent, and an estimated 6.7 million jobs were lost with the closure of approximately 67,000 factories (de Haan 2010: 72).

Underlying the optimistic commentaries on the implications of the current surge in the economic (and thereby geopolitical) power of China, and to a lesser extent India, is an arguably over-simplistic notion. Based upon a misreading or an ignorance of history, it has often been assumed that the present remarkable growth patterns of China and India in contrast to those of the United States, Japan, or Western Europe, are unique or at least unparalleled in the recorded past. This is a flawed notion, as during the late seventeenth century both China's and India's relative wealth and geopolitical power far surpassed that of the Western world. In the early 1800s, for example, the two countries contributed nearly half of the world's income. As Dalrymple (2007: 1) pointed out, 'historically South Asia was always famous as the richest region of the globe …. At their heights during the 17th century, the sub-continent's fabled Mughal emperors were rivaled only by their Ming counterparts in China'. He further suggested that it was colonialism which 'slowly wrecked the old trading network and imposed with their cannons and caravels a Western imperial system of command economy' (Dalrymple 2007: 1). Thus, rather than being a new phenomenon, the current economic growth in both China and India represents little more than a 'return to the traditional pattern of global trade' (Kelly, Rajan and Goh 2006; Mahbubani 2008).

Whilst Dalrymple's thesis (2007) is questionable, as the present global economic environment is far more complex and interconnected than in earlier periods, the current economic growth in China and India should be perceived as a resurgence in their global prominence rather than a completely new phase of economic development. In recent years the joint contribution of China and India has amounted to approximately a fifth of global income, although there are predictions that it will reach one-third by 2050 (Gupta, Govindarajan and Wang 2008). Table 1.1 provides some comparisons between the gross domestic product (GDP) of China and India compared with the US and Europe between 1000 and 1950. As the Table demonstrates, India and China have re-emerged as significant global economic forces, albeit from a low base in the early 1900s.

The key themes of this chapter and throughout the book are:

- The diffusion of macro level strategies to enterprise levels in China and India.
- The re-emergence of China and India in the context of the recent global financial crisis.
- A strategic focus on bilateral collaboration, linking one-third of the global population and a quarter of the world's talent.
- Future Chinese and Indian collaboration through human resource development and research and development.
- Trust and learning as the bases for cooperation in building new industries and innovative capacities.

Economic growth indicators in China and India

Whilst at least some of the exaggeration surrounding the developments has been driven by the self-promotion (or wishful thinking) of authors from these two

Table 1.1 World GDP statistics (in percentages)

Year	*US (plus other Western offshoots)*	*Europe (including from USSR)*	*China*	*India*
1000	0.7	13.4	22.7	28.9
1500	0.5	23.9	25.0	24.5
1700	0.2	29.7	22.3	24.4
1820	1.9	32.3	32.9	16.0
1913	21.7	46.6	8.9	7.6
1950	30.6	39.3	4.5	4.2

Source: A. Maddison, 2005, *The World Economic Historical Statistics*, Paris: OECD.

Table 1.2 China and India transition statistics (2010)

	China	*India*
1 Percentage of global population	21%	17.5%
2 Percentage of global trade	8%	1.5%
3 Total number of English speakers (in millions)	10	232
4 Global ranking of the economy	2nd	12th
5 Global ranking of purchasing power parity	2nd	4th
6 Per capita income (in US dollars)	3,180	1,032

Source: Compiled by the authors from various including the CIA *World Factbook* and *The Economist*.

neighbouring countries (Ramesh 2005; Huang 2010), many external observers have also noted their above average development and economic growth statistics. Table 1.2 compares some of these pertinent indicators.

A 2008 report by the Bank of New York Mellon (Anonymous 2008a: 4), for example, concluded that '… the two economies will account for up to 50 per cent of global consumption … combined, China and India will be the largest world-wide producers and consumers of coal, steel, cement and non-ferrous materials'. A more recent report in *The Economist* predicted that 40 per cent of world economic growth would derive from the two countries (Anonymous 2010a), and the International Monetary Fund (IMF) suggested that 'Asia – spurred on by booming exports and the rise of China's and India's middle class – would become the world's biggest economic region by 2030' (Yeates 2010: 3). The IMF's graduated growth rates differentiate between China and India, with China's rates predicted to be 8 per cent (2010), 12 per cent (2020) and 22 per cent (2030) respectively, whilst India's are considerably smaller – namely, 2 per cent, 4 per cent and 5 per cent (Yeates 2010). This latter prediction is somewhat at odds with the figures for the third quarter of 2009 (in the midst of the GFC) during which period India achieved nearly 8 per cent growth, transforming itself 'from a land of elephants and snake charmers to that of an information technology powerhouse and an emerging economic giant' (Gupta and Wang 2009a: 86).

Other indicators of China's impressive economic growth and transformation: it is the second largest global economy now with a GDP greater than Japan; GDP has 'multiplied tenfold' in 30 years to almost US$ 9 trillion; since 2000, it has displaced the US to absorb the largest amount of exports from Korea and Japan, especially textiles, garments and electronics; and it is rated twenty-seventh in the World Economic Forum's competitiveness index. Further, China contains the world's biggest car market (14 million sales annually); it consumes a fifth of all global energy and 46 per cent of the world's coal, together with double the amount of crude steel of the EU, US and Japan combined. Finally, it is the world's largest producer of IT products, the biggest microchip market, and has developed growing expertise in solar cell and semiconductor manufacturing, shipbuilding and biomedical technology (compiled from various sources, including Anonymous 2010c: 9; Ferguson 2010: 21; Green and Kliman 2011: 37; Lee and Kim 2011: 56, 59; Park

2011: 15; Zhang 2011: 23). These optimistic predictions and prognostications should, however, be treated with some caution because of the often inaccurate or misleading statistics provided by Chinese (and other) agencies, and the contestable bases upon which they are built, together with the plethora of their underlying assumptions. As Dixon (2011: 3) explains,

> China is so big that its economic success is applying a brake to further progress. Not only has this helped push up the price of commodities, which are hugely important for China's manufacturing-orientated economic model .... two (other) big challenges ... the need to switch gears to a new consumption-led economic model, and the quest for social stability.

Whilst India's economic indicators are not quite as remarkable as in China, there are also important signs of its growth and development, including the presence of many large Indian companies in *Forbes* 2010 Top 500 companies (Indian Oil, Reliance Industries, the State Bank of China, Bharat Petroleum, Hindustan Petroleum, Tata Steel and Tata Motors) and even more in the Global 2000 companies. Indian multinationals employ more than 200,000 people in their global operations (for example, Patni Computer Systems, Ranbaxy Labs, Tata Tea, Dr. Reddy's Labs, GHCL and Bharat Forge – Chatterjee 2010). With respect to the growth in intra-regional trade between China and India, the indicators are just as impressive – approximately US$ 60 billion in 2010 – which was 230 times greater than in 1990 (Anonymous 2010a, b). Table 1.3 illustrates the comparative growth in external FDI outflows between China and India.

However, whilst China's 'competitive edge is shifting from low-cost workers to state-of-the-art manufacturing, India is creating "world-class innovation hubs" ' (Nelson and Choudaha 2006: 2). China 'has (also) managed to convert the advantage of a growing workforce into a virtuous loop of creating productive jobs that lead to higher savings, investment and growth' (Kucukakin and Thant 2006: 10). Some factual comparisons and contrasts between China and India both highlight their similar and different characteristics and suggest implications for their potential collaboration or competition in regional and global environments. Thus, both China and India have large land masses (China is 9.5 million and India is

Table 1.3 Foreign direct investment outflows from China and India (in billions of dollars)

	2000	*2001*	*2002*	*2003*	*2004*	*2005*	*2006*	*2007*	*2008*
China	1.0	6.9	2.7	2.9	5.5	12.3	21.2	22.5	52.1
India	0.3	0.8	0.4	0.9	2.2	2.5	14.3	17.3	17.7

Source: J. Zhan, 2010, *World Investment Report 2010: Investing in a Low-Carbon Economy*, United Nations Conference on Trade and Development (UNCTAD).

Note: UNCTAD also reports that the amount of foreign investment in China in 2010 was almost US$ 500 billion, employing approximately 16 million workers – Anonymous, 2010g.

3.3 million square kilometres); and similar population sizes (1.4 million versus 1.1 million); but there are significant discrepancies with respect to GDP real growth (11 per cent versus 9.5 per cent); GDP per capita (US$ 7,800 versus US$ 3,800); relative export income (US$ 974 billion versus US$ 112 billion); and research and development expenditure (2.5 per cent GDP versus 1.5 per cent GDP) (Y. Huang 2008). As Murthy (2009: 250) observed:

> Every year, China produces 600,000 engineers while India produces 450,000. In comparison, USA produces 70,000 engineers a year. Several global corporations have consequently realized the importance of sourcing this global talent. For example, General Electric (GE) has set up an R&D laboratory, the largest of its kind outside the USA, in Bangalore; over 1,000 GE researchers work on leading-edge solutions out of this facility. Microsoft has established R&D facilities in China and India.

China and India – cooperation or collaboration?

An important underlying notion which requires some exploration is the concept of 'Chindia', first coined by an Indian politician, Jairam Ramesh, in his 2005 book entitled *Making sense of Chindia: Reflections on China and India*. Whilst Ramesh's interpretation of Chindia is quite loose and broad, involving a blend of economic agreements, joint ventures and collaborative economic projects, subsequent observers have extended his vision to higher levels, ranging from basic facts to more extreme predictions. Thus, some observe that China and India have complementary economies – 'China, through its burgeoning factories, is the world's workshop. India, with its fast-growing IT and outsourcing firms, is becoming the world's back office. With Chinese hardware providing the orchestra and Indian software writing the score, surely they can make beautiful music together?' (Sen 2005: 1).

Other authors present a more complex view, suggesting that formal agreements between the Chinese and Indian governments to preserve their present niche industry expertise – for example China's specialization in fabricated products versus India's strength in raw or semi-processed commodities – would be mutually beneficial. China's export-oriented industrial production versus India's commercial services (Anonymous 2007b; Holslag 2008) – together with the acceptance of competition in other industry sectors (automobiles, machine tools) – may represent a form of pragmatic collaboration (or merely a China–India Free Trade Agreement) which 'prioritizes the attraction of investments and the access to foreign markets, with stability at the borders as a precondition' (Anonymous 2007a: 5). Most of these authors acknowledge the crucial pre-conditions of stasis in the division of labour between China and India, and a stable mutual political and military relationship in the pursuit of these objectives, neither of which seem likely in the foreseeable future.

Optimistic observers have suggested that Chindia could lead to 'a division of labor … that is mutually beneficial, optimizes the effectiveness of production and stimulates commercial exchange' (Holslag 2008: 2), or that the economic and political relationships between China and India will transform into a form of intra-regional symbiosis (Anonymous 2007a). What is significant in the concept of 'Chindia' is the suggestion of complementarity between China and India. However, with complementarity comes competition. As an example, with an original US$ 200 million investment from Toyota, the Indian auto components industry has become a global player second only to China. As Meredith (2007: 91) observes, '... India's auto parts exports have been growing by 25 percent a year and are expected to rival China's by 2015. Every auto parts factory opened could mean hundreds of new jobs for India's ranks of unskilled workers'. In more recent times, there have been alternative conceptions such as 'Chimerica' (Aiyar 2009) or 'Amerindia', reflecting both the recognition of the global economic prominence of China and India, and the apparent psychological need for some form of bilateral relationship between Asia and the US. It appears however, that China's geopolitical imperatives are more concerned with multilateral than bilateral cooperation, 'a vision which competes directly with the US (and Indian) approaches' (Choi 2011: 45).

Unfortunately, these notions fail to factor in the historical and current difficulties in the relationships between China and India – for example, the dynamic changes taking place in industry structures in both countries; their diverse demographics and socio-cultural characteristics; frequent tensions and conflicts; and global power imbalances which exist between the two nations. The seeds of future dissonance may lie in the very ideological, geopolitical, economic, social and cultural factors which are inherent in the apparent complementary characteristics. As both countries continue to develop in similar competitive (rather than collaborative) directions, heavily dependent on the injection of FDI from Western and other wealthy Asian economies, a mutually beneficial strategic relationship between China and India looks fragile at best. At the macro-political level, Sino-Indian relationships have been and remain problematic. Tensions associated with such issues as the 1962 Sino-India war; China's vote against India's desire to join the UN Security Council; China's ties to Pakistan; the US–India nuclear agreement; and strains over Tibet, Kashmir and the Dalai Lama all persist – 'two Asian giants facing each other over a disputed border' (Anonymous 2010e: 9).

At the economic level, the growth trajectories of both countries are heading in some similar directions, leading to almost inevitable competition for the same global marketplace. Thus, both require similar resources for their future development (iron ore, gas, water), desire increasing amounts of FDI from largely the same sources (US, Europe), are moving away from low-tech to high-tech manufacturing industries and on occasion towards off-shoring activities, and are experiencing significant cost increases in wages, raw materials and other production costs. There are already signs in both China and India that low-tech manufacturing may move to regional neighbours with lower labour costs – 'increasingly, you'll see factories move out of China and go into places like Vietnam and Malaysia' (Bita and Sainsbury 2010: 4).

In addition, there are mutual suspicions between the two countries. As examples, the 2008 Pew Research Center's Global Attitudes Survey revealed that 24 per cent of Chinese respondents ranked India as a threat to China, whilst a 2009 *People's*

Daily (China) poll indicated that 90 per cent believed that India threatens China's security (Malik 2009: 1). In this context, it appears that competition rather than collaboration is a more likely outcome (Sen 2005; Anonymous 2007b; Holslag 2008; Malik 2009; Aiyar 2009).

At the domestic political level, at least some of China's economic success can be attributed to its strong socialist ideology and the central role of the state, whilst India's colonial history, combined with its post-colonial democratic system, have arguably constrained its parallel economic development – 'a tumultuous democracy, ensnared in the challenges of being the world's largest democracy in economic transition. Its political environment is riven with instability' (Kucukakin and Thant 2006: 16). As a consequence, any suggestion of a wholly collaborative and cooperative bilateral relationship is highly questionable, with regional and global competition, accompanied by a degree of pragmatic agreement, as a more likely outcome – 'increasingly, regional, political, economic and business leaders are pointing out that Sino-Indian relations are at their best and getting better. The extent to which China and India can strengthen and expand cooperation will be a key factor in their ability to succeed in the global marketplace' (Anonymous 2008a: 1). The following section of this chapter considers the demographic, social and industry changes occurring in both countries with respect to their management and human resource management implications.

Demographic and infrastructural challenges

Apart from the macroeconomic issues discussed earlier in this chapter, the growing global spread of their power and influence is also reflected in both countries' social and demographic factors and their participation in overseas acquisitions and mergers on almost all continents. These latter activities have been spearheaded by Chinese companies but closely followed by Indian entrepreneurs, and have been simultaneously lauded and feared by internal, regional and global observers alike. With respect to social and demographic factors, both countries have, to a different extent and with differing degrees of success, focused on poverty reduction, infrastructure redevelopment, rural–urban migration, industrial diversity, improved workplace legislation and regulation, educational enhancement and technological development. Given the diverse nature of their histories, ideologies, stages of economic development and racial and religious compositions, such governmental strategies and policies have achieved disparate outcomes. Thus, whilst China 'has embarked on a more classical development path through manufacturing exports … India's growth has been startingly service-driven, a very new mode of development' (Anonymous 2008a). Or, as Kulkarni (2010: 4) observed, 'both China and India face similar problems, but have chosen absolutely diverse solutions. It is difficult to predict which approach is better at producing long term sustainable growth and poverty reduction without causing large social disruptions'. Similarly, India has been slower than China to modernize its ageing infrastructure (especially roads, railways, utilities, ports), but its banking system is more transparent and reliable, with a central bank (Reserve Bank of

India) which has 'clear rules for safeguarding the stability of the financial system' (Kucukakin and Thant 2006: 14), and is thus more attractive for foreign investors who may mistrust the 'strong influence of government bureaucracy and mandates' (ibid.) in China. The role of the respective governments in nurturing entrepreneurship is also significantly different in China and India. In the former, the government spearheads entrepreneurial activities whilst in the latter it is primarily driven by the private sector (Khanna 2007).

China has attempted the 'largest poverty reduction program in human history' (Anonymous 2007b) according to some observers, resulting in between 5 and 10 per cent of people still classified as under the poverty line (Anonymous 2007a), and through its economic development China has spawned a middle class (1 per cent) with 10 per cent of its urban disposable income. Despite these successes, some commentators suggest that China 'is becoming one of the most unequal societies in East Asia' (Warner and Zhu 2010: 286; Chen and Miller 2010: 24) based on the Gini Coefficient. Economic growth has, however, been accompanied in China by massive unemployment following the rationalization and modernization of the old state owned enterprises (SOEs), with some conservative reports suggesting that it has now reached 8 per cent of the workforce, with a projected need for the creation of a further 35 million jobs between 2006–2015 (Holslag 2008).

These developments undoubtedly contributed to the formulation of the 'harmonious society' (*jiànshè héxié shèhuì* 建设 和谐 社会) vision, initiated by Hu Jintao, and endorsed by the Central Committee of the Chinese Communist Party in 2006. In recognition of the growing disparity between rhetoric and reality, the Chinese Communist Party's twelfth Five Year Economic Plan (2011–15) consciously addressed these inequities. Thus, it promoted 'accelerated restructuring, reforming technologies and institutions, ensuring and improving the people's welfare and livelihood, and reducing energy consumption and protecting the environment' (Zhang 2011: 23). The main features of the plan included the expansion of domestic consumption, the development of new growth industries, the management of urbanization and the development of regional and inland economies. Sub-goals embraced upgrading science education and human resources, globalizing the Chinese economy and promoting prosperity, equality and justice (ibid.). The 'people-centred' focus of the plan was paralleled by a strong emphasis on innovation, specifically 'market innovation, management innovation and technological innovation' (Zhang 2011: 27).

Some more cynical observers have suggested that the 'harmonious society' concept is little more than a veneer for more sinister motives. Citing such recent government actions as reported imprisonments of prominent lawyers, dissidents and artists, the 'Great Firewall of China', which effectively blocks critical Internet websites, and the associated People's Liberation Army's 'blue army' of cyber-warriors, together with the obstructive Chinese legal system, they have suggested that Hu Jintao's 'social management' policy is little more than a smokescreen for 'a retrospective catch-cry for the slow-burning crackdown on (the government's) most public critics, tied with a fresh zeal for censorship, particularly online' (Sainsbury 2011a: 12). Others discuss the 'renaissance of the Mao cult' (Hille and

Anderlini 2011) especially amongst older Chinese, exemplified in the rise of such patriotic websites as Utopia (www.wyzxsx.com), Mao Zedong Flag (www.maoflag.net) and Red China (www.redchinacn.com) which nostalgically yearn for a mythical time when 'people were more equal and many things were free or subsidized' (Tatlow 2011).

Successive Indian governments have been less successful in poverty reduction, infrastructure development and the combination of capitalism with improved social outcomes as it has been unable to curb population growth as successfully as China, and remains the country with the 'largest number of poor people, infant deaths in childbirth, and highest child malnutrition in the world' (Aiyar 2009: 1). With respect to infrastructure reform, the Indian government has often been criticized for its under-investment in transportation, energy, water and sanitation in contrast to China – 'public transport is a disgrace. Many of the country's workers spend hours each day stuck in traffic. Their firms are hobbled by the country's infrastructure: back-up generators, water-treatment plants … And India's demographic dividend will not count for much for the unemployable' (ibid.). Tables 1.4 and 1.5 illustrate the similarities and differences between India and China with respect to their telecommunications and transportation infrastructures. India's literacy rate is rising but it is still far behind China's (Anonymous 2010d: 3). However, in recent years the government has spent more than US$ 70 billion on infrastructure development in order to redress some of these issues. In addition, as Kulkarni (2010: 2) noted, 'in *soft* infrastructure India seems far ahead of China. India has a fiercely independent free press … a much vaunted, independent judicial system … rule of law ... (and) the banking infrastructure is robust'.

One of the major drivers of economic growth, especially in the technology, health and financial sectors in both countries, has been a significant emphasis on the development of secondary and higher education (for further discussion, see Chapter 6). This is evidenced in both growing literacy rates and tertiary graduations. With respect to literacy levels, China is ahead of India (70 per cent versus 52 per cent), with lower teacher:pupil proportions (19:1 versus 34:1), and significantly lower male youth illiteracy rates (1 per cent versus 20 per cent) (Kucukakin and Thant 2006: 11). In 2011, Shanghai secondary school students excelled in the OECD's (Organization for Economic Development) most recent global Program for International Student Assessment (PISA), with 'more than one-quarter of Shanghai's 15-year-olds demonstrating advanced mathematical thinking skills to solve complex problems, compared to an OECD average of just 3 percent' (OECD Secretary-General, Angel Gurria, cited in Marginson 2011: 12). However, these findings need to be treated with some caution as they may be skewed towards only the best schools in Shanghai. At the tertiary level, some authors have suggested that India has 'an annual output of half a million engineers, a quarter of a million doctors, and at least one hundred thousand management and business school graduates' (Chatterjee and Nankervis 2003: 45), many of the latter educated in the series of prestigious Indian Institutes of Management (IIM) sprinkled across the sub-continent. The American Academy of Sciences reported that Chinese universities graduated more than 600,000 engineers in 2004, compared with only

Table 1.4 Telecommunications infrastructure

Country	*Electric power consumption (kWh per capita) 2006*	*Internet access to information*	*Internet users (per 100 people) 2008*	*User growth (2000–2008)*	*Users (%) in Asia*	*Penetration (% population)*	*Personal computers (per 100 people) 2006*	*Accessibility of digital content*	*Internet bandwidth (hard data)*	*Cellular (in millions)*	*Mobile phone subscribers (per 100 people) 2008*	*Main lines in use (in millions)*
China	2041	Controlled	16	12.244	0.453	0.224	5.6	5.53	4.79	547.286 (2007)	42	365.4 (2007)
India	503	Open	7	15.2	0.123	0.071	3	4.5	0.31	362.3 (2009)	21	37.75 (2009)

Source: UNCTAD, 2008, Internet World Stats, 2008, Global Information Forum, 2009.

Table 1.5 Transportation infrastructure

	Airports	*Airports with paved runways*	*Heliports*	*Railways*	*Roadways*	*Ports and terminals*[1]
China (2008)	477	413	35	75,438 km	1,930,544 km (2005)	16 major and about 130 open to foreign ships
China (2010)	502	502	48	77,834 km	3,583,715 km (2007)	
India (2008)	345	251	30	63,221 km	3,316,452 km (2006)	12 major and 187 minor and intermediate
India (2010)	352	249	40	64,015 km	3,3320,410 km (2009)	

Source: CIA, 2008, 2010, *World Factbook*.

70,000 in the United States (Carron 2008: 1), and that this number has grown sharply since then, but there are concerns that at least some of these are 'not up to par with the western engineers' (ibid.).

Although the quantum of higher education provision has been noticeably enhanced, the quality of some Chinese tertiary institutions and their graduates has come under more scrutiny in recent years with broad allegations about cheating, plagiarism and fake qualifications amongst Chinese academics, their students and even prominent business leaders. As some observers have suggested, there is serious concern in China about copyright infringement (Green and Kliman 2011: 37) and 'rampant academic fraud and lack of honesty and credibility in mainland society as a whole, and against the mainland authorities' feeble attempts to tackle the issue' (Wang 2010: 3). Recent cases of fake degrees involved the former President of Microsoft China, who is alleged to have falsely claimed to possess a doctorate from the California Institute of Technology (Caltech), and an Executive Director from Megniu Dairy (China), Ding Sheng, who admitted that he did not complete an MBA that he had earlier claimed (ibid.). These aberrations do not necessarily detract from the quality of education provided by the large number of prestigious Chinese universities, but they do demonstrate the difficulty of monitoring and regulating such an immense national system. Regardless of the quality of tertiary education in China and India, as perceived by Western observers, it is indisputable that education levels in both countries are rising significantly and are contributing to their economic growth. As one author explained, 'the more I read about higher education in India and China, the more I believe that Chindia is going to drown us under a tsunami of brilliant young PhDs of any possible kind. Why? Because they have the crowd and they try harder' (Carron 2008: 1).

A growth in internal consumption is consciously nurtured in China's twelfth Five Year Plan, partly as a long-term economic strategy, and partly in response to the increased expectations and purchasing power of its escalating middle class. In the short term, it is a response to the effect of the GFC on decreased exports. A recent Economic Intelligence Unit (EIU) report on Chinese consumers found high consumer optimism (91 per cent of 2,651 respondents); growing expectations for motor vehicles, real estate and computers; concerns about quality healthcare (60 per cent in urban areas, and 84 per cent in rural areas) and a 'desire to keep up with the Zhangs' (Deming 2010: 11). To a lesser extent, and in the absence of such an explicit political strategy, the Indian government has also recognized the growing demands and power of its own affluent middle class, together with the advantages of a joint export-led and internally-driven economy. However, these consumer demands (as in many Western countries) are tempered by concerns about pollution (54 per cent) and other environmental issues (ibid.). Similar issues have been raised by Indian observers (for example, Anonymous 2010d, e, f; Choi 2011). In both countries there is a heightened awareness of non-materialistic aspects – 'improving people's livelihood doesn't only mean eating braised pork in brown sauce or wearing pretty clothes … a healthy spiritual life is also very important' (Bo Xilai, Party Secretary, City of Chongqing, cited in Deming 2010: 39) an ironic comment perhaps in light of the observer's recent difficulties. Indian observers report even greater emphases on these issues (Chatterjee 2010; Cappelli *et al.* 2010), together with the greater commitment of employees to their companies' values and philosophies.

Social and demographic indicators aside, perhaps the most pertinent reflections on the resurgence of China and India as regional and global players lie in their microeconomic or institutional characteristics. As some observers have noted, China's competitive edge is 'shifting from low-cost workers to state-of-the-art manufacturing' (Nelson and Choudaha 2006: 1); and 'MNCs [multinational corporations] are attracted to India not just because of the less expensive resources it offers for production activities, but also because of its vast potential markets' (Cooke and Saini 2010: 476).

Guruswamy and Singh (2010: 46) suggest that China's population is predicted to increase from 812 million (2000) to 921 million (2020) and then reduce to 824 million (2050); whilst India's population will increase from 599 million (2000) to 824 million (2020) and 962 million (2050), thus resulting in what has been described as India's 'demographic dividend'. The cohort in the productive phase (15–60 years) is currently significantly behind China but is expected to move ahead over the next few decades because of the ageing of the population and the 'one child' policy in China. In addition, China's fertility rate is declining, notably in urban areas such as Beijing, Liaoning, Shanghai and Tianjin but less so in the countryside (Evans-Pritchard 2011). But the significant question is how to convert this 'demographic dividend' to the national advantage and it will depend upon how education, innovation, investment and market creation can absorb and utilize this additional cohort.

Economic and industry restructuring – implications and opportunities

China

The breadth and scope of China's and India's relatively recent entry onto the world stage as entrepreneurs, joint venturers and merger and acquisition (M&A) specialists were unimagined. In essence, both countries have adopted expansionary regional and global business strategies, either as deliberate governmental geopolitical strategies (China) or as serendipitous opportunities (India). In the latter case, apart from its well-publicized development of information technology software and associated services at the higher end of the economic scale, India has also developed extensive outsourcing services (call centre and back office services: 'trade in tasks' – US$ 48 billion in 2006) at the lower end (Brown 2008). Major Indian companies such as Tata Consultancy Services, Wipro, Infosys and Satyam (see Chapter 7 for more detailed discussion) are involved at both ends of these markets (ibid.). Others, such as Flextronics and Ranbaxy Laboratories have established multiple subsidiaries across Europe and the United States (ibid.).

Other Indian companies, with the support of their government, have ventured also into other manufacturing specializations such as aerospace, military and space and consumer durables including automobiles and appliances. This trend is exemplified in Hindalo's acquisition of Novelis (the largest North American sheet aluminium company); and the Oil and Natural Gas Corporation and the State Bank of India (SBI) engaging in acquisitions, as has Dr. Reddy's in pharmaceuticals, and Mafatlal and Raymonds in fashion and garments. In addition, there has been limited industry diversification advanced by international acquisition and mergers. As examples, Mittal Steel acquired Arcelor of Luxemburg (Europe's largest steelmaker) in 2007; Tata Steel acquired Corus; Tata Motors attempted unsuccessfully to take over Jaguar and Land Rover (UK); and United Breweries (India) bought the UK's Whyte & Mackay's whisky distillery (Brown 2008). This has been defined as the 'Brand India' mindset (Chatterjee and Nankervis 2003), which was described by Jack Welch, the former chief executive officer of GE thus: 'The real treasure of India is its intellectual capital. The real opportunity of India is its incredible skilled workforce. Raw talent here is like nowhere in the world' (Chatterjee and Nankervis 2003: 6). Apart from the large companies discussed above, lesser known examples include Bollywood's 1,000 films produced annually; Kingfisher beer; and the Narayana Hrudayalaya hospital which has 'turned heart surgery into a Wal-Mart business' (Anonymous 2009a: 1).

In contrast, Chinese companies have ranged more widely across continents (Africa, South America, the United States, United Kingdom, Southeast Asia, Europe) in different ways. For example, Lenovo moved its headquarters to North Carolina; Huawei, Chery, Sinopec and CNOOC expanded their operations to Europe; the Shanghai Automotive Industry Corporation (SAIC) bought Rover's designs in order to better penetrate the European market; and there are now more than 800 Chinese firms spread across Africa (Brown 2008). Chinese international expansion has, however, sometimes met with some resistance. For example, CNOOC's attempt to purchase Unocal, and Haier's proposed takeover of the American firm Maytag were eventually thwarted. Despite these setbacks, some 113 Chinese companies and 56 Indian companies joined *Forbes Magazine*'s 2000 world's leading companies in 2010 (De Carlo 2010). Apart from these high profile global companies, the plethora of small and medium size (SMEs) companies which form the foundation of both countries' industrial landscapes should not be disregarded. Whilst they are not as well known, and rarely documented, it is likely that they will spearhead the future growth of both economies, albeit with less flair and in a more informal manner.

Thus, by any measures, both the Chinese and Indian economies can be considered to be resurgent (whether at the macro or micro levels) based upon demographic, social and individual company indicators. However, each country has achieved these outcomes independently and in pursuit of their own economic and/or geopolitical goals. Whilst there may be synergies between them, there are also considerable tensions, challenges and competitive characteristics, both historic and contemporary, which may constrain the 'Chindia' ideal discussed earlier in this chapter. As Sen (2005: 2) suggests,

> the closer integration of China and India is not inevitable, nor is it even certain that both sides should want it … Indians are always quick to contrast

> China's single-minded pursuit of its own interests with their own messy democratic floundering. But in China's dealings with India it is not clear that either side knows yet where its long-term interests lie.

China has variously been classified as 'an economy in transition', a 'coordinated market economy' (Robins 2010), or even 'network capitalism' (Boisot and Child 1996). Described as 'crossing the river by feeling for the stones' (Collins, Zhu and Warner 2012: 1), the so-called 'third way' (ibid.) between Western-style capitalism and Russian-style socialism has progressed through several developmental stages to the twelfth Five Year Plan which commenced in 2011 and was discussed earlier in this chapter. Some observers suggest that China's recent economic development has been propelled by what has been called the 'Beijing Consensus', which involves 'financial support for the state sector, restrictions on private sector development and tight controls' (Huang 2010: 33). Other authors note that China's transition to its present phase of economic growth has been 'a top-down policy development under the control of an authoritarian, centralized, party-state apparatus, enjoying a monopoly of political power' (Boisot and Child 1996: 25). In other words, China's economic success has been largely the product of what might be termed bridled (as opposed to 'unbridled' Western) capitalism.

The pillars of this 'third way' to economic growth are China's strong political control and direction and its consequent ability to make rapid and wide ranging economic decisions; its emphases on innovation and experimentation (Boisot and Child 1996); its encouragement and facilitation of FDI, especially through the creation of wholly owned foreign enterprises (WOFEs) by the Foreign Investment Law (Collins, Zhu and Warner 2012); and its willingness to dismantle and rationalize former inefficient organizational structures such as the SOEs. In the latter case, the central government has presided over the demolition of the SOE sector, with massive reductions in their number and in associated employment by more than 40 per cent (Robins 2010), resulting in significant innovations and greater efficiencies. Huang (2010: 31) explained the underlying philosophy of successive Chinese governments thus: 'if state ownership of firms promotes economic growth, why privatize? If the one-party system works well in generating growth in gross domestic product (GDP) why democratize? If state financial controls are effective in resource mobilization, why liberalize?'

Within these parameters, this socialist market economy is driven by direct government control of the strategic directions and often even the operations of business – 'the state remains deeply involved in the detail of commercial activity' (Robins 2010: 35). However, sustaining economic growth and buttressing China's burgeoning global stature in the future will be challenged by many aspects of its infrastructure, social, cultural and labour market factors. These include (but are not restricted to) the transparency and effectiveness of China's banking, legal and administrative systems; the ability to continue to attract FDI; greater diversification of industrial sectors and external markets; ongoing poverty reduction campaigns; and dynamic labour market issues, such as the disparity between rural and urban employees' rights and working conditions. It will also be evaluated on the geopolitical strategy underpinning its economic growth – specifically, whether its external economic expansion represents a threat or a 'peaceful rise' (Brown 2009; Choo 2009; Zhen 2009; Buzan 2010) to the Asian region and globally. These issues are canvassed later in this chapter.

China's entry into the World Trade Organization (WTO) in 2001 brought with it many new opportunities for Chinese state and private sector enterprises, not the least being their access, individually or in mergers or acquisitions, to a host of new global markets. Their successes in this regard are discussed earlier in this chapter and throughout the book. However, WTO membership also entails reciprocal responsibilities, including adherence to international financial, legal, quality and employee protection standards and regulations. Whilst some of these expectations have been conscientiously met by both the Chinese government and by individual enterprises, neither the overall legal or banking systems currently reflect fully the characteristics of modern global economic systems, and may eventually hinder the ongoing development of the Chinese economy. As discussed earlier, the four state banks in China control more than half of the total assets of the banking system (Kucukakin and Thant 2006) contrasted with only 2.16 per cent held by foreign banks (Robins 2010: 34), and are in turn controlled by the state.

As a consequence, the transparency of banking systems and regulatory procedures is far from assured. Robins (2010: 25) points out that 'China's banks still have lots of non-performing loans and are characterized by party-influenced management and lending decisions'. Similarly, although there has been considerable development in the extent of China's legal and administrative systems relating to business, 'nobody claims that contemporary China experiences the rule *of* law. At the same time, positive steps away from arbitrary rule towards rule *by* law are steadily being taken' (Robins 2010: 29). Despite these encouraging developments, some observers suggest that there are still many examples of the subversion of WTO expectations with respect to trade restrictions, technical requirements and quarantine regulations (Rudman 2006). Contemporary administrative regulations and systems are in a similarly transient phase, with remnants of excessive bureaucracy and inflexibility. In summary, as the OECD expresses it: 'China's challenge now is to develop a more transparent business environment with a clear legal and regulatory framework. That should help to attract higher-quality investments that are focused on the long-term, high technology, (and) capital-intensive projects' (Chatterjee and Nankervis 2007: 39).

To these ends, China has been actively seeking increased FDI in order to further develop its infrastructure and consequently to support its economic growth (Holslag 2008; Brown 2009; Callahan 2010). It currently attracts 19–38 per cent of Asia's total FDI (Holslag 2008). The rationalization of the former SOEs, the encouragement of multiple joint ventures, and the creation of the wholly foreign owned enterprise (WFOE) sector were all undertaken with at least a partial focus on the attraction of FDI (Warner *et al.* 2005; Collins, Zhu and Warner 2012), an outcome which brings with it a significant degree of economic vulnerability, not only during short-term global crises such as the GFC, but also in the longer term. The certainty of continuing FDI in China is, therefore, by no means assured, and is inevitably linked to China's adherence to WTO and global financial transparency standards. Table 1.6 shows China's relatively greater success than India in attracting FDI. As Wei (2005: 734) explained, this is likely on account of its 'larger domestic market and higher international trade ties with OECD countries'.

Whilst foreign investors in China have been provided with some protections, flexibilities and assurances, together with taxation and other benefits (especially if operating in the special economic zones), there are also expectations imposed upon them, as the Chinese government '… does not distinguish between the business entity, the government, and the society … joint ventures are also expected to serve all these stakeholders' (Chatterjee and Nankervis 2007: 46). These implicit requirements may inhibit the achievement of foreign investors' profit expectations, especially in the low-cost manufacturing sector. There are also significant indications that this sector is undergoing significant transformation as the result of WTO requirements, growing industrial unrest, and difficulties associated with the employment conditions of largely rural workers in urban factories. The lustre of low-cost manufacturing for foreign investors may well be fading, with accordant advantages for neighbouring countries such as India, Vietnam and Malaysia.

As part of its broad geopolitical strategy, the Chinese government has consciously combined the attraction of FDI with active external investment both directly and indirectly. As a global diversification imperative, these ventures have been generally quite successful in terms of their broad geographic penetration (Africa, Asia, Europe, the United States, United Kingdom, South America, Australasia – Brown 2009; Choo 2009; Wang 2009; Buzan 2010; De Carlo 2010; Yeates 2010). They also illustrate the gradual diversification of industry sector interests, with Chinese companies involved in resources, automobiles, white goods and information technology software and hardware, as well as more basic manufacturing.

It is, however, China's management of its dynamic labour market landscape which will inevitably facilitate or constrain its ongoing economic success, as in India, if for different reasons. China has a large, readily available and predominantly low-cost, actual and potential workforce – the world's largest manufacturing labour market, the so-called 'docile, diligent and dirt cheap' workers (Anonymous 2010g), the majority of which (60 per cent) is of employable age (Holslag 2008). In addition, the increasing number of Chinese engineering and MBA graduates (Carron 2008; Anonymous 2010g) provides complementarity at both ends of the labour market, notwithstanding the alleged difficulties with some of these systems and their graduates, and associated skills (Wang 2010). The 'open door' policy which commenced in 1978 embraced a broad export orientation, together with the associated establishment of several important major labour market revisions – namely, the development of a new labour contract system, a 'floating wage' mechanism (performance-linked rewards), contributory employee social insurance, and the dissolution of the guaranteed lifetime employment system (Warner 1995, 2005; Collins, Zhu and Warner 2012).

Legislation such as the Labour Law 1994 provided for new forms of individual (*gèrén* 个人 合同) and collective contracts (*jítǐ hétong* (集体 合同 – Warner 1995, 2008a: Collins, Zhu and Warner 2012), whilst the 2007 Labour Contract Law

Table 1.6 Inward FDI flows: China and India 1970–2008 (US$ millions)

Year	*China*	*India*	*FDI developing economies: Asia*	*World FDI*	*China as % of developing economies in Asia*	*China as % of world FDI*	*India as % of developing economies in Asia*	*India as % of world FDI*
1970	0	45	854	13,346	0.0	0.0	5.3	0.3
1971	0	48	796	14,282	0.0	0.0	6.0	0.3
1972	0	18	1,423	14,933	0.0	0.0	1.3	0.1
1973	0	38	1,648	20,646	0.0	0.0	2.3	0.2
1974	0	57	−1,665	24,127	0.0	0.0	−3.4	0.2
1975	0	85	5,265	26,567	0.0	0.0	1.6	0.3
1976	0	51	1,605	22,002	0.0	0.0	3.2	0.2
1977	0	−36	3,031	27,139	0.0	0.0	−1.2	−0.1
1978	0	18	3,919	34,358	0.0	0.0	0.5	0.1
1979	0	49	2,146	42,292	0.0	0.0	2.3	0.1
1980	57	79	543	54,076	10.5	0.1	14.6	0.1
1981	265	92	13,329	69,567	2.0	0.4	0.7	0.1
1982	430	72	17,136	58,059	2.5	0.7	0.4	0.1
1983	916	6	10,894	50,268	8.4	1.8	0.1	0.0
1984	1,419	19	11,557	56,839	12.3	2.5	0.2	0.0
1985	1,956	106	5,419	55,887	36.1	3.5	2.0	0.2
1986	2,244	118	9,299	86,345	24.1	2.6	1.3	0.1
1987	2,314	212	13,426	136,548	17.2	1.7	1.6	0.2
1988	3,194	91	18,058	162,834	17.7	2.0	0.5	0.1
1989	3,393	252	16,992	196,617	20.0	1.7	1.5	0.1
1990	3,487	237	22,660	207,273	15.4	1.7	1.0	0.1
1991	4,366	75	24,164	155,686	18.1	2.8	0.3	0.0
1992	11,008	252	32,956	166,594	33.4	6.6	0.8	0.2
1993	27,515	532	56,022	222,408	49.1	12.4	0.9	0.2
1994	33,767	974	68,289	256,785	49.4	13.1	1.4	0.4
1995	37,521	2,151	80,114	341,144	46.8	11.0	2.7	0.6
1996	41,726	2,525	94,186	390,443	44.3	10.7	2.7	0.6
1997	45,257	3,619	105,814	485,808	42.8	9.3	3.4	0.7
1998	45,463	2,633	95,302	705,330	47.7	6.4	2.8	0.4
1999	40,319	2,168	111,537	1,078,606	36.1	3.7	1.9	0.2
2000	40,715	3,585	148,561	1,381,675	27.4	2.9	2.4	0.3
2001	46,878	5,472	113,936	820,430	41.1	5.7	4.8	0.7
2002	52,743	5,627	101,185	629,675	52.1	8.4	5.6	0.9
2003	53,505	4,323	116,928	565,160	45.8	9.5	3.7	0.8
2004	60,630	5,771	172,910	734,892	35.1	8.3	3.3	0.8
2005	72,406	7,606	213,751	973,329	33.9	7.4	3.6	0.8
2006	72,715	20,336	282,127	1,461,074	25.8	5.0	7.2	1.4
2007	83,521	25,127	331,425	1,978,838	25.2	4.2	7.6	1.3
2008	108,312	41,554	387,828	1,697,353	27.9	6.4	10.7	2.4

Source: UNCTAD, WIR, 2009.

extended worker protections, including 'mandatory written contracts, restrictions on temporary labour, and more difficult layoffs'. A new labour mediation law was promulgated in 2008. These reforms precipitated the removal of the unproductive 'old irons' of the former socialist regime – the 'iron rice bowl' (*tiěfànwǎn* 铁饭碗), which provided lifetime employment guarantees for all Chinese employees; the 'iron wage' (*tiě gōngzī* 铁工资), inflexible wage structures; and the 'iron chair' (*tiě jiāoyǐ* 铁交椅), which based employee selection on political rather than work performance factors (Ng and Warner 1998; Collins, Zhu and Warner 2012) and heralded the demise of the SOE sector, with its associated mass redundancies. On the positive side, these innovations encouraged 'increasing autonomy of management, issues such as the rights to hire and fire, performance evaluation, managerial decisions on standards and the way of conducting evaluation, performance-related matters, such as pay and promotion' (Collins, Zhu and Warner 2012: 17). These actions and their effects are discussed in more detail in other chapters.

However, many of the workers displaced from the SOEs drifted from rural to urban areas seeking employment, and have subsequently both contributed to the low-cost manufacturing so attractive to many foreign investors in China, and arguably to the multiple problems identified with rural–urban worker migration (approximately 130 million workers, or one-third of the total urban workforce in Anhui, Chongqing, Guangdong, Hebei, Henan, Hubei, Jiangsu, Shanghai, Sichuan, Zhejiang (Meng *et al.* 2010: 1), rural migrants' working conditions, and the current threats to the future of manufacturing growth in China. As Cooke (2010: 27) explained, 'Chinese workers in the export-oriented manufacturing firms remain largely unorganized and unprotected, have little bargaining power and often work in sweatshop conditions'. Thus, whilst in theory all workers, including those rural workers who have migrated to urban-based factories, receive equal protections (access to jobs, welfare, minimum wages and maximum hours) under the Labour Contract Law 2008 (Meng *et al.* 2010: 48), the reality is that many employers flout the law and force their employees to work long hours, fail to provide minimum wages, employer insurance contributions, adequate safety standards, or equal access to basic education and healthcare services.

A recent example of the abuses of protective employee legislation and regulations include a study of employee conditions in some Shenzen factories which found that the average monthly salary for migrant workers was 1800 Yuan (approximately 47 per cent of the average income); more than half of them worked between 9–24 hours extra weekly overtime; and most lived 'in cramped, basic dormitories … with more than six people sharing a tiny room' (Tam 2010: A4). More extreme cases include the 13 worker suicides at the Shenzen Foxconn factory, attributed to their desires to send home the company's financial compensation; alleged corrupt practices and disregard of employee safety standards within the toy manufacturing sector, together with continued use of child labour (Tsang 2010: 1, 3). Foxconn has subsequently doubled its pay rates in an attempt to deal with its problems (Sainsbury 2010: 17).

Cai Fang, from the Chinese Academy of Social Sciences, has recently argued that not only are Chinese workers demonstrating more assertive and confrontational behaviours, but they are also becoming scarcer (Anonymous 2010c). He suggested more broadly that 'labourers can impose stress on employers through voting with (their) feet' (ibid.: 2), whilst others point out that the foreign multinational companies can choose similar options should rising wages and enhanced benefits lead to reduced profitability and growth. As recent examples, there are labour shortages in Fujian, Guangdong and Zhejiang provinces. Employers in these regions have been forced to adopt non-traditional measures to ensure employee retention – Apache Footwear (Qingyun), for example, has built high quality employee apartments (rather than traditional dormitories) and organizes weekend films and social occasions; Haier has set up a 24-hour hotline and a support group for employee emergencies (see Chapter 7 for more detailed discussion); and GM pays its workers relatively higher wages, whilst replacing some with robotics (Roberts 2005: 1–3). The essential issue here is whether China will be able to maintain its global competitive advantage and attractiveness to foreign investors in the low-cost manufacturing sector, given WTO requirements, rising union and worker expectations, and both regional and broader economic competition.

The foregoing discussion has highlighted some of the main factors which may constrain the projected continuing growth of China's economy, and which it must address if it is to maintain its prominence within the Asian region and globally. A further issue which will undoubtedly underpin its sometimes problematic relationships with neighbouring countries (most notably with India) is that of China's strategic intentions. This dilemma has been expressed as a choice between 'China threat' theory and the so-called 'peaceful rise' (*hépíng juéqǐ* 和平 崛起'), 'peaceful development' (*hépíng fāzhǎn* 和平发展), or 'harmonious world' (*héxié shìjiè* 和谐世界) concept (Choo 2009: 392; Warner 2008a). China threat theory has been progressively developed and nurtured by Western countries (notably the United States) whose economies have been challenged by the resurgence of China, and other countries (especially India) with whom China has had a troubled diplomatic or military history. The contrary 'harmonious society/world' view (Choo 2009: 397) was promoted by President Hu Jintao in China during August 2004 and reiterated later at the United Nations in September 2005, and was subsequently echoed by Premier Wen Jiabao (Callahan 2010: 1). It represents official Chinese Communist Party policy as it was ratified at the sixth Plenum of the Sixteenth CCP Central Committee (11 October 2006), and was explained thus: 'social harmony is the intrinsic nature of socialism with Chinese characteristics and an important guarantee of the country's prosperity, the nation's rejuvenation and the people's happiness' (Warner *et al.* 2011: 3).

Whether this is pure rhetoric, a smokescreen for more sinister motives, or a genuine attempt to adopt a 'third way' in the integration of economics and geopolitical strategies, remains to be seen. Another (and possibly more realistic) interpretation is provided by Callahan (2010: 3) who suggests the pragmatic notion of *tiānxìng* (天性) – that is 'a grand geopolitical struggle where competition between nations is natural and good … a zero-sum game where victory and defeat are total'. This is akin to the resource-based theory, and is not unlike Michael Porter's 'competitive strategy' (1985) applied at the regional or global levels. Buzan (2010: 35–6) suggests, finally, that

> peaceful rise is possible, but it will not be easy, and it will require new thinking from China. At the forefront of that new thinking must be three things … a clearer vision of China's own identity … a clearer vision of what kind of international society China wants to promote … and a strategy for creating a proper reconciliation with Japan

(and arguably India as well). The next section of this chapter considers the challenges and opportunities facing India in its economic growth surge, as well as its comparisons and contrasts with China.

India

India differs from China in many aspects, including its land mass (approximately one-third of China's), its population growth rates (1.6 per cent versus 0.8 per cent), GDP real growth rates (9.5 per cent versus 11 per cent), GDP per capita (US$ 3,800 versus US$ 7,800), export volume (US$ 112 billion versus US$ 974 billion), and research and development expenditure (1.5 per cent versus 2.5 per cent GDP) (Chatterjee and Nankervis 2007). India's workforce is also considerably more rural-based than China's, which may constrain its parallel industrial transformation. In historical, political and socio-cultural arenas, they are worlds apart despite sharing a common border and a similar resurgence in their economic growth and regional influence. Arguably, China's recent development in these areas has been more impressive than that of India, because ironically of the combination of its socialist (rather than democratic) political traditions; its higher literacy rates; India's fragmented and sometimes confrontational social, religious and cultural landscape and more rigid legislative framework (Kucukakin and Thant 2006). Some observers even claim that 'India is decades behind China' (Gupta and Wang 2009b: 1), pointing, inter alia, to its lower comparative standard of living, its ageing infrastructure and maze of confusing legislation and regulations (Anonymous 2007a).

However, 'with a population of over a billion people and a strong democratic tradition, institutional stability and a large pool of talented employees, (India's) performance gap is inevitably destined to be bridged' (Nankervis, Chatterjee and Coffey 2006: 44). Goldman Sachs, for example, predict that India's GDP will reach US$ 1 trillion by 2011 and US$ 2 trillion by 2020 – 'in terms of GDP India will overtake Italy by 2016, France by 2019, UK by 2022, Germany by 2023, and Japan by 2032' (ibid.: 45). Whilst these projections were made prior to the GFC, and may, therefore, be aspirational rather than realistic, they do indicate the scale of India's current economic growth. Successive Indian governments, supported by the Indian Ministry of the National Development and Reform Commission, have urged Indian companies to be 'outward-oriented' in their financial development strategies (Holslag 2008). The success of many of them in these endeavours has been discussed earlier in this chapter. As evidence of this, Cooke and Saini (2010b) pointed to the dramatic success of Indian multinationals globally and the effective restructuring of public sector agencies.

Domestically, optimistic observers have suggested that India is being 'slowly transformed from a land of spiritual *swamis* and impoverished rural masses to a modern intellect-leveraged corporate society' (Chatterjee and Nankervis 2003: 64). More pragmatic authors merely indicate the growing importance of the information technology software sector and the outsourcing/off-shoring of international call centre services. However, India's economy is not restricted to these two sectors. As has been earlier noted, it is also developing expertise in such areas as aerospace, military, space and consumer products, automobiles, steel production, oil and gas, banking and insurance, the media and entertainment, pharmaceuticals and fashion (Chatterjee and Nankervis 2003).

In the corporate sector, there are five significant organizational types – namely, family conglomerates, (as examples, Tata is in communications, IT, engineering, cars and construction, consumer products, hotels and housing, energy and chemicals; others include Reliance Industries, Aditya Birla, Bajaj, Thapars, Mahindra and Mahindra and Amalgamations); the so-called 'born-global' IT companies such as Infosys and Wipro; multinationals including Hindustan Lever, Coca Cola, IBM, McKinsey, Sage Publishing and Price Waterhouse; large government–owned and controlled infrastructure corporations (airlines, shipping, mineral exploration, railways, postal services, steel plants, oil and gas); and finally, entrepreneurial Indian small and medium enterprises. Thus India's industrial landscape is significantly more complex than China's, and is characterized by a greater amount of associated legislation within the political context of rambling and often unmanageable democratic traditions. It also faces a range of bewildering challenges which threaten its continuing economic growth – 'fragmented pluralism, polemical transformation and adaptive labour market flexibility' (Nankervis, Chatterjee and Coffey 2006: 47).

India's current economic surge has been popularly attributed to its recognized expertise in the research and development of information technology software, on the one hand, undoubtedly spearheaded by its returning diaspora from the United States and Europe; and on the other hand, to its growing 'trade in services' such as call centres and publishing support functions built upon its well-educated English-speaking graduates. Certainly, the IT sector is a significant contributor to the Indian economy. In 2008 it alone earned US$ 72 billion or 4 per cent of GDP, and created two million direct, and over eight million indirect jobs, from a total workforce of seven hundred million people (Gupta and Wang 2009a: 1). The IT sector has strengthened 'Brand India' (Nankervis, Chatterjee and Coffey 2006: 52), but it has also shifted the geocentric centre of power in India from Mumbai to other centres such as Bangalore, Chennai, New Delhi and Secunderabad (Chatterjee and Nankervis 2003: 78). In addition, it has nurtured a new generation of educated Indian entrepreneurs, provoked significant challenges to the traditional Indian management culture, and, on account of expectations of long-term economic growth, 'blunted some of the political opposition to India's gradual integration with the world economy' (Chatterjee and Nankervis 2003: 80). This has been strengthened by the Indian government's National IT Taskforce that was established in 1998 and which has consciously nurtured a 'new strategic paradigm in Indian's managerial culture' (Chatterjee and Nankervis 2003: 77), with tariff and duty reductions on imported IT equipment, taxation exemptions and a relaxation of foreign investment and exchange controls.

Some more cynical observers suggest that the contribution of the IT sector to the growth of the Indian economy has been over-estimated. As Gupta and Wang (2009b: 7) note, whilst the IT sector has provided public relations support to the perceived resurgence of India, it is 'little more than a tiny, though highly visible, niche in the Indian economy'. There is also an increasing fear in India that China's software engineers may soon catch up with their expertise (Sen 2005). Similarly, the lustre of the 'trade in services' sector, especially in relation to call centres, seems to be fading because of international customer resistance, parent country government opposition and the growing use of technological options. In these scenarios, India may be forced to return to competition with China in the manufacturing arena both at home and abroad.

Apart from these actual and potential challenges to the Indian economy, there is a plethora of other factors which may threaten its future growth. These include the need to upgrade its ageing infrastructure; its massive urban–rural disparity; its increasing demand on the world's resources consequent on its burgeoning population; the rigid governmental control of its financial system and labour market; the quality of its public services (Anonymous 2007a); and of course its fragmented political, cultural and religious fabric. With respect to its infrastructure, especially in relation to ports, railways, public administration, water and electricity, India's expenditure on upgrading is reportedly only one-seventh of China's. Other observers report that China spends 40 per cent of its GDP, compared to only 19 per cent in India (Anonymous 2008a: 2). Starting a business takes 71 days in India (compared with 48 days in China) and exporting, 36 days compared to 20 in China (Anonymous 2010a: 6).

As in China, there is a significant imbalance in the income, employment and overall quality of life between India's vibrant cities and its huge rural population, although the rural–urban drift is not nearly as pronounced as in China. In addition, India's population is growing at twice China's rate (Kucukakin and Thant 2006). As a consequence of its democratic political system and colonial legacies, India's legislative framework and banking system regulations are far more developed but considerably less flexible than their counterparts in China, leading on occasion to constraints on innovation and entrepreneurialism. Differing regulatory requirements between states adds a further layer to this administrative complexity, slowing down scrutiny and approval processes. Similarly, whilst India's banking system is more transparent and accountable than China's, there is still an urgent need to 'reduce government regulation, ownership and "privileged borrowing", and to reform restrictive labour laws' (Anonymous 2007a: 3).

With respect to the latter, Indian labour legislation is seen to be protective of labour and amongst the most restrictive and complex in the world, and there are clear disparities between the 'organized' (unionized) and 'unorganized' (non-unionized) segments of the workforce (Cooke 2010a: 5). The organized segment is represented by a host of general and industry-specific unions, including the All India Trade Union Congress (affiliated with the Communist Party of India); the Centre of Indian Trade Unions (affiliated with the Communist Party of India–Marxist), the Indian National Trade Union Congress (affiliated with the Indian National Congress), the Hind Mazdoor Sabha (affiliated with the Bharatiya Janta Party); the All India Bank Employees Union and the All India Railway Workers Union (the most powerful trade union in India) (Nankervis, Chatterjee and Coffey 2006: 48). In the 'unorganized' or informal segment 'wages and working conditions are inferior, largely insecure and mostly devoid of social security benefits' (Cooke 2010a: 5).

Unlike China, India is characterized not only by its colonial traditions and its democratic systems, but inextricably by the fragmentation, disparity and eclectic nature of its socio-cultural and religious landscape. This provides a considerably more complex and esoteric dimension to its opportunities for future growth and clearly differentiates it from the challenges facing China.

In addition, the perceived traditional division of labour between China and India – export-oriented industrial production versus commercial services – is neither static nor equal. The reality is, as Holslag (2008: 7) suggests, that this division of labour is actually, 'a hierarchy of labour in which China (has been) more successful to generate jobs and to reap export revenues … India and China also vie for access to the same countries and regions for exports and attracting investments'.

One of the principal contemporary advantages of a resurgent China, especially for foreign investors in search of inexpensive and uncomplicated labour relations, is its relatively unitarist industrial relations system compared to India's complex and adversarial framework. However, a more pluralist system may be more compatible with its market economy imperatives. The growth in worker demands for higher wages and improved workplace conditions expressed through increased industrial action may (or may not) support this view. A counter view is encapsulated in Huang's (2010: 31) proposition that the so-called 'Beijing Consensus' is 'committed to experimentation and innovation … eclectic and pragmatic', implying continued Chinese government control over trade unions and associated industrial action. Indian governments, on the other hand, are unlikely to be able to exercise similar controls, given its industrial relations traditions of an 'industry-wide membership basis with local, regional and national affiliations with powerful political parties … minimum wages, payment of wages, working conditions, gender equity in pay, industrial safety and policies on redundancy' (Chatterjee and Nankervis 2003: 89).

Conclusion

This chapter argues that India and China have followed divergent growth strategies. China has adopted a 'top to bottom strategy', combining large scale FDI, mass manufacturing and impressive government infrastructural initiatives. In contrast, India's recipe has been much more organic and driven mainly by the private sector. The various strengths and weaknesses of each country with respect to both their individual and collective economic and geopolitical influence in the likely future are canvassed. In this regard, Gerhaeusser *et al.* (2010) summarized the initial similarities and differences of India and China as follows; their similarities included 'the advantage of backwardness' (based on their initial low per capita incomes), large domestic markets, the 'demographic dividend' (although India is the greater beneficiary here), ICT networks, the early roles of state governments, the move towards 'an outward-looking strategy based on international division of labour, and a gradual approach to reform (2010: 2–9); whilst their differences included the roles of local governments, India's 'culture of entrepreneurship' compared with China's lack of such, their manufacturing versus services focus, and China's earlier growth (2010: 9–12).

The chapter suggests that China will likely be the dominant partner in any conceivable strategic partnership. China has arguably greater geopolitical reach than India on account of its WTO membership and broader direct penetration of global markets. It also appears to have a competitive advantage in attracting FDI because of its focus on inexpensive and flexible manufacturing, supported by its 'bridled capitalism' ideology and practice, its rapidly developing infrastructure, increasing literacy and generally successful poverty reduction programme. On the other hand, India's democratic traditions and post-colonial global connections; together with its IT, 'trade in services', English language expertise, and its transparent banking and labour market protection legislation, make it attractive to both local and international investors. In addition, India's technological prowess is highly valued, although there are signs that China is rapidly catching up. Certainly, China is financing its infrastructure and technological development at a greater rate than India.

When we look at the overall panorama of both the Chinese and Indian economies, it is necessary to keep a sense of proportion. There is a tendency to emphasize the positive in the financial press in order to spin out a narrative of Eastern expansion and Western decline. Although long-term growth rates have been impressive, it is by no means certain that these can be extrapolated far into the future. Some economists believe that China will indeed be slowing down over the next half decade. A related question is how truly accurate existing reported growth rates have been. Whilst both of these economies have been growing at a relentless pace over recent decades, development has been skewed in favour of the urban, and in some cases, coastal areas. Correspondingly, the agricultural interior has been relatively neglected, although in the case of China this seems to be changing, with a new surge of investment and jobs in the 'frontier' provinces of the west.

With respect to the much vaunted complementarity of Chinese and Indian economies, this chapter suggests that this is a dynamic situation, with increased industrial action in the former leading to inferences that Chinese labour costs may render it uncompetitive for foreign investors, and that competition rather than collaboration is more likely in their future economic scenarios.

Acknowledgement

Parts of this chapter were previously published in an earlier journal article: A. Nankervis and S. Chatterjee (2010), 'The resurgence of China and India: Collaboration or competition?' *Human Systems Management*, 29 (1–2): 1–17. The authors wish to thank the publishers for their permission to reproduce the material.

2 Cultural and traditional legacies, leadership values and human resource management principles

Introduction

Two of the world's most ancient and rich traditions have for centuries shared their philosophical and material foundations. It is remarkable that there have been so few contradictions between such divergent societies (*shìjiè dàtóng* 世界大同) 'viewing the world in a harmonious state' in China, and *vasudhaiva kutumbakam* 'the world is one family' in India). This semi-spiritual unity of the two civilizations, now embracing more than 40 per cent of the world's population, is also reflected in their mutual acceptance of ideas, their absorption of religious practices and above all, their participation in regional and global trade and commerce. Trade through the Silk Route reflected the two countries' openness to outsiders, their spirit of enterprise and the relative absence of administrative barriers. These factors are arguably unprecedented in the history of the world. As some recent commentators have suggested,

> one has only to visit the caves of Ajanta or see the murals of Dunhuang (敦煌) in China to see the capturing through the eye of the artist, of this vision of unity – with their depiction of various nationalities thronging royal processions or expressing their grief before a dying Buddha.
>
> (Rao 2011: 3)

Numerous ideas and principles which underpin contemporary management and human resource management practices emerged from China and India, and mirror those supporting Western-style systems (Wang *et al.* 2008; Nilekani 2008)). The concept and practice of bureaucracy, for example, guided organizational form in China thousands of years before Max Weber (1864–1920) popularized it in the European context (Sahang 1971). Ethical precepts for leadership behaviour advocated by Confucius informed the ideals of the Indian emperor Asoka in the third century BC, and the *Sreni* system of management was widespread in India by 800 BC. This system guided the institutional managerial ideas of commercial, military, governmental and religious organizations (see more discussion later in this chapter), and preceded the Roman proto-corporations by centuries (Chatterjee 2009a). The first known treatise on management in the world (*Arthashastra*), written around 300 BC by Kautilya Chankya, formulated principles of good governance and encouraged the emergence of complex bureaucratic systems with strong centres and delegated authority (Rangarajan 1992). In similar vein, the Chinese imperial civil service examination which originated later (sixth century AD) 'built up a critical mass of certified individuals with knowledge and skills able to run large organizations. It trained scholars and bureaucrats for over 1300 years' (Warner 2011b: 397). During the eight century AD the elite Hanlin Academy was established in Beijing, continuing until its demise in 1911 (ibid.).

China has had a continuity of common culture over a longer period than any other, whilst the history of India by contrast is beset with invasions and assimilations from the Persians in 540 AD, the Greeks in 325 AD, the Arabs in the fifteenth century, the Portuguese and French in the sixteenth and seventeenth century and subsequently British domination for two hundred years until Independence in 1947.

This chapter highlights some of the traditional influences on the leadership dynamics and human resource management principles of modern Chinese and Indian organizations. In order for these global companies to compete effectively and to contribute to the well-being of humanity, contemporary management and leadership concepts need to be complemented by their rich indigenous wisdoms and cultural traditions. Such a cross-vergence of ideas, ideals and realities is likely to shape their future directions and impact.

National contexts for paradigm shifts in China and India

It is evident that over the past three decades the impressive economic growth in India and China (see Chapter 1 for more discussion) has revealed multidimensional challenges for both countries in the areas of global and corporate leadership strategies and roles, ideologies of institutional development, human resource management principles and practices and their respective governance systems. The legacy of communist ideology in China and the colonial administrative heritage followed by parliamentary democracy in India have featured prominently in the transformations taking place in both economies. As discussed in Chapter 1, China has recently overtaken Japan as the second largest global economy, and within Asia it has become the main trading partner of both Japan and India. Such developments have required China to employ pragmatic philosophical perspectives. It is argued that the paradigm shift in economic relations within Asia brought about by China can be attributed at least in part to its adherence (or return) to Confucian values. Thus, one explanation for China's priority in building up enormous foreign exchange reserves may be associated with Confucian values.

It should also not be ignored that over the past two decades global Chinese companies on the *Fortune 500* list have risen from 0 to 61 in 2011 (see Chapter 7 for information on particular companies), while similar Indian company representation has been considerably slower, rising from one to only eight over the same period (*Fortune* 2011: 18). In addition to this growth in the global recognition of indigenous Indian and Chinese companies, there is intense competition from multinational companies to locate their research and development, and manufacturing facilities in both countries. This is particularly evident in industrial sectors such as aerospace, biotechnology, sustainable energy systems, green technologies, pharmaceuticals and healthcare, where Chinese, Indian and third country scientists, managers and knowledge specialists come together within very diverse leadership cultures. The mutual benefits to the two countries through such revivals of regional collaboration were highlighted in 2002 by the former Chinese Premier visiting India who remarked that 'you are the first in software, and we are the first in hardware. When we put these two together, we can become the world's number one' (*The Economist* 2004: 49). The ideological implications of such statements are significant in understanding the paradigm shift consequent on China's possible ascension to world's largest economy status within the next decade. On the road to such a goal, in 2010 China became the world's biggest manufacturer, displacing the US.

Continued economic success will, however, be dependent on moving away from narrow interpretations of *shèngshì* 盛世 (or 'harmonious Chinese glory') by emerging leaders at every level. It is important to realize that Chinese culture has evolved without a specific focus on plurality. The Han ethnic group comprises almost 95 per cent of the population and its written language can be traced back more than 3,500 years. In contrast, the ethnic and linguistic diversity of India is arguably greater than in the whole of Europe. There are more than 20 recognized languages and over 1,500 living dialects. The social structure of the Chinese heritage lacked strict divisions between the elite and commoners, and social mobility was not uncommon, in contrast to the clear delineations of hierarchy and social order in Indian traditions. The caste system defined (and to some degree still does) one's place in society permanently (Sinha 1980).

The Ethical School founded by Confucius strongly opposed internal as well as external conflict. His opposition to war was eclipsed by the rise of Qin who emphasized legalism and the necessity of conflict. However, the subsequent ascendancy of the Han in 207BC revitalized Confucianism but without its opposition to war. Marxism and Maoism both reinforced the importance of ethical and ideological forces. Perceptions of war and conflict differ between China and India, with associated implications for leadership, corporate management and industrial relations. In China, they were perceived as the domain of strategy and tactics, whereas in India war has usually been considered a ritual within which codes of chivalry and heroism were clearly understood. The warrior class (*khsatriya*) was entrusted to demonstrate valour (*shourya*) through their diplomacy and alliance skills, unlike the Chinese preoccupation with strategic actions and plans. Transparency in the deployment of technology, as well as communication between warring parties in ancient India were considered the most essential elements of *neeti* or ethics (Chatterjee and Nankervis 2007).

Chinese traditions and perspectives of leadership

Leadership traditions drawn from cultural roots have been the visible pillars of the Chinese state owned enterprises and family businesses. Their applications in large private sector organizations are more subtle and nuanced with more contemporary political and social influences (Li, Tsui and Weldon 2000; Gupta and Wang 2009c). In addition, the influences of tradition are reported to be waning among generations X and Y employees (see also Chapters 1, 5 and 6). In particular, there appear to be more individualistic and less conformist behaviours in employees' work-related interactions (Ralston *et al.* 1997). Despite these observations, *guānxì* is still an important factor in employer–employee relationships. Some authors (e.g. Chatterjee 2001) have argued that these apparent contradictions explain the relative under-development of managerial autonomy and innovation, and the persistence of collectivism in many spheres of work organization (Chatterjee 2009).

Despite the persistent critiques of Chinese cultural traditions during the Cultural Revolution (1966–76) and associated attempts to redirect the duty orientation away from the family towards the Communist Party leadership, there now appears to be a resurgence of traditional leadership forms in many Chinese organizations. These cultural legacies can be traced back three thousand years, and have coalesced around an amalgam of Taoism, Confucianism and Buddhism. The Taoist School, espoused by Lao Zi, highlights spiritual reasoning linking actions and their consequences, and has had a particular relevance in the contemporary debate about the relationship between man and nature. Confucian precepts are often characterized into the two elements of *rén* (仁) and *zhōngyōng* (中庸). Buddhist influences are much deeper and imprinted on the mindscape of the Chinese worldview. Table 2.1 summarizes the main Chinese cultural traditions and leadership frameworks which derive from these influences.

The Table illustrates the key precepts, together with the human, social and organizational value domains which in turn underpin contemporary leadership

Table 2.1 Cultural traditions and leadership frameworks in China

Precepts	*Tradition-anchored belief system*	*Leadership emphasis*
Human values	• *rén* 仁 (Benevolence) • *zhì* 智 (Wisdom) • zhōngyōng中庸 (Harmony) • xìn信 (Trustworthiness) • *guānxì* 关系 (Particularistic social relationship)	• Paternalism • Higher values jūnzǐ君子 • Long-term orientation
Social values	• miànzi 面子 (Importance of honour and reputation) • wǔlún五伦 (Rules, hierarchy and authority structure)	• Dominance of relationship • Acceptance of social network • Avoidance of loss of face • Hierarchy of social order
Organizational values	• décáijiānbè德才兼备 (Integrity and competence) • Bā Róng Bā Chǐ八荣八耻 (Reverence for education and morality)	• Loyalty to leadership • Organizational collectivism • Respect for age

philosophies and practices in Chinese institutions. It should also be noted that Confucianism has a rich history of 'precept–practice' linkages by emphasizing a preference for the uses of science and technology rather than the processes of their discovery. Important inventions were driven by the need for solutions to specific problems. For example, the invention of the compass was linked to the concept of *fēngshuǐ* (风水) as well as solving navigational problems. Similar practical purposes underpinned the applications of mathematics and astronomy to agriculture, gunpowder for the army, printing for knowledge storage and even medicine for human well-being. It was not clinical experimentation but empirical validation that guided the development of medical science. In spite of its exceptional ingenuity, no theoretical explanation of the working of the compass is available in the ancient literature (Needham 1956).

The 'two force' and 'five element' theories popularized by Confucian scholars have long been the guiding philosophy and scientific methods have been the logic of social sciences. The two forces *yīn* (阴) and *yang* (阳) highlight the antagonistic yet complementary aspects of ideas and practices, and the five elements (namely: wood, fire, earth, metal and water) dominated early Chinese worldviews. It was widely held that the two forces and five elements fitted together to construct a cosmic system that was the foundation of not only the rule of the empire but also all forms of organizations and groups. The ideas of balancing opposites and searching for harmony through the synthesis of *yīn* and *yang*; as well as the cosmic notion of five elements of the world were incorporated in the Book of Changes. These concepts highlighted man as an integral part of nature, and maintaining harmony as the most important imperative. The five element concept of Confucian tradition is an holistic tradition integrating natural phenomena in human endeavours, at a time when managerial and administrative work was primarily nature-dependent. The well known five virtues of Chinese tradition – namely: kind heartedness (*rén* 仁), righteousness (*yì* 义), etiquette (*lǐ* 礼), wisdom (*zhì* 智) and purity (*shèng* 圣) – originated from the five elements (R. Huang 2008; Warner 2011a).

It is somewhat paradoxical that, in terms of the content of Chinese culture, the ethics orientation originating with Confucius was always a dominant characteristic of all aspects of life. Rather than pursuing a preoccupation with analytical theories, Chinese thinkers tended to emphasize the development of (prescriptive) guiding frameworks for government actions and the social activities of their citizens. The generation of science, technology and ideas seldom received the same degree of respectability as the scholarship of literature, politics and ethics. Many observers (for example, Yeung 2009) point out that this subordination of science and innovation to social and political pursuits may be one of the reasons for China's failure to honour international patent laws.

In essence, the relevance of the core Confucian values is undeniably a very powerful force in shaping the leadership culture in China. Such ideas have served as a proxy for a legalistic approach and a less adversarial mode of organizational dynamics. It represents an interesting alternative to both individualistic capitalism and collective socialism, and may provide evidence that a non-individualistic and non-Western form of modernity is not only conceivable but also practicable (de Bettignies and Tan 2007). Thus Table 2.1 may be reinterpreted in terms of the widespread adoption of the market economy and the Confucian dependency on the 'wisdom of virtuous men', that mature and experienced leaders who understand the holistic imperatives of organizations appear to be mostly taken for granted. Many Chinese organizations resolve this duality of holistic concern and market economy by promoting paternalistic management systems. These may be evidenced in terms of housing, medical care, children's schooling and even arranging employee marriages.

It is interesting to note that it was a deliberate choice of the reformist leadership in China to adopt Western managerial ideas and then to adapt them to the local context. As one of the most authoritative voices on Chinese management explained, the four choices faced were:

> first, leave things unreformed; second, evolve new indigenous forms; third, straightforwardly adopt Western types of management; or fourth, adapt the latter more specifically to its own local environmental conditions, using Western knowledge to implement an evolutionary change process but within the context of Chinese values. They chose the fourth of these options; and in doing so, looked to their cultural roots.
>
> (Warner 2008b: 772)

In spite of subsequent significant achievements, the breakdown of the certainties in terms of work security, education and health provisions brought about by the impressive post-Mao reforms have not yet been satisfactorily resolved. The existence of millions of low-skilled agricultural workers, miners and public servants, and significant gender issues, are examples of formidable managerial challenges that face China (Cooke 2005, 2009; see also Chapters 1 and 3).

Leadership ideals of the Indian tradition

It has often been suggested that Indian leadership ideals have drawn heavily on spiritual–religious doctrines, in sharp contrast to their secular and pragmatic Chinese counterparts. This general view of the Indian heritage has, however, been vigorously refuted by many leading scholars (for example, Thapar 1990; Singh and Krishnan 2007; Basham 2007; Virmani 2007). Nobel Prize winning scholar, Amartya Sen, on the other hand provided systematic evidence to argue that analytical and rationality-based reasoning was at the core of Indian tradition. In his widely known work, *The Argumentative Indian*, Sen argued with copious and cogent evidence that the concepts of 'rationality', 'liberalism' and 'justice' had been the core of Indian heritage long before they became popular in the West (Sen 2005). His most significant evidence was that India had welcomed and absorbed leadership ideas from around the world over many centuries. Trade and commerce flourished with many nations, with international linkages refreshing ideas of social, business and public administration.

Ashoka, who is often considered the greatest and most idealistic Indian emperor, propagated democratic and inclusive leadership principles, in sharp contrast to the teachings of Confucius (Sen 2005). During his reign, pillars depicting moral and ethical precepts, behavioural codes, human and animal welfare, as well as wide-ranging managerial and leadership ideals were erected from Thailand in the east to Northern Afghanistan in the west of Asia. Inscriptions on these pillars emphasized universal human values of secularity and inclusiveness, within which the rights of women, tribal and marginal people as well as animals were enshrined, many centuries before they became popular in the West. Table 2.2 illustrates some of the important precepts and traditional belief systems underpinning Indian leadership frameworks.

Confirmatory evidence exists of the ancient Indian management system called '*sreni*' which was the main form of organization for business, the armed services, and local government (Thapar 1996). This system was based on occupational guilds and is arguably the earliest example of managerial leadership systems. *Sreni dharma* specified complex organizational structures and detailed rules guiding supervisors, managers, kings and emperors. It was based upon both philosophical and procedural foundations, and was widely employed during the Buddhist era of Indian history. *Sreni* required a general assembly of all organizational members which entrusted managerial leadership roles to the anointed leaders, called *Jetthaka*, *Pamukha* and *Sreshthi*. All of these appointments were merit-based, and the leaders were supported by cabinet-type teams of experts referred to as *Karya chintakh*. The concept of the legal authority of corporations was a sacred obligation, and managerial practices included the use of incentive pay, elected managerial leaders and a strong requirement for corporate loyalty. The most significant feature of the *Sreni dharma* was its democratic spirit and focus on training and development (Chatterjee 2009a: 270). *Sreni* ideals continued

Table 2.2 Cultural traditions and leadership frameworks in India

Precepts	*Tradition-anchored belief system*	*Leadership emphasis*
Human values	• Centrality of *dharma* and *Neeti* (Duty orientation) • Cosmocentrism (Acceptance of diversity) • *Loka Sangraha* (Obligation to society)	• Wisdom of virtue • *Shourya* (Courage) • Holistic concern
Social values	• *Nish Kam Karma* (Effort focus not outcome orientation) • Patronage (Personal loyalty) • Bond of *Sradha-sneha* (Respect and affection – residual colonialism)	• Paternalism • Nurturant • Social mission
Organizational values	• *Udyoga* (Entrepreneurship as a spiritual exercise) • *Seva* (Service)	• Long term • Rule orientation • Family culture

to be evident in the management of social organizations in India until the arrival of Islam around 1000 AD (Khanna 2005).

Indian value systems were developed and nurtured in a number of global universities in ancient India. Taxila University in the north and Nalanda in the east drew scholars and students from all over the world and particularly from China. As the oldest international university in the world, Taxila had on its faculty the greatest strategic thinker of the time, Kautilya (also known as Chanakya) as a professor. His book on public management entitled *Arthashastra* was written a thousand years before Machiavelli's *The Prince*, and provided detailed philosophies, tools and techniques guiding the management of all types of organizations. His idea of a complex bureaucratic model in which the welfare of all stakeholders was paramount underpinned many subsequent empires and continued for centuries. The first pan-Indian empire of Maurya enlisted Kautilya as its prime minister and he was thus able to translate his concepts into practice.

Nalanda University, which is currently being revived in order to reignite the spirit of Indian values (Buncombe 2010), became famous for its holistic ideas incorporating the diversity of traditions and its links with the great scholars of China and Southeast Asia. Such famous Chinese scholars as Fa Hsien, Xwan Zang and others have provided elaborate details of Nalanda university life including its dormitories, classrooms, libraries, faculties, course content, pedagogical methods and the beautiful buildings and gardens of the campus. Legendary Chinese scholar, Heiwn Tsang, went to Nalanda to study law and, after obtaining his Masters degree, served as its Vice President for almost 20 years.

The arrival of Islam from the tenth century AD together with multiple invasions and conquests by the Persians, Afghans and Turks significantly eroded these Indian traditions. Perhaps the only exception to this trend occurred during the rule of the great Mughal emperor Akhbar whose attempt to revive indigenous concepts saw renewal in the palimpsest of traditions. Over subsequent centuries, the pluralistic and community orientation gave rise to a culture of patronage. Many scholars claim that this system reflected a return to centralization and personality-based practices which reinforced the traditional bureaucratic structures within which managers at the lower echelons were unwilling to respond to their stakeholders (Sinha 1980; Sen 2005).

The subsequent British domination of Indian economic life for two centuries extracted a heavy price with respect to the demise of successful local industries and their subservience to colonial economic interests. As examples, the importation of cotton and silk from India was legally banned during the 1700s, and many laws unfavourable to the growth of local industries were later enacted. This legislation was accompanied by the importation of many Western managerial and leadership concepts both at national and institutional levels. It is interesting to note that the British colonial period also saw a continuance of many of the tradition-bound systems and practices (Basham 2007). The reliance on family, caste and trading compatriots survived colonialism and were evident in business houses after Independence. As examples, the houses of Tata, Birla and later Reliance (see Chapter 7 for further discussion) led the economic life of India until the period of economic liberalization and the global ambitions of Indian MNCs.

A new group of business role models, whose global visions and inspirational practices have been instrumental in the rise of India internationally, are transforming the Indian management landscape. Interestingly, this transformation derives mostly from visions founded on collective endeavours. A recent study of leadership in contemporary Indian business suggested that:

> the era of charismatic CEOs with personal brands and high profiles in the outside community stands in stark contrast to the India Way leaders who expect to be role models in their behavior for individual employees. These differences help explain why India Way companies focus on long-term customers because those relationships are at the heart of the organization, why they see themselves as extended families with mutual obligations, and why they bang away at hard, persistent challenges until they crack them.
>
> (Cappelli, Singh, Singh and Useem 2010: 206)

The new emerges from the old

The preceding sections of this chapter attempt to portray in broad societal terms a variety of influences from the cultural traditions of China and India. Most strikingly, these experiences not only reframe discussions about emerging trends in managerial leadership and human resource management models and practices in the two countries, but also the very purpose of management itself. Whilst such systems and practices continue to reflect contextual nuances, they increasingly also have relevance globally. This book explores the latter issue in considerable detail (see in particular Chapter 8). Long traditions of self-sufficient agricultural economy complemented by centralized rule and elite mandarin systems of public management ensured the continuity of the 'Chinese' (as opposed to the 'Indian') Way. A serious challenge to this tradition was mounted by Chairman Mao in 1955 through his collectivization of farming, and later in 1958 through China's expansion into the 'Great Leap Forward'. The Cultural Revolution unleashed during the 1960s attempted to demolish China's civilizational continuity and to generate a new ideology based primarily on Mao's Thoughts.

It is, therefore, instructive to note that the economic reform subsequently initiated by Deng Xiaoping aimed to reconnect with the 'Chinese way'. As Meredith (2007: 17) explained, 'China began its economic reforms not by building the factories and skyscrapers visitors marvel at today but by changing the countryside'. In contrast, the Indian village-based economy of self-sufficiency and anti-industrialization promoted by Gandhi during the freedom struggle with the British never became serious policy options for India. After four decades of planned quasi-socialism and serious suspicions of foreign direct investment (FDI), India is re-emerging as an economic power initiated by entrepreneurship and the global vision of corporate leaders. Despite the fact that the earliest stock market in Asia was in India in 1875, the government controlled price setting discouraged private companies from raising capital through such arbitrary and unfair price determinations. Since the 1991 reforms, Indian stock markets have played a significant role in economic resurgence.

The contrasting traditions of centralized control in China from the Han Dynasty in 200 BC and the heterodoxy and plurality tracing back to the Mauryan Empire in India have had significance in the leadership psyche of the two countries. The path for 'the new to emerge from the old' lies in the quest for 'mutualism' to develop in all spheres of economic, social and cultural life. As Khanna (2007: 7) astutely noted:

> The different paths taken by the two countries have another profound implication, only now becoming manifest: China and India together could have a stronger impact on each other and the world than either country could alone. What China is good at, India is not, and vice versa. The countries are inverted mirror images of each other. This complementarity creates grounds for an economic cooperation that has already begun, as native entrepreneurs tap into each other's backyards in a reprise of their long-term historical cooperation rather than their recent four decades of hostility. This mutualism is there for the world to benefit from, not only for native Chinese and Indians.

This concept of 'mutualism' which underpins aspirations of 'Chindia' (as discussed in detail in Chapter 1) would demand much deeper levels of harmonious relations and enlightened self-interest than those which currently exist in either country (Engardio 2007). The reality of such visions will likely be heavily dependent on the development of significant collaboration, trust and creative leadership in particular industrial sectors, rather than between the countries as a whole. The rise of the software industry in India, for example, illustrated traditional values and visions of India and has had beneficial effects for China. On the other hand, the relatively poor performance of the Indian textile industry in comparison with China has benefited neither. Interestingly, whilst this sector dates back to the pre-colonial era, and was then one of the most prosperous, India's share in the global export of textiles was approximately 4 per cent in 2010, compared to China's 40 per cent (Dhir 2011). Similarly, while the Chinese textile industry employed twenty million workers directly, and another hundred million indirectly during this period, Indian textile manufacturers have never employed more than half of this number (ibid.).

Earlier comments about the software and manufacturing sectors highlight the role of traditional legacies. While post-independence India promoted elitist concepts including a preference for investment in tertiary rather than primary or secondary education, communist ideological imperatives led China down a diametrically opposed path. More recent legacies have also had major but different effects in both countries. For example, the 'one child' policy in China is predicted to result in a shrinking future workforce (see Chapter 1 for further discussion) with the oldest population in the world by 2050, whilst India's 'demographic dividend' from its youthful workforce is of considerable competitive benefit

(Nankervis and Chatterjee 2011). These paradoxes are complicated by consideration of the comparative literacy rates in both countries. Thus, while India boasts of having the second largest university-trained labour market in the world after the US, estimated to generate more than half of the world's English-speaking engineers by 2050, its illiteracy rate of 34 per cent will be a significant barrier for its future competitiveness.

The emerging models of management and human resource management from China and India are designed in the 'hemispheric holism of imagination'. This holistic imagination allows strategies, processes and techniques that energize people and align resources to emerging opportunities and challenges. The synergy of systematically innovating new horizons of engagement in the external world, and at the same time shaping rapid performance improvement through the reform and readjustment of managerial mindsets in the internal world, provide the context of the search for this elusive model. The holistic imagination offers the possibility for the first time for corporate leaders to enhance the performance of their human and other resources, but through extensive employee participation. It demands designing platforms of performance within which responses to unexpected opportunities and challenges are built into the institutional architecture.

Implications of socio-cultural traditions for human resource management principles in China and India

The response to performance demand, generated by the economic and social reforms over the past several decades in China and India, has generated interest in exploring the models of success. It is surprising that the 'performance dividend' has been noticeable in all types of industries. The well known success of the product-based economy in China, as well as the impressive transformation of the knowledge-based service sector in India, are illustrative of this performance dividend. It can be argued that the traditional 'experience curve model' of performance improvement has been replaced by the 'participation curve', suggesting that with increasing numbers of trained employees (participants), there are significant individual (and collective) performance improvements. The recognition that work motivation may have a strong collective underpinning is in stark contrast to the individual 'hierarchy of needs' espoused by Maslow (1968). The debate on the applicability of Maslow's hypothesis to the collectivist cultural contexts of countries such as China or India has been unresolved for decades (see, for example, Wabba and Bridgewell 1976; Cianti and Grambel 2003). Some evidence from both countries on the effect of the 'participation curve' questions the context-neutrality of societies, organizations and human resource management systems implicit in the individual-organizational interface. Denial of autonomy and holistic choices to individual workers implicit in the Maslow framework are in sharp contrast to the realities of post-reform work organizations in China and India. The theory that organizational performance is a simple aggregation of individual performance has become untenable as it ignores the complex traditions of these two countries and the consequent role of holistic human resource synergy.

In contesting Maslow's framework, Sharma (2007) presented an alternative model drawn from the Indian tradition, His 'Basket Model' provided choices and contextual anchors not present in the mainstream theories originating in the Western context (Sharma 1996, 2007). Sharma also introduced the dynamic element of how needs are expressed through human interactions called 'needs intensity'. He contended that, 'in the context of organizations, different types of needs find their expression in different forms. For example, psychological and sociological needs find their expression in the formation of formal and informal groups. Further, political needs find their expression in decision-making processes' (Sharma 1996: 103). In essence, the experiences of China and India demonstrate a very complex and multi-dimensional underpinning to human resource management. Figure 2.1 draws on a number of seminal ideas from China and India and suggests a modified form of the 'basket' approach in conceptualizing 'human resource synergy' as the most critical element in responding to the macro-level reform and global relevance.

The model outlines the six key needs that underpin work-related motivation in the workplace. Needs such as physiological, instrumental and relational forces have been recognized universally, but the three other needs in the 'basket' which impact significantly are the 'subjective space need', learning and developmental needs and spiritual needs.

In an empirical survey of Asian managers in ten countries (including China and India), the learning and development need was identified as the primary goal across all countries and all demographic levels, with the minor exception of female managers between the ages of 30–40 in Malaysia (Chatterjee and Pearson 2006).

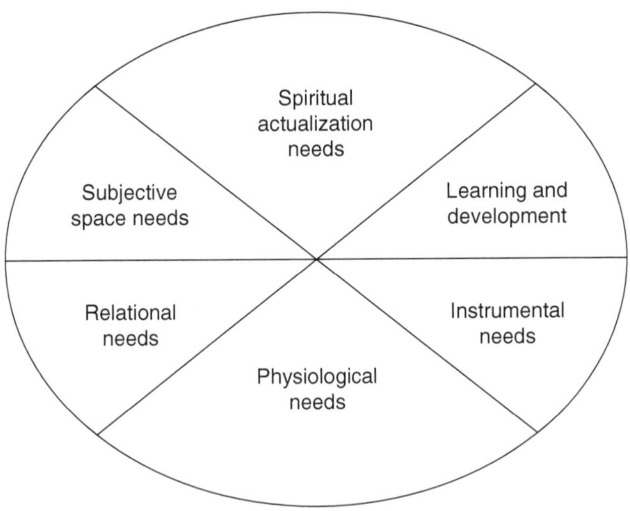

Figure 2.1 The human resource 'needs basket' model.

Source: Modified and extended from seminal ideas of S. Sharma, 1996: 103.

The subjective space need is another important component underpinning the cultural context which is expressed through employees' identity needs. Employees' ideas about themselves are significantly shaped by the cultural context and the resulting need for identity changes from organization to organization as well as across demographies and subcultures (Knippenberg *et al.* 2004; Gao *et al.* 2011). In spite of considerable convergence occurring in the workplace roles, the performance experience is inevitably situated within a culture and the need for a craving for a holistic identity defines this experience (Nankervis, Chatterjee and Coffey 2006). As has been suggested, Indians are, according to this view, sociocentric as opposed to egocentric, which is to say that they ostensibly place community and family interests at the centre of their universe rather than the individual, in contrast to the West. The need for the subjective domain to construct an identity is interlinked to the 'collective belongingness'. Deriving personal meaning in a work context requires embedding oneself in a network of relationships. It can be suggested that individual achievement, autonomy and choice coexist in workplace settings, thus demonstrating a curious cross-verging trend (Knippenberg *et al.* 2004; Luyckx, Vansteenkiste, Gossens and Duriez 2009).

The sixth element of the Basket Model focuses on the non-material domains guiding work- related engagement. As pointed out in the opening section of this chapter, the search for harmony between traditional and global work roles remains a powerful item for both Chinese and Indian employees. Both Chinese and Indian heritages highlight one's spiritual connection to work rather than mere performance. The employee organizational linkage has witnessed a quantum shift over the past three decades. The transformation created by the pressures of global integration, the relentless redesign of work roles, as well as environmental sustainability, is profoundly affecting both identity and performance (Giacalone and Jurkiewicz 2003). The Basket Model suggests that workers are frequently searching for a 'purpose' in their employment. As employees spend increasing amounts of their time at the workplace, the traditional sources of inner fulfilment through faith and religion have been replaced by their work organizations.

Human resource management (HRM) is generally considered a 'Western' paradigm which underpins employee contributions at the workplace from the perspectives of 'outside in' where forced systems, structures and procedures dominate. The spiritual domain has the potential to enlarge autonomy by the experience of 'inside out' that is consistent with Chinese and Indian cultures and traditions. There are many organizations from China and India in which values and mission statements act as the mobilizing factor, encouraging their employees to engage purposefully (Gupta and Wang 2009c; Kumar 2009; Kim *et al.* 2010; also see Chapter 7). These companies have successfully deployed and managed large cohorts of employees in delivering increasing value-driven performance. Li, Tsui and Weldon (2000), for example, reported on a virtual organization design and production network in China with 10,000 global partners.

In India, Infosys mastered the HRM architecture, as they were able to 'hire, train and deploy hundreds of programmers in an unfamiliar site and in an unfamiliar country (very) quickly. Certainly it is faster than any non-Indian multi-national operating in India and possibly faster than its leading Indian rivals' (Khanna 2007: 126). The building of this HRM architecture was only made possible through the superimposition of a socially-inclusive purpose linking the messages – 'a better Infosys leads to a better India' and 'a better India produces a better world' (Murthy 2009).

The need for clarity of purpose and cohesion is indeed critical in a global business delivery model requiring fast turnaround with many employees from diverse countries and cultures operating in different locations. The overall orientation to the unique values that drive Infosys (for example) is reinforced to global recruits at a training facility termed the 'Taj Mahal of Training Centres' by *Fortune* magazine. The training infrastructure which Infosys provides for global and Indian recruits includes

> … two helipads, a professional grade cricket stadium, an employee centre with a laundromat, a medical centre, supermarket, bank, book store, hair salon, movie theatres, basketball, tennis, badminton and squash courts, an 8 lane Brunswick bowling alley, snooker tables, yoga classrooms, meditation rooms, a steam bath and a swimming pool. The training facility has 10,000 rooms, 250 classrooms and several large and small conference halls.
>
> (Subramaniam, Misra, Jayachandra and Singh 2008: 257)

Such examples represent an amalgam of Western HRM practices (for example, Microsoft, HP) with traditional Indian paternalistic influences.

Similar examples of the pervasive influences of cultural traditions can also be observed in the Chinese Internet company Alibaba. The growth of the Alibaba group from its humble beginnings to a multinational organization can without doubt be attributed to its strong emphasis on people and values. In addition, a willingness to embrace change, a passion for innovation, and a commitment to company culture are some of the essential requirements for its new recruits (see also Chapters 5 and 6). Many commentators have expressed their surprise about the way in which these values have been woven into the fabric of the Alibaba group in its recruitment, motivation, evaluation, promotion and rewards systems (Liu 2010). Taobao, a fully-owned Alibaba company explicitly adopted the mystical weapons of the iconic martial arts novels. These weapons called the 'divine sword of six vines' are customer first, team work, embracing change, enthusiasm, integrity and dedication. Both employees and customers identified with the characters of the novels by Master Jing (Einhorn *et al.* 2009: 49–50).

The 22,000 employees of Alibaba in 70 cities and regions are recruited, nurtured and inspired by constant reminders of their roles and responsibilities. The well-publicized requirements for people to be successful at Alibaba are intimately connected to the corporate vision and work culture. The key human resource characteristics are reportedly driven by 'dreams', a willingness to share values, energy and above all team orientation.

The corporate vision of the work environment highlights openness and transparency (blue sky), society-focused (solid ground), the encouragement of organizational expertise over functional specialization (free flowing ocean), innovation driven (green forest) and the ability to engage others in organizations to share values (harmonious community) (Williamson and Zheng 2009). The latter element chimes with the Chinese government's espoused 'harmonious society' imperatives (see Chapters 1 and 3). Interestingly, the philosophy of focusing on employees, innovation, learning and values in serving customers, are inevitably the driving force of the new age companies in both China and India (Nayar 2010).

Conceptualizing a new frame of reference of HRM originating from Chinese and Indian experiences can only begin with the recognition that energizing human creativity in organizations is a contextually-based challenge. The role of knowledge and complexity of the product, process or service may vary in significance, but they need to be in line with the characteristics of the human capital. For example, the concept of the India Way espoused by Cappelli *et al.* (2010); or the *hè-hè* (和-和) philosophy of HRM advocated by Huang (2010); demonstrate powerful frameworks. As has been noted,

> the essence of *hè-hè* (和-和) philosophies is peace and harmony, an exploration of the balance between nature, society, human relations, the inner being and civilization. It is the quest for continually perfecting process, the pursuit to define what is good and what is bad, and the research into its standard.
>
> (Huang 2008: 8)

Political leaders in China often claim the combination of harmony and holism as a Chinese innovation. For example, former vice-chairman of the National People's Congress, Cheng Siywan, contended that

> … we define harmony as the co-existence of heterogeneous factors, while 'unity' refers to the fusion of such heterogeneous factors. The combination of 'harmony' and 'unity' emphasizes the complementarity and cohesion of different beings. This is a representation of the dialectic and systemic philosophy of the Chinese nation.
>
> (Huang 2008: 10)

Perhaps this can be categorized as a high involvement, trust-centred human resource model, as evident in companies like the Alibaba group and others in China, and Infosys and others in India. These companies use a series of practices that develop the special bonding of individuals and their organizations through training, teamwork, strategic imagination, participation, empowerment, wellness programmes and other such initiatives.

It has been suggested in a number of HRM research studies that traditional Chinese culture acts as a double-edged sword with regard to teamwork (Chen and Francesco 2000; Goodall *et al.* 2006; Wang, Yi, Lawler and Zhang 2011; Warner 2011a). Such contradictions arise because on the one hand the cultural imperatives like *guānxì* (关系) and harmony may foster teamwork for a broad and overall corporate purpose, on the other hand 'the Confucian emphasis on rigid social hierarchy and upward deference to leaders encourages a top-down control and creates a strong barrier to teamwork' (Wang *et al.* 2011: 2435). This interpretation, that a culturally specified cohesion can work as a double-edged sword, may not reflect the overall societal force that provided team velocity. It is not the dichotomous but a trichotomous worldview between two contradictory opposites through which an intermediate perspective can be located. Chinese tradition contends that without this intermediary, stability and harmony cannot be established. The Confucian precept argues that

> … people observe rites and institutions, accept their status in the family and societal hierarchy, and obey power and authority for the sake of social harmony. The past two thousand years of development in China have been realized and sustained by traditional *hè-hè* (和-和) philosophy, which can still give a valuable inspiration today.
>
> (Huang 2008: 9)

New HRM frameworks for China and India?

Asia's decline in its share of global GDP over many centuries, and its current resurgence, have profound implications for the ways in which human resource capabilities are being harnessed. As evidence, Asia's contribution to 'global' GDP in the first century AD was 76.3 per cent, by 1000 AD it had declined to 70.3 per cent, by the year 2000 it was only 37.2 per cent; and yet by 2010 China and India's collective contribution to global GDP was greater than that of Japan. As Mahbubani (2008: 51) pointed out, 'for the vast majority of recorded history, Asia, with the greatest share of the world's population has had the greatest share of the world's economy'. Such economic indicators may reflect the contemporary resurgence of China and India, but it is the extent to which their progress is shared which will make the journey sustainable. China's success in integrating its human resources from both rural and urban areas began with Mao, who instilled a sense of pride and inclusiveness amongst the peasants. This strategy assisted the post-Mao reformers to engage with a broader range of the rural population. India, on the other hand, has been much slower in drawing from a larger labour pool on account of its tradition-bound mindsets and associated practices such as the caste system and the barriers of poverty. With respect to the latter, perceptions of the poor in the minds of Indian corporate leaders are changing as a new generation of ethically-empowered and competent managers devote organizational resources towards broad social responsibility imperatives (see Chapter 7 for some specific examples). Some recent empirical research investigating the effects of social responsibility in Chinese companies has suggested that linking HRM practices to broader social concerns can generate greater organizational commitment and effectiveness (Shen and Zhu 2011).

The diffusion of the benefits of corporate growth more widely, through poverty alleviation and economic engagement, needs to be compatible with the principle of merit. Merit was inherent in the Chinese national examination for senior bureaucratic positions based on Confucian principles, as it was in the Indian civil service examination introduced under British rule. Contemporary entry to elite universities in China and India is as competitive as to Western universities such as Harvard, Oxford and Cambridge. The recruitment process for applicants to the top Chinese and Indian companies is no less competitive. The merit-based selection procedures of GE, IBM and McKinsey are comparable to those employed by Chinese and Indian corporations such as Lenovo, Infosys, Tata and Huawei (see Chapter 7). Emphases on merit, cultural sensitivity and a deep connection to society, call for a new cadre of managers with a cross-verging mindset of 'inner coherence'. As Kase, Slocum and Zhang have suggested:

> it still seems unrealistic that a simplified universalistic management model such as the American model will be able to dominate the globalizing business world, even though it is still gaining market share. The Japanese management and the emerging Chinese management .... demonstrate this divergent way of viewing the managerial world.
>
> (Kase *et al.* 2011: 147)

The argument espoused in their book is not merely that the universalistic perspective of HRM is no longer tenable, but also that nation-based paradigms lack robustness. As human resource practices become more globally diverse and a wider range of local concepts gain acceptance internationally, mutual learning through frequent interactions becomes an imperative for success in the global arena.

It is interesting to note that most corporations from China and India depend upon highly abstract general goals in creating a 'world view' for managers and their employees, based upon work as a cohesive relationship between individual employees and their work groups. The basic design and control philosophy of traditional Western organizations with underlying aspirations of continuous growth and profit may not be as powerful in harnessing human capital within culture-bound contexts. Chinese and Indian companies, on the other hand, are well-placed to leverage their traditional heritages in order to design alternative HRM models to those rooted in industrial organizations of previous centuries. These issues are discussed in more detail in subsequent chapters, and particularly in Chapter 8.

Conclusion

Fifty years of tension and distrust following the border war of 1962 between China and India after two thousand years of mutual learning, are being assuaged by a resurgence of commercial relationships in recent years. In addition, a number of global companies have been actively facilitating this mutuality by investing significantly in building a strong synergy between these two neighbouring countries. For example, GE has been a success story by synergistically using Indian software talents through intelligent recruitment methods as well as obtaining a unique cohort of hardware engineers in China. Innovative healthcare equipment is created in Bangalore but assembled in China. The human resource advantage to GE through this use of parallel groups of talents is unique.

This resurgence of traditional synergies and of the capacity to re-engage with each other is a challenge that needs a new beginning. The insular experience of China, together with foreign dominance and socialistic experimentations in India over the past century, have tipped the trajectories of these countries in diverging directions. The embracing of new capacities for engaging in each other's cultures and traditions may well define how corporate strategies, and in particular HRM practices, may emerge. The end result of the powerful process of mutual learning began through entrepreneurs and corporate leaders, but this needs a wider diffusion. While China has closed the educational gap with the West in a significant way, India has not been as strategic in this area. While China has more than 20 universities in the world's top 500, India only has one. English language and information technology, skills where India previously had an advantage, are now key priorities for Chinese leaders with the provision of remarkable power and telecommunications infrastructures (see Chapter 1 for further discussion of these issues).

Deng Xiaoping summarized this process of mutual resurgence in his famous seven point wisdom principles. These may explain many of the developments guiding the management and HRM perspectives of ancient virtues. The traditional virtues of partnership and pragmatism were summarized as follows:

1 *Lěngjìng guānchá* (冷静观察): Calm observation, analysis and reflection of issues
2 *Chénzhuó yìngfu* (沉着应付): Acceptance of and responding to changes with a systematic and confident approach
3 *Wěn zhù zhèn jiǎo jué* (稳住阵): Ensure that conformity with the Chinese way is maintained
4 *Tāoguāngyǎnghuì* (韬光养晦): The practice of humility in developing capabilities and expertise
5 *Sshànyú shǒuzhuō* (善于守拙): Maintaining a focus on the challenges rather than assuming a higher profile
6 *Juébù dītóu* (决不低头): Avoid the limelight and false glorification
7 *Yǒusuǒ zuòwéi* (有所作为): Engage in disciplined work to achieve goals (Mahbubani 2008).

These principles are in stark contrast to the relatively simpler 'bottom line' imperatives of some Western organizations. When leaders highlight a higher meaning in work, a sense of community and perceived social cohesion, organizations reflect a more spiritual focus (McKenna *et al.* 2009). Deng Xiaoping's call for an emphasis on holistic imperatives rather than a reliance on micro-level analytical and objective thinking underlines such ideas, and influences the psychological climate and individual performance (Nisbett *et al.* 2001). More broadly, the ontological origins of Indian and Chinese thoughts are fundamentally divergent from the Western traditions inherited from Plato and Aristotle.

Like the service of the monks in ancient Buddhist temples, which required long apprenticeships, the collaborative synergies need to be carefully studied. The Buddhist monks entered the monasteries with permission from their parents and were entrusted with duties as they gradually progressed not only through their internships and wise mentoring, but also by meticulous study of the scriptures and the rigorous practice of rituals and observances. A dedicated commitment to a higher cause ensured their attainment of priesthood and freedom of movement across monasteries and the holding of senior positions. The following chapters explore the implications of these cultural and spiritual traditions on the design and implementation of HRM systems in a range of organizations in China and India.

3 Human resource management in transition

Introduction

The transformation of the economic policy and structure in China and India since the 1980s coincides with the advent of the concept of human resource management (HRM) in the American–Anglo context and the ensuing development and promotion of a wide range of HRM techniques across the world. Both countries have been going through a period of internationalization and modernization, although the process and speed vary across different industrial sectors and ownership forms. The need to improve productivity in light of the rise of young and relatively more competitive private sectors has forced their public sectors to make radical changes and implement new HRM practices which depart significantly from those in their former centralized economies. As discussed in Chapter 1, the changing demographic profile of their labour markets; and the different cultural values, career aspirations and workplace expectations compared with the older employees; add further pressure on employers to adopt HRM practices in order to attract and retain young talent. These issues are discussed in more detail in Chapter 5.

In this chapter, we examine the extent to which changes have taken place in the approaches to people management in India and China. By reviewing empirical studies, we identify the types of (Western) HRM practices that are considered effective in the oriental context, as well as the similarities and differences between HRM systems in China and India. We also present the perceptions of different groups of employees on these HRM practices and assess the varying impacts on their organizational commitment and engagement.

Transitions towards a strategic approach to HRM

In the previous chapters and the chapters that follow, we highlight the demographic changes in the labour markets in China and India. We also observe major changes in the business environment in which firms have to compete in the post state-planned era. Given these significant changes and the challenges to talent management, are Indian and Chinese firms becoming more strategic in managing their human resources? Are we witnessing a level of convergence of HRM practices in these indigenous firms towards more Western-styled HRM practices?

Earlier studies of Chinese firms found that they tended to be less strategic than their Western counterparts in their approach to HRM (e.g. Warner 1993; Child 1994). As the competition for talent has intensified, some Chinese firms are reported to have become more strategic in linking their HRM practices to organizational performance (e.g. Law *et al.* 2003; Wei and Lau 2005; Zhu *et al.* 2005; Wang *et al.* 2007). Many are now more market-oriented, with growing evidence of the adaptation of Western HRM techniques (e.g. Ding and Akhtar 2001; Zhu and Dowling 2002; Cooke 2012a). Some of these companies and their HRM systems are discussed in further detail in Chapter 7.

Studies by Wei and Lau (2005) and Wang *et al.* (2007) found that the differences in key HRM practices amongst firms of different ownership forms in China are diminishing, indicating a trend towards convergence in the HRM practices adopted by foreign-invested and Chinese owned firms. There is a continuing trend away from traditional Chinese HRM practices towards Western-styled HRM practices, and the gaps in the HR competence between Chinese owned private firms and MNCs are closing. According to Wang *et al.* (2007: 699), '[t]he pattern of the organizational goals and HR practices linkage reflects that private-owned enterprises are more aggressively utilizing their HR functions to accomplish their organizational goals'. This is in spite of the fact that they have adopted fewer high performance HRM practices than the foreign-invested companies.

In India, the opening up of the economy since 1991 has led to the dramatic rise of a number of privately owned Indian firms that have been growing into globally competitive MNCs. Meanwhile, heightened market competition has resulted in public sector enterprises restructuring their organizations and reconfiguring their business strategies (e.g. Khanna 2007; Som 2007). This requires new ways of managing their human resources. Som (2007), for example, argued that heightened competition due to liberalization has forced Indian firms to adopt HRM practices which foster creativity and innovation among employees. A major HR challenge widely observed has been the shortage of skilled/professional workforce and their high attrition rate, particularly in the BPO (business process outsourcing) industry (e.g. Budhwar 2009; Kuruvilla and Ranganathan 2010; Stumpf *et al.* 2010). Firms are increasingly involved in the 'war for talent', as discussed further in Chapter 5. According to Stumpf *et al.* (2010), the rapid growth of the BPO sector has in part contributed to the sharp rise in wages in India, estimated as more than 15 per cent annually between 2002 and 2007. Despite this, companies are encountering an attrition rate of 15–30 per cent amongst young professionals.

A number of HR techniques, such as performance management, training and development, diversity management and employee recognition, have been implemented by some Indian companies as key HR initiatives to attract and retain talent (Bhatnagar 2007a – see also Chapter 6). As Singh (2003) observed, there has been a growing awareness of the importance of HRM as a key driver of business performance in India. Similarly, Lange *et al.*'s (2010: 2439) study found that intrinsic job rewards are playing an increasingly significant role in HRM in the liberalized Indian economy, with greater emphasis on satisfying individual employees' ambitions, needs and aspirations.

Based on the growing body of empirical evidence discussed here and elsewhere (e.g. Budhwar and Bhatnagar 2009; Warner 2011c), it might be argued that HRM practices in India and China are, in general, becoming more mature, systematic, relevant to organizational needs and reflective of contemporary labour market conditions. Illustrations of such practices include the adoption of more sophisticated recruitment methods such as assessment centres and psychometric tests; the introduction of mentoring and coaching schemes; and the use of performance management systems and employee financial participation, as a high performance, but not necessarily a high commitment, model of HRM. In addition, there is some evidence that well performing domestic private firms in both countries are adopting decision making HRM practices (e.g. Ding *et al.* 2001; Bhatnagar 2007a; Ngo *et al.* 2008). Here, the ability of firms to understand and align their HR strategy with the employees' expectations appears to be a crucial factor in managing talent effectively.

The apparent increasing incidence of the adoption of Western-styled HRM practices and the development of HR competence in China and India, especially in globally-oriented firms, have been facilitated by a number of institutional actors, including but not restricted to the state, trade unions and employer associations, at both the national and local levels. The new economic and labour market environments have also incorporated new actors, for instance, employment agencies and HR consultancy firms, and new roles for the traditional actors. They play varying and at times overlapping roles within their respective national institutional frameworks.

It is interesting to note that there are considerable differences in the level of state power and, relatedly, the level of market openness for HR professional associations and consultancy businesses in the two countries. For example, in China the state continues to play a central role in facilitating the adoption of specific HR initiatives that are informed by the ideological values that the state seeks to promote, namely, to build a knowledge workforce and a harmonious society. They are also designed to meet the needs which have arisen from the evolution of the economic model. These new forms of interventions, both hard and soft, are designed to fulfil the state's continuing role. That is: to foster unity, to promote national economic and social development and stability, and to redistribute wealth. In spite of the opening up of the market, it was not until the early 2000s that foreign funded employment agencies and HR consultancy firms were allowed to operate independently without a Chinese business partner (often in the form of joint ventures). This has to some extent restricted the level of importation of Western HRM practices.

By contrast, in India the inability of the state to take actions to improve employment environments and workplace practices appears to be a key feature (see Chapter 4 for a more detailed discussion of these factors). Nevertheless, the limited state intervention has given other institutional actors more scope to operate. Foreign owned as well as indigenous HR consultancy firms are highly active in the Indian market. Compared with China, India also appears to have much more developed HR professional associations, such as the HRD Networks, and industry-based employers' associations, such as NASSCOM (National Association of Software and Services Companies) (India's association of software and service providers). These institutional actors play a crucial role in disseminating HRM practices and sharing knowledge. For example, NASSCOM has been instrumental in surveying HRM practices, highlighting problems and disseminating good practices in the IT-based BPO industry. Some of the best practices adopted by indigenous small and medium sized BPO firms in performance and career management are so cutting edge that they are setting standards even for firms from developed economies (Stumpf *et al.* 2010, also see Chapter 6).

It is important to note that enthusiasm in embracing Western-styled HRM initiatives for strategic people management is not yet widespread amongst indigenous firms. This is particularly the case in smaller private businesses (e.g. Saini and Budhwar 2008; Cooke 2012a). For those that are adopting Western-originated HRM initiatives, the key questions to ask are: do Western-derived HRM practices have any impact on organizational performance in the Indian and Chinese context? And do they have a uniform impact across different groups of employees in different types of firms and business sectors? We address these issues in the following sections.

HRM practices and organizational performance in the Chinese and Indian contexts

Proponents of high performance/commitment models of HRM have argued that recruiting competent employees, providing them with training and career development opportunities, extensive employee involvement in decision making and high levels of reward incentives are considered to be the key HRM practices in enhancing organizational performance. These Western-developed theories and empirical studies have been applied and extended to the Asian context in the last decade (e.g. Lawler *et al.* 2000; Singh 2003).

Indeed, a growing number of studies have found a positive relationship between various types of HRM practices and enhanced HR outcomes, such as increased motivation, job satisfaction, commitment, organizational citizenship behaviour and reduced turnover intent in the Chinese context. For example, Lam *et al.*'s (2009) survey study of a Sino-Japanese joint venture in China found that retention oriented compensation and formalized training were positively related to organizational citizenship behaviour which in turn discourages job quit intent. Similarly, Akhtar *et al.*'s (2008: 15) study of professional and managerial employees identified 'a valid set of strategic HRM practices (training, participation, results-oriented appraisals, and internal career opportunities)' which 'affect both product/service performance and financial performance'. In addition, they found that employment security and job descriptions contribute uniquely to product/service performance but not financial performance, whereas profit sharing contributes uniquely to financial performance but not product/service performance or new product development (Akhtar *et al.* 2008). A possible explanation is that managers are more motivated by short term financial gains and behave accordingly at the expense of the long-term development of the organization. Based on their research evidence, Akhtar *et al.* (2008: 15) regarded these practices as 'the "core" of strategic HRM in Chinese enterprises because they are common in explaining variance in the two performance indices'.

Akhtar *et al.*'s (2008) findings were supported by those of Zhang and Li (2009) who investigated the relationship between high performance work practices and firm performance in a number of pharmaceutical companies in China. They found that high performance HRM practices as prescribed in Western HRM literature such as extensive training, employee participation, detailed job definition, results-oriented performance appraisal, career opportunities and profit sharing were significantly related to a firm's market performance. Equally, Qiao *et al.*'s (2009: 2326) survey study of 1,176 employees in six manufacturing firms in two cities showed that the perceived existence of a high performance work system was positively correlated to organizational commitment.

In their study of 241 firms in southern China in order to 'identify unique patterns of HR practices and business strategy that are posited to be maximally effective', Chow *et al.* (2008: 687) found that 'HR configurations are significantly related to effect in predicting overall outcome performance and turnover, but not significantly related to effect on sales growth and profit growth rates'. In addition, their study found that 'a commitment HR configuration (i.e. investment in training and development, opportunity for internal career progression), compared with other HR configurations, has a significantly positive effect' (Chow *et al.* 2008: 702). In one of the few studies on psychological contract of 200 senior executives in China, Bao *et al.* (2011: 3373) found that 'a violation of psychological contracts for Chinese executives has a strong negative relationship with organizational commitment'.

Similarly, the growing number of studies on HRM practices in India not only reveal a number of common characteristics, but also highlight the relevance of strategic HRM in enhancing organizational performance. For example, Budhwar and Khatri's (2001) study found that while Indian organizations have a unique internal labour market that is based on social relations, political contacts, caste, religion and economic power, there is evidence that private firms are beginning to focus on competence and performance in their HRM policies. Singh's (2003) study revealed that firms with strategic HR orientation perform significantly better than those with a lower HR emphasis. Paul and Anantharaman's (2003) study of Indian firms in the IT industry showed that training, job design, compensation and incentives have a direct impact on operational performance outcomes such as employee retention, employee productivity, product quality, speed of delivery and operating cost.

Chand's (2010) study of the Indian hotel industry showed that good HRM practices have positive impact on service quality which leads to enhanced customer satisfaction and hotel performance. Tymon *et al.*'s (2010a) study of over 4,000 professional employees in the BPO sector showed that the intrinsic rewards experienced were critical to employee retention, satisfaction with the organization, and career success. Key elements of the intrinsic rewards include the social responsibility of the employer, pride in the organization, manager support and performance management. Other studies highlight the importance of organizational climate on employees' psychological well-being and organizational commitment. For example, Bhatnagar's (2007b) study found that within a psychologically empowering climate, the strategic role of HR facilitates organizational learning capabilities, which leads to higher organizational commitment.

Biswas and Varma's (2007) survey study of firms in both public and private sectors in India revealed that individuals' perception of the psychological climate in the organization has a significant positive impact on their willingness to engage in organizational citizenship behaviour, as well as on their job satisfaction levels. Further, organizational citizenship behaviour and job satisfaction levels have a significant impact on individuals' performance. Biswas and Varma's (2007: 664) findings suggest that 'Indian organizations need to pay attention to employee perceptions of the work environment, and that human resource strategies should go beyond establishing policies and procedures to fostering an employee-friendly work environment that promotes both in-role and extra-role performance'.

A consensus from these studies in the Indian and Chinese contexts is that strategic HRM does contribute to enhanced employee commitment to, and behaviour towards, the organization and ultimately organizational performance. There is clear evidence that firms that adopt good HRM practices benefit from doing so. As Law *et al.* (2003: 263) argued, 'good HRM does matter to firm performance in a transitional economy'. This is suggestive of two possibilities. One is that there is a relatively high level of universality of SHRM as a guiding principle, though specific practices, their function and impact may differ according to societal and organizational contexts (Kim and Bae 2005). Another possibility is that there are stronger external HR attributions in the Asian countries which share a collectivistic culture (e.g. Japan, South Korea, China and India) than in countries characterized with individualistic cultures (e.g. Nishii *et al.* 2008). In addition, it may so happen that these Asian nations with a collectivistic culture are under great pressure to catch up as latecomer global economic players (e.g. India and China) or to maintain competitive edge (e.g. Japan and South Korea). Therefore, the perceived need to respond to external pressure is so paramount that employees are more ready to accept HRM practices as a progressive given and adapt their attitudes and behaviours towards the organizational goals accordingly (Nishii *et al.* 2008).

Context matters in HRM

The adoption of high performance/commitment-oriented HRM practices by firms in India and China is undertaken in a vastly different social, economic and cultural context than that found in the United States, where the notion of high performance work system (HPWS) and many of the related HRM initiatives emerged. As Appelbaum and Batt (1994) observed, the HPWS concept emerged in the late 1980s as an alternative production system to the Tayloristic mass production system in the manufacturing sector in the capitalist United States against the backdrop of heightened global competition and the discovery of the perceived competitive advantage created by Japanese management techniques. Job security, empowerment, autonomous teamwork and group-based rewards are seen as some of the most powerful practices for an HPWS.

By contrast, state owned and collectively owned Chinese firms were forced to move away, since the late 1980s, from the state socialist personnel system that was characterized by employment security and extensive welfare, in order to compete in the market. Their company history and management styles are fundamentally different from those of the private firms that have primarily emerged since the 1980s following the opening up of the economy. Similarly, Indian state sector firms have been highly protected and are now having to compete (to some extent) with the newly emerged private firms that are more strategic, performance driven and without the legacies and constraints of the state sector (Cooke and Saini 2010b). Despite major organizational changes, key characteristics that define public sector firms may persist, albeit continuously diluted by market forces. These differences, compounded with industrial and regional factors, influence the types of HRM practices that are adopted, the way they are implemented and the perceived outcomes.

Influences of ownership forms and industrial sector in HRM practices

Differences in HRM practices specific to ownership and sectoral forms have been observed in studies in the Indian context (e.g. Budhwar *et al.* 2006). For example, Budhwar and Boyne (2004) found that while the public and private sector firms share some similarities in their HRM function and practices, there are also key differences amongst them in compensation, and training and development. In comparison, private firms have adopted a more rational and systematic approach to HRM (e.g. formal assessment in recruitment, job evaluation, training needs analysis, training evaluation and performance-related pay) than their public sector counterparts.

Similarly, Shrivastava and Purang's (2011) study of the Indian banking industry revealed the continuing constraints of the public sector which can neither lay off poor performing employees, nor increase the salary of good performers for recruitment and retention purposes. By contrast, private banks have made significant progress in a short period of time, adopted aggressive strategies and become highly competitive. In particular, Shrivastava and Purang's (2011) study showed that employees in the private sector banks expressed a higher level of satisfaction with their performance appraisal system than their public sector counterparts. The former perceived their appraisal system to be fairer than the latter on a number of factors, including: 'raters' knowledge to conduct the process', 'well set and explained performance expectations', 'accurate ratings and well-explicated rating decisions', 'constructive feedback' and a 'well-placed appeal system' (Shrivastava and Purang 2011: 644). Kumar's (2005) study of the banking industry also found that the organizational climate of new privately owned and foreign owned banks in India is perceived as significantly better than that in the public sector banks.

The difference is seen on a number of HRM aspects including: leadership, communication, motivation, decision making, goal setting and control process.

Stumpf *et al.*'s (2010: 367) study of 'the role of HR practices for individual and organizational success via a survey of 4,811 employees from 32 units of 28 companies operating in India' revealed that Indian owned firms are using professional development more strategically to enhance employee performance than foreign owned firms. The same study also found 'a stronger relationship between performance management and career success in service firms than in manufacturing or IT', suggesting that services firms may be more sophisticated in their deployment of HRM practices (Stumpf *et al.* 2010: 367). Nevertheless, Stumpf *et al.* (2010: 367) concluded from their study that 'there is not a consistent, simple pattern of effects of HR practices across geographic footprints or industry sectors'.

Taylor *et al.*'s (2011: 15) study of the experience of work of workers in the Indian call centres that serve the domestic market found that 'India's domestic sector is distinct from its offshore counterpart in important respects', mainly because of the difference in client base. The domestic sector relies primarily on the newly emerged Indian middle class and the revenue margins 'are significantly lower than that in international operations' (Taylor *et al.* 2011: 15). This translates into 'lower salaries and inferior conditions and the extension of working hours are the outcomes' (Taylor *et al.* 2011: 15). Worse still, authoritarian management styles, a lack of autonomy and denial of employee voice and representation are common characteristics amongst the smaller domestic call centres, where a higher proportion of female workers are employed, than those operating in the international market.

Amongst all industries, the IT and BPO industries have perhaps presented the most serious HR challenge and attracted the most research attention in India. The IT and BPO industries have risen in India in the last two decades as the leading industries that drive the Indian economy. Many firms in these sectors have become major global players and are presenting challenges to well-established MNCs from the Western economies. The explosive growth of these two industries also triggers severe skill shortages and retention problems. Empirical studies on these two industries have identified a common set of HR challenges including a shortage of IT professionals with a sufficient level of skills and competence, managing globally distributed teams, poor HR systems and processes, lack of commitment, high staff turnover rate and problems associated with the deployment of contract staff. Monotonous job design, absence of work–life balance and a lack of training and development opportunities are the major causes of attrition (e.g. Mathew and Ogbonna 2009; Holtbrügge *et al.* 2010; Stumpf *et al.* 2010; Agrawal *et al.* 2011; Sengupta and Gupta 2011). Krishnan and Singh's (2010: 433) study found that employees who lack engagement with the organization tend to spend a long time in the café, update their CV in working hours, 'networking actively outside the workplace for possible openings, providing information to newcomers to the organization/team that may not be motivating, and spending more time on self development'.

In China, research evidence shows that, compared with their counterparts operating in the labour intensive sector, MNCs in the high-tech sector are far more proactive and developed in their HRM initiatives to manage their talent. However, these interventions are high performance oriented often underpinned by financial rewards. The emphasis on financial incentive and performance-related pay reflects the high growth nature of these businesses on the one hand and the growing expectation of the employees to share organizational gains on the other.

More specific studies at the firm level revealed the interplay of ownership, industrial sector and local institutional factors in shaping HRM practices and outcomes. For example, Morris *et al.*'s (2009) study of foreign owned garments and consumer electronics factories in China showed that the pursuit of a high quality product strategy in these firms has not led to the adoption of HRM practices in line with those promoted to support the quality enhancement strategy (e.g. job security, extensive training, employee involvement, performance-based reward). This is because, as Morris *et al.* (2009) argued, the Chinese plants were only engaged in the labour intensive part of the production chain which is prone to intensive global price competition. A different HRM strategy may well be pursued to support a quality enhancement and innovation strategy in other industries, such as automotive, in other parts of Asia, such as Hong Kong and Japan. Morris *et al.* (2009: 368) further revealed that in a number of cases in their study, the same firm 'was pursuing different HRM strategies at different points in the commodity chain and at different locations'. Based on their findings, Morris *et al.* (2009) concluded that strategy (e.g. cost reduction versus quality enhancement) and industrial sector (e.g. a mature industry with a low level of innovation versus a new industry with rapid innovations) are more important than nationality in the adoption of HRM practices in foreign MNCs in China. In other words, MNCs may not be interested in adopting or transferring good HRM practices if they are pursuing a cost reduction strategy in a mature industry such as garments and electronics.

Gong and Chang's (2008) study of employment security and internal career mobility in 478 firms in different ownership forms, and the impact of such practices on employee and organizational outcomes, found that there was a greater level of employment security in the state owned than non-state owned firms. By contrast, employees in the latter enjoyed more career advancement opportunities than those in the former. The study further revealed that the provision of career advancement opportunities was positively related to employees' organizational commitment, citizenship behaviour and firm performance. Similarly, employment security was positively related to employees' organizational commitment, but not to citizenship behaviour or firm performance. They concluded that 'employment security is not as effective as career advancement' as an HRM practice to enhance organizational performance (Gong and Chang 2008: 45). This suggests that job insecurity in the non-state owned firms may force employees to respond with a greater level of performance and citizenship behaviour in order to remain employed. By contrast, reduced job insecurity in the state owned firms also reduces employees' motivation to excel.

Similarly, Ngo *et al.*'s (2008) study of Chinese firms from various industries and regions showed that the levels of adoption of strategic HRM and HRM practices were lower in SOEs than in foreign-invested enterprises and privately owned enterprises. They found that both strategic HRM and HRM practices have direct and positive effects on financial and operational performance and employee relations climate. However, 'the moderating effect of ownership type was significant for financial performance only' (Ngo *et al.* 2008: 73). Ngo *et al.* (2008) further argued that employee involvement and cooperation is crucial for Chinese firms to gain competitive advantage, as suggested in the literature on the high performance/ commitment model of HRM. In short, research evidence points to the fact that state owned firms are generally less advanced in their HRM practices than well performing private firms and MNCs, although the gap is closing; and that there is much room for improvement if SOEs are to increase their competitiveness.

The continuing relevance of societal culture in HRM

Studies on international HRM and comparative employment systems (e.g. Rubery and Grimshaw 2003; Harzing and Pinnington 2011) have highlighted the enduring influence of societal culture in the configuration of national HRM and employment systems. Whilst a culturalist approach may run the risk of overplaying the significance of cultural factors and overlooking the crucial role of political, economic and institutional factors, it remains a valid perspective and is highly relevant to the study of HRM practices in the Chinese and Indian context (e.g. Frenkel and Peetz 1998; Westwood *et al.* 2004; Budhwar 2009; Cooke and Saini 2010a). This is because the 'socio-cultural context informs perceptions of, attitudes towards, and responses to the employment relationship, giving rise to cross-cultural differences' (Westwood *et al.* 2004: 366).

In addition, as noted earlier, the political and social contexts of China differ significantly from those found in the United States and Britain where much of the debate on the HPWS has taken place. China, as a political regime, is state-centric and authoritarian and the Chinese people are collectivist in their socialization. The current emphasis on social harmony in the state political ideology is arguably a renewed acknowledgement of the Confucianist egalitarianism and humanism under the disguise of socialism (see Chapter 1 for additional discussion of this issue). By contrast, the contemporary political economy of the United States and Britain is informed by neo-liberalism in which the pursuit of individual rights and interests is a democratic given. According to Westwood *et al.* (2004: 365), employment relations in Western economies 'are characterized by a model of impersonal rational economic exchange', whereas 'Chinese employment relations remain more fully embedded in the wider socio-cultural system of which reciprocity is a vital and integral part'. However, there is evidence that the rational economic model of thinking is permeating the Chinese business system.

The high-commitment model of HRM promoted in the United States and Britain has been heavily criticized for being deceptive, unitarist and failing to recognize the pluralistic interests of labour and management/capitalists (e.g. Legge 1994; Ramsay *et al.* 2000; Godard 2004). Attempts to implement these unitarist HRM practices have therefore been found to encounter strong resistance from the unions and employees (e.g. Wood and Albanese 1995; Wood and de Menezes 1998;

Delaney and Godard 2001; Godard 2004). In contrast, it is arguable that the collectivist and paternalist culture (e.g. employee care and obedience to authority as part of the paternalist expectations) and the weak institutional position of the trade unions vis-à-vis the employers may actually create a more conducive environment in the private sector in China and India for the adoption of a unitarist approach to HRM than Western societies that emphasize individual rights and interests. For example, Lange *et al.* (2010: 2447) observed that, despite the growing desire for intrinsic rewards, 'extrinsic job rewards such as relative pay and congenial work environment retain their importance in predicting Indian employees' job satisfaction'. The same study also revealed that collectivistic work values, for example, technical, social and financial support from colleagues, continue to have significant influence in employees' job satisfaction.

Raghuram's (2011) study of organizational identification of young software engineers in India revealed that those who perceived a higher level of paternalism tended to display a stronger positive relationship between job challenge and organizational identification. Saini and Budhwar's (2008) study of small and medium sized firms showed that indigenous practices in people management help employers win loyalty from their workers, which in turn enables the former to maintain a unitarist approach to HRM. The indigenous practices identified by the authors include Indian traditions at the workplace, such as celebrating key festivals, sending gifts on festive occasions, employee recognition, providing interest-free loans to workers, and using employee referral schemes for recruitment. In addition, Saini and Budhwar (2008) observed that the unitarism exhibited in these firms is not one that is built on pure authoritarianism, as is often found in paternalistic societies. Rather, it contains elements of consent, care and employee involvement. The authors argued that it is this kind of indigenous and paternalist management practices that play a key role in achieving a relatively harmonious capital–labour relationship at the workplace. Chapter 2 discusses these (and other) cultural influences in India in more detail.

Social relations and interpersonal interventions continue to play a key role in the supervisor–subordinate relationship in India. A good supervisor is expected to get to know the employees' personal life and to provide support for their family problems if the supervisor is to win the trust of the employees and to motivate them (Cooke and Saini 2010a). In addition, managers are expected to display a level of lenience and tolerance towards poor performing employees. For example, Varma *et al.*'s (2005) study on the role of interpersonal effect in performance appraisal showed that supervisors in India tend to inflate ratings of poor performers, suggesting that local cultural norms may be operating as a moderator.

Studies of the organizational behaviour of Chinese employees and managers have revealed some interesting differences between them and their counterparts in other countries, indicating the influence of culture in moulding these behaviours. For example, Bu *et al.*'s (2011) study of 279 young professionals in China regarding the relationships between employees' turnover intention and a broad range of potential behavioural indicators of such intention revealed some unique Chinese cultural characteristics that were attributed to behavioural patterns. Based on their findings, the authors cautioned the generalization of behavioural explanations found in studies conducted in the Western context to the Chinese setting. Similarly, Cai *et al.*'s (2011: 3245) survey study of Chinese organizations showed 'a strong "group orientation" and a great emphasis on "soft factors" such as seniority, loyalty and connections in many HRM areas'. Based on the findings, they concluded that whilst certain aspects of Chinese HRM are converging towards the Western model, 'the influence of traditional Chinese personnel practices remains strong' (Cai *et al.* 2011: 3245).

Cai *et al.*'s (2011) observation is shared by findings of Fu and Kamenou's (2011) study of HRM in MNCs in China. In particular, Fu and Kamenou (2011) found that *guānxì*, valuing seniority, and the importance of 'human factor' were the three Chinese cultural values which could affect HR policies and practices. They argued that these 'Chinese cultural values are far more sophisticated than the ones being conceptualized in previous literature', as they 'appear to be interlinked and be embedded within the Chinese collectivist culture' (Fu and Kamenou 2011: 3270).

In their comparative study of employees in Germany, Romania and China on the influence of cultural differences on employees' commitment and its impacts, Felfe *et al.* (2008: 230) observed that 'employees with a collectivistic orientation appreciate being part of a group and have a stronger striving to belong to a social entity'. This desire of social belonging fosters positive relationship building behaviours in the organization and 'leads to a stronger affective commitment' (Felfe *et al.* 2008: 230). Felfe *et al.* (2008: 230) also found 'a clear relationship between collectivism and normative commitment' and argued that 'persons who generally tend to accept norms, obey rules, and value loyalty to the group also experience a stronger duty and obligation to fulfil organizational requirements'.

Similarly, Wang's (2008: 916) study that investigated 'the contribution of the emotional bond a Chinese worker has with his supervisor and with his co-workers in accounting for employees' organizational commitment in foreign-invested enterprises', highlighted the importance of 'personal relationships in shaping the linkage between employees and firms in China'. Similar findings were also yielded in other studies on the relationships between the employees and their supervisors and their impacts on organizational commitment (e.g. Hui *et al.* 2004; Gamble and Huang 2008).

The strong desire of social belonging and its associated behaviours in positive relationship building of employees in a collectivist society like China is not confined to in-group employees. When examining the role of collectivist orientation, interpersonal affect, and *guānxì* in relation to the host country nationals' (HCNs) willingness to support expatriates, Varma *et al.* (2009: 199) found that 'HCNs' perceived relationship quality with the expatriate has a significant impact on their willingness to provide assistance' and social support to expatriates. An implication of this finding for managing expatriates in foreign MNCs in China is to develop the cultural awareness of the expatriate employees in order for them to develop a quality relationship with local employees.

In many ways, Varma *et al.*'s (2009) study is nothing new, nor is its management implication confined to the Chinese context. Indeed, the need for cultural adaptation has been found crucial to expatriate management and successful international assignments in different societal contexts (e.g. Forster 2000; Sparrow *et al.* 2004; Selmer 2006). What is emphasised here is that cultural awareness is particularly important to positive relationship building in a society that highly values social relationships in all aspects of work and life. As Child (2009) observed, HRM in China is essentially human relationship management (also see Warner and Goodall 2010).

Equally, whilst existing studies have highlighted the continuing effect of societal culture in shaping HRM practices and employees' perceptions of their effectiveness, it is important to note that the cultural distance between Western society and China is somewhat shrinking in part on account of globalization. As mentioned in other chapters and earlier in this chapter, the Chinese employees' cultural values and personal goals are evolving as the economic and social reform of the country deepens. A number of studies have also pointed to the fact that certain HRM practices may actually have a more general applicability than they have been given credit for. For example, Taormina and Gao's (2009: 102) study of acceptable performance appraisal (PA) criteria in Chinese firms concluded that 'it is possible to identify PA criteria that are generally acceptable to employees from a variety of industries, and that organizational socialization can influence the acceptance of PA criteria'.

Finally, the positive relationship between the collectivist culture and organizational outcomes found in the empirical studies discussed so far may not be widely generalizable in China on the one hand because of significant differences across the firms, industrial sectors and regions, and may need to be seen in relative terms against the national context on the other. For example, Hong and Snell's (2008) study of Chinese employees and Japanese expatriates in Japanese subsidiaries in China found that the former lack enthusiasm in problem solving and are less likely to adopt collaborative team-working behaviour than their Japanese counterparts. Chinese employees may adopt a compliance rather than commitment approach to organizational goals, values and culture. The brand reputation of the company (e.g. prestigious foreign MNCs) may be a reason for employees to stay with the firm instead of organizational loyalty elicited by high commitment types of HRM practices. Similarly, Felfe and Yan's (2009: 448) study of absenteeism and turnover intent showed that compared to Germany, workgroup commitment is more powerful in the Chinese (collectivist) context and that employees 'in this cultural environment are more willing to behave on behalf of the group'. An implication for HRM is that firms in China may wish to focus on the development of workgroup commitment of the employees as this commitment is closely associated with organizational commitment.

The influence of demographics on HRM outcome

Demographic characteristics are important factors in influencing the career opportunities and labour market outcomes of individual workers. In particular, age and gender may have strong bearings on individual employees' perception of HRM practices in the organization. For instance, in both the Indian and Chinese contexts, research has found that the younger generation of the workforce has a stronger preference for performance-related pay than the traditional seniority-based pay, and that performance-based reward plays a crucial role in motivating and retaining managerial and professional employees (e.g. Budhwar and Boyne 2004; Holtbrügge *et al.* 2010; Cooke 2012a, also see Chapter 6 for more discussion).

Li *et al.*'s (2008) survey of 316 Chinese employees found that older workers, managers, better educated workers and male employees tend to hold more traditional work values than younger, less well-educated, non-managerial and female workers. This finding has important implications for employers because many of them tend to discriminate against older workers during recruitment and in the selection for redundancy without realizing the extra value they may get from the older workers. Li *et al.*'s (2008) study further revealed that neither generation of the workers feel satisfied because the younger employees are often considered less experienced and the older employees are led to believe that they are of less value to the organization. In the same vein, Qiao *et al.*'s (2009: 2311) survey study of 1,176 workers in six manufacturing firms in two Chinese cities revealed that the perceived existence of HPWSs is correlated with organizational commitment. In particular, 'age, marital status, and education, but not gender, correlated significantly with organizational commitment'; and interestingly, 'male and unmarried Chinese employees were significantly more affected by the existence of HR practices than female and married employees' (Qiao *et al.* 2009: 2311).

By contrast, Peng *et al.*'s (2009) study of 582 employees in Beijing showed significant gender differences in organizational commitment with women displaying a lower level of commitment than their male counterparts. Female informants in this study clearly felt a level of discrimination. They reported that they were assigned to less challenging tasks and were 'engaging in a low level of leader–member exchange' (Peng *et al.* 2009: 323). It is this perceived discrimination and lack of opportunities, rather than their marital status and family commitment, which contributed to female employees' lower level of organizational commitment relative to their male counterparts.

The social and economic status of the workers and the way they have been treated in their society also affect workers' preference to, and perception of, HRM practices. For example, Frenkel *et al.*'s (2011: 1) study of migrant workers in two manufacturing plants found that a 'strong HR system – perceived by workers as distinctive, attractive and consistently implemented – fosters perceptions of distributive, procedural and interactive justice'. However, the authors also found that migrant workers 'view economic aspects of work as primary and intrinsic aspects as secondary' and that they are 'more concerned with distributive justice than with procedural or interactional justice' because they are not accustomed to the latter (Frenkel *et al.* 2011: 20). Cultural and institutional context, status of the migrant workers and type of workers (semi-skilled, manual) were attributed to this finding.

Similarly, the role of age in affecting HRM outcomes has been observed in the Indian context. According to Kuruvilla and Ranganathan (2010), the annual turnover rate in the BPO industry is commonly estimated as 30–40 per cent. Dissatisfaction with the immediate supervisor (the 'lousy boss syndrome') is an important reason. This is partly to do with the lack of leadership skills of the supervisors who have been promoted prematurely because of the rapid expansion of the industry and the shortage of managerial talent. The changing work values and expectations of the younger generation of the workforce is also a factor attributed to superior–subordinate conflicts. The nature of work of the call centres and the absence of career prospects are two further major reasons for the attrition (Kuruvilla and Ranganathan 2010, also see discussion earlier and in Chapter 5). As Taylor and Bain (2005) noted, half of those who leave a call centre exit the industry altogether. Many of the HR interventions introduced to combat retention problems in the BPO industry are specifically designed to suit the young and educated workforce. These include job rotation, lateral movement, career and leadership development programmes, and the creation of a joyful environment with recreational facilities like that of Google's (Kuruvilla and Ranganathan 2010).

Conclusions

This chapter has outlined changes and continuity in the HRM practices in India and China since they opened up their economies in the 1980s. Both countries have relatively young and increasingly highly educated workforces, although there are significant differences as well, as illustrated in Chapter 1. However, both are facing worsening skills shortages at the same time, a problem exacerbated by brain drains. According to Baruch *et al.* (2007), whilst both China and India have been experiencing a brain drain of young talent to developed countries where they pursued higher education, Indian graduates are more likely to stay in (or return to) their home country than their Chinese counterparts on account partly of the comparatively smaller cultural distance of the former than the latter. The dramatic rise of the IT-based BPO industry in India as a result of outsourcing and off-shoring of firms from the developed countries adds further strains to its skilled labour market.

Research evidence suggests that an increasing number of firms in China and India are becoming more systematic and strategic in their HRM. It is clear that they are aware of the labour market changes, particularly the erosion of organizational loyalty amongst the younger and well-educated workforce, and have started to adopt high performance HRM practices to align the interests of the employees with those of the firm. Nevertheless, empirical studies have highlighted the enduring influence of societal context in the configuration and implementation of Western-prescribed high performance HRM practices (e.g. Gamble and Huang 2008; Morris *et al.* 2008). In particular, ownership form, industrial sector, cultural values and the changing demographic profile of the workforce have been found to be influential.

Research evidence further suggests that the transition from the traditional style of people management to a more strategic and progressive approach to HRM remains uneven in pace, process and substance between the private and public sector, between traditional and new high-tech industries, and between firms that are connected to the global value chains and those that serve primarily the domestic market competing on cost. Organizations in different ownership forms carry with them different legacies and characteristics. Compounded with the characteristics of industrial sector and the local institutional environment, firms' approach to HRM tend to differ and the same HRM practices may not yield similar effects across firms and regions. What is clear is that organizations that wish to enhance their competitiveness through effective HRM need to develop HRM practices that are sensitive to demographic differences in their workforce.

Interestingly, whilst the younger generation of the workforce is keen to have individualistic practices on performance management, reward and career development, it values a collectivistic social relationship in the workplace at the same time. Benevolent paternalism remains a key feature in leadership in privately owned indigenous firms in both countries (e.g. Saini and Budhwar 2008; Cooke 2012a). Such a style is not only a natural inheritance of the cultural traditions of these societies, but is also seen as an effective technique to attract, motivate and retain people to enhance organizational performance.

The transition of the HRM system in China and India can be described as from paternalistic HRM to paternalistic-based and market driven HRM. It is Western, yet Eastern, capitalist, yet socialist, particularly in the case of China (Warner 2011a). In both countries, moral motivation, a key feature of paternalistic HRM (Farh and Cheng 2000), remains an essential ingredient in the HRM philosophy.

Acknowledgement

Part of this chapter draws from Chapter 10 in F. L. Cooke (2012a) *Human resource management in China: New trends and practices*, London: Routledge.

4 Transformation in industrial relations

Introduction

Industrial Relations (IR) in China and India have undergone significant changes as their economic reforms deepen. In this chapter we examine how the changing institutional contexts and conditions are impinging upon the IR systems and the evolving role of the state and the trade unions as key institutional actors in both countries at the national level. We also consider the impact of globalization and employers' strategy on IR at the firm level. The chapter begins with an overview of the characteristics of the labour markets of both countries to highlight the changing demographics of the labour force and their relative bargaining power. This is followed by an examination of the evolution of the regulatory frameworks, both legislative and administrative, for labour protection. The understanding of the labour market characteristics and labour regulations is important because they are, at least partially, outcomes of the state economic and social policies that reflect its political ideology. It is also within these broader contexts that the trade unions' role is assessed, although the functioning (or not) of the trade unions also shapes the employment environment.

The changing characteristics of labour markets

The labour markets of China and India have experienced significant changes over the last two decades, despite the continuing influence of the state-planned economy characteristics. In India, the labour market is divided into two sectors: the organized and unorganized. According to Hill (2009: 403) the 'organized sector' refers to all public sector organizations and all non-agricultural enterprises in the private sector employing ten or more workers; whereas the 'unorganized sector' refers to business entities in the non-agricultural sector employing fewer than ten persons. Workers in the former are privileged with relatively extensive coverage of labour regulations, whereas those in the latter remain largely unprotected (see D'Souza 2010 for more detail, as well as other chapters in the book). The proportion of employment in the organized (but not necessarily unionized) sector is low compared with that in the unorganized sector. It is estimated that only about 8 per cent of the Indian workforce was employed in the formal economy in 2000

(Venkata Ratnam 2009; also see Harriss-White 2010 for a detailed account on the informal economy). According to Candland (2007), organized labour not only has an effect on the political regime type but is also affected and constrained by it (also see below).

Female workers are concentrated in the informal sector, 'where wages and working conditions are inferior, largely unsecured and mostly devoid of social security benefits' (Venkata Ratnam and Jain 2002: 279; also see Hill 2008, 2009). In 2004, the share of women in wage employment in the non-agricultural sector was 18 per cent in India, compared to 40 per cent in China (The World Bank 2006a). According to Hill (2009), poor Indian women have always worked but have until recently been ignored by official statistics. The rapid development in the offshore BPO sector since the 2000s has led to an increasing proportion of women working in this sector. This is in part as a result of the amendment of the Factories Act to allow women to work on night shifts to combat skill shortages (Cooke 2010b).

Female employment in the domestic call centre industry has also experienced considerable growth. Taylor *et al.*'s (2011) study of call centre workers in the domestic call centre industry revealed that a higher proportion of women were found in domestic than international call centres. However, women's experience of work has not been as positive as expected, to say the least, and their career prospects were reported to be bleak on account of harassment, discrimination and poor working conditions.

Similarly, the Chinese labour market contains two major segments of the labour force: those with urban residential status and those who hold rural residential status but have migrated to urban areas to seek employment, often known as the rural migrant workers. Rural migrant workers are found in both the formal and informal sector, the terms and conditions of which are generally better in the former than in the latter. Whilst rural migrant workers are often classified as in 'informal employment', their terms of employment are in fact far more formal than that found in many other developing economies in terms of their employment packages and organizations. According to Xu (2009: 439), informal employment ('flexible employment' is the preferred government terminology) in China 'is much more organized and less "informal", with more government intervention than equivalent employment in many other developing countries'. As such, informal employment is an indicator of one's (inferior) employment status as much as (the precarious) nature of one's work.

It is important to note that not all of those who are engaged in informal employment in China are rural migrant workers. A considerable proportion of the SOE employees who were laid-off by their state owned employers in the period between the late 1990s and early 2000s and some urban residents entering the labour market for the first time, can also be found in the informal employment category. Two factors have contributed to the growth of the informal employment category in the Chinese labour market. One is the relaxation of the *hukou* (residential status) system since the mid-1980s which had previously restricted the mobility of the rural residents from entering the urban area to live and work.

The other factor is the large scale downsizing and privatization programme which was carried out in the state sector since the mid-1990s. In 1978, approximately 78 per cent of urban workers were employed in the state sector. This figure was reduced to less than 21 per cent by 2009 (National Bureau of Statistics of China 2010a). It is estimated that, by 2009, 30 per cent of the urban labour force, and two-thirds of the 150 million rural migrant workers in urban areas were engaged in informal employment (Cai and Chan 2009).

In comparison, Chinese women make up a higher proportion of the total workforce than their Indian counterparts. Chinese women comprised more than 37 per cent of the urban (full time) workforce in 2009 (National Bureau of Statistics of China 2010a), despite the slight decline since the mid-1990s. The majority of Chinese married women tend to work full time and work continuously throughout their working life, having only brief maternity breaks; whereas a higher proportion of Indian married women are full time housewives and for a longer period in order to accommodate their family commitments (Cooke 2010a).

Within the formal employment sector, India and China share some similar characteristics in that their labour workforces are relatively young and an increasing proportion of them are well-educated to university degree level, making them highly attractive to firms, as both countries are experiencing severe skill shortages (see Chapter 5 for further discussion). These young workers carry with them different career outlooks and work attitudes from their older counterparts, presenting new challenges to employers in IR and HRM, as explained in the following chapters.

Labour regulations

As in other national IR systems, labour regulations play an important role in the Chinese and Indian IR systems. The labour laws of India, most of which were introduced prior to its independence in 1947 with subsequent moderate amendments, are considered to be 'extremely protective of labour' (Kuruvilla 1996: 650). They are also regarded as 'among the most restrictive and complex in the world' and 'have constrained the growth of the formal manufacturing sector where these laws have their widest application' (The World Bank 2006b; also see Saini 2009, and Chapter 1 for more details on these laws). Legislation that is aimed at providing an enhanced level of labour protection may actually prove to be counterproductive, especially when the laws are only applicable to certain sectors (e.g. the organized sector), industries and occupational groups. In particular, restrictions in lay-off and retrenchment have not only led to inefficiency, but have also discouraged employers from creating employment with a better job quality in the formal sector, thus trapping millions of Indian workers in poor jobs in the informal sector (see Sen Gupta and Sett 2000 for an insightful overview of the Indian IR laws and the role of the key institutional actors).

There are a small number of labour regulations that cover workers in the unorganized sector, including the Unorganized Workers' Social Security Bill that was passed in 2008. However, their enforcement of them remains patchy or almost non-existent (Hill 2009).

Within the organized sector, the pro-labour government stance has not been equally applied across all groups of employees, notably those in the public sector (e.g. Mathur 1966; Subramanian 1973; Sen Gupta and Sett 2000; Venkata Ratnam 2009). Here, the tensions caused by the multiple roles of the Indian government as an employer, an economic manager and a legislator and policy maker were borne out in full force. For example, strikes by certain groups of public employees (e.g. government employees and those providing public services) might be considered by the government as unlawful, with some facing dismissal consequences (e.g. Subramanian 1973; All India State Government Employees Federation 2003). In addition, the labour laws were enacted in a way that suggested that the state is the only arbiter of industrial conflicts (Sen Gupta and Sett 2000; Venkata Ratnam 2006, 2009).

Contrary to India's complex and detailed labour legislative framework, the regulation of the labour market and employment relations in socialist China has until the mid-2000s relied primarily on administrative regulations and policy guidelines issued at the central, regional (provincial) and local (municipal and township) level. For example, the Enterprise Minimum Wage Regulation (enacted in 1993 and revised in 2004) was essentially a national administrative regulation that provides only a framework. It is up to the local governments to decide the level of minimum wage and coverage.

The first major piece of labour legislation was only promulgated in 1994. This was followed by three major pieces of legislation passed in 2007 – namely, the Employment Promotion Law, the Labour Contract Law and the Labour Disputes Mediation and Arbitration Law. In 2011, the Social Security Law was enacted to provide further protection to (rural migrant) workers by making the social security contribution portable when a worker moves from one place to another. In general, all the laws are applicable to all employing organizations and groups of workers unless specified otherwise. Whilst laws are legislated by the central government to be enforced by the regional and local governments, the latter often develop local policy regulations and guidelines to dilute the impact of the laws in order to prioritize their economic development agenda (e.g. Taylor *et al.* 2003; Cooney 2007; Cooke 2012a).

Both the Indian and Chinese labour disputes laws specify the procedures and processes of dispute settlement – conciliation, arbitration and adjudication in India as specified in its Industrial Disputes Act (1947); and mediation, arbitration and litigation in China as specified in its recent Labour Disputes Mediation and Arbitration Law (2008). In both countries, a voluntary approach is emphasised, or at least encouraged, by the government as a cooperative way of resolving the conflicts. The inefficacy of the dispute resolution system appears to be a common characteristic of both countries (e.g. Chandrashekar 1970; Taylor *et al.* 2003; Venkata Ratnam 2006; Cooney 2007; Saini 2009). In India, governments have been widely criticized for their discretionary power to overrule adjudication instead of accepting and implementing the rulings.

In China, local governments have been found to force labour dispute cases back to the workplace and to request employers to resolve the dispute internally 'for the sake of building a harmonious society', although resource constraints to handle the rising number of cases may actually be the key reason for this (Cooke 2012a).

Industrial relations in transition

The IR systems of India and China display some similar as well as some distinctive characteristics. They have evolved over the decades in different ways mainly as a result of their distinctive political systems in contemporary history. The Indian IR system began to take shape after the Russian Revolution in 1917 and prior to its independence in 1947 (see Dufty 1965 for an overview). It is believed that the ILO (Indian Labour Organisation) 'has had a significant influence in the shaping of the Indian IR system' (Dufty 1965: 41). The early years of post-independence IR until the early 1960s was marked by 'the rise and dominance of state-sponsored unions', whose influence on terms and conditions was only exerted indirectly 'through their political links with ruling parties' (Bhattacherjee 1987: 248).

The ensuing two decades saw 'the phenomenal rise of strikes and lockouts due to rivalries between unions affiliated to different political parties' (Bhattacherjee 1987: 248). Inter-union competition in a given workplace also made it impossible to establish a stable partnership relationship between the union and management for collective bargaining (Venkata Ratnam 1993). Union militancy in the 1960s and 70s gave way to a gradual decline in the 1980s, when the unions realized the need to cooperate in the wake of firms' growing pressure to improve productivity and business performance (Mankidy 1995).

The 1980s and 1990s was characterized by incremental changes and the adaptation of the Indian IR driven by 'endogenous forces of party politics, government policy, class segmentation, demography and geography' as well as by 'exogenous forces of globalization or by the functional requirements of a particular industrialization strategy' (Bhattacherjee 2001: 261). The 1990s witnessed the growing power of the employers in IR and, for the first time, employers felt that the state was on their side (Venkata Ratnam 1993, also see below). Still bounded by the rigid labour policy, employers launched a number of strategies, with tacit support from the government (D'Souza 2010), to overcome legislative constraints on labour deployment in order to increase productivity and to reduce cost.

As Kuruvilla and Erickson (2002) noted, public sector firms introduced early retirement schemes and the private sector embraced numerical flexibility in order to cut labour costs (see also Venkata Ratnam and Verma 2011). The 1980s witnessed 'a significant shift in employment from an organized to an unorganized sector' through the growing use of casual and contract employment and subcontracting (Sen Gupta and Sett 2000: 148). In addition, union avoidance policies were increasingly adopted by employers, such as developing greenfield sites and promoting workers to above a certain rank so as to take them out of the legislative protection (Mathur 1993; Venkata Ratnam 1993; Kuruvilla and Erickson 2002). According to Hensman (2010: 111) workers' rights in India have been weakened since independence, particularly since the late 1970s. Employers' attack on the trade unions, in the form of the informalization of employment, and the government's pursuit of a neo-liberal economy policy were attributed to this decline.

In both countries, political interests have tended to be the main concern of the unions at the national level rather than the pursuit of economic and labour movements, although interests in any one of the three can rarely be achieved without the suppression or mobilization of the other two. It needs to be noted that, given the inter-union differences in their political stance, and strategy and resources that are also linked to local political views, it would be a gross simplification to describe Indian unionism as one national pattern, as was argued by Bhattacherjee (2010). Both the Chinese and Indian governments have played a vital role in shaping the IR climate. For example, under the Industrial Dispute Act of India, 'the government enjoys the full discretionary power of whether or not, when, and how to intervene in an industrial dispute – actual or threatened' (Sen Gupta and Sett 2000: 145). The government also has the power to refuse lay-offs, retrenchments or the closure of certain firms under the Industrial Disputes Act 1947 (Gopalakrishnan and Tortell 2006; Saini 2009). The state dominance in the Indian IR was attributed to the legacy of its colonial past, which successive post-independence Indian governments have failed to reform in line with their democratic political systems and industrializing economy (Sen Gupta and Sett 2000; also see Bhattacherjee 2001; Hill 2009; Bhattacherjee and Ackers 2010, for overviews of the evolution of Indian IR).

In China, state dominance as the policy maker and employer spanned the entire period of the state-planned economy and the first decade of the ensuing reform period. The strong state intervention is associated with its socialist ideology and the need felt by the government to keep a tight grip in order to maintain its authority. As such, there is no real 'partnership' between management and the trade union, or 'employee voice' in management–labour relations. While unions may appear to be sympathetic to the plight of employees, their lack of autonomy from the state prevents any concerted actions designed to influence the government (Frenkel and Peetz 1998). The one-party system means that the Chinese Communist Party (CCP) is able to hold down the only officially recognized union – the All-China Federation of Trade Unions (ACFTU) – as its junior partner in the party–union relationship (see below for further discussion). However, the dominance of state influence in the state owned sector, and the weakness of the trade unions in IR as a whole, do not always guarantee a unilateral determination of employment practices by the (state) employers. During the state-planned economy period, conflict between management and workers as a result of the dominance of the CCP within enterprises has been 'a far more common feature of industrial life in China than is generally recognized' (Sheehan 1999: 2).

By the early 1990s, there were growing incidences of 'wildcat' strikes without any union presence or organization, especially in foreign funded (including and especially in Hong Kong, Macao and Taiwan funded) enterprises (see Chan 2001; Lee 2007). These industrial actions by unorganized workers (or unrecognized unions) reflect both the ability of enterprises to prevent unionization and the failures of existing official unions (Frenkel and Peetz 1998).

In 1994, the number of officially recorded labour dispute cases brought before arbitration panels was 19,098. However, by the end of 2007 this number had risen to 350,182 (National Bureau of Statistics of China 2008). Major issues of disputes involve wage payments, labour contracts, social insurance and welfare and work injuries. This has led to the enactment of the Labour Contract Law and the Labour Disputes Mediation and Arbitration Law in 2008, as noted earlier. The promulgation of these two laws has led to a dramatic surge of officially recorded labour disputes, with 693,469 cases in 2008 and 684,379 cases in 2009 (National Bureau of Statistics of China 2010a). This is in spite of the fact that some employers were reported to be taking the law seriously (Park and Cai 2009).

The evolving role of the state

Developments following the opening up of both countries' economies, and the ensuing globalization of production and markets, have been the major driving forces for the changes in the IR systems experienced by India and China. As a legislator, the two governments are expected to respond very differently. While the Chinese government has been subject to pressure to develop a more comprehensive regulatory framework in order to provide greater protection for its workers, the Indian government has been facing growing pressure to 'de-regulate' IR to allow employers more freedom to operate. However, numerous attempts to reform the labour laws in India since its independence have mostly ended up in inaction (e.g. Sen Gupta and Sett 2000; Hill 2009; Venkata Ratnam 2009). Despite the pressure of rising competition, the Indian government has been considered to be slow in responding to the pressing need to relax the strong hold of the labour legislation, to entrust union recognition and to promote a labour disputes resolution system independent of the state executive (Sen Gupta and Sett 2000; Kuruvilla and Erickson 2002). Nevertheless, it should be noted that, since the 1980s, 'concomitant changes in the government's labour policy tended to become increasingly supportive' and even 'in favour of employers', as the government desperately needed private investments to stem its economic crises and revitalize the economy (Sen Gupta and Sett 2000: 149). In addition to favouring employers, political parties in power also mobilized their affiliated trade unions to assist workplace restructuring (Sen Gupta and Sett 2000; Bhattacherjee and Acker 2010).

As economic managers, the two governments choose to play two rather different roles, although privatization has been a common strategy in the reform in both countries. As Khanna (2007) argued, the Chinese government is often the entrepreneur itself in its current vigorous economic growth. Governments at all levels continue to be heavily involved in businesses and the largest and best performing firms tend to be state owned/invested. Chinese owned multinational corporations (MNCs) are also mostly state owned or supported by the government. By contrast, entrepreneurship in India is driven mostly from the private sector and civil society, staying away from government interventions. It should be noted here that a countervailing view holds that the ever-present state intervention has been precisely the obstacle to the development of a strong private sector in China (e.g. Nolan 2001;

Y. Huang 2008), whereas the absence of government intervention has led to the growth of a number of highly internationally competitive Indian private firms. The presence or absence of government involvement, directly or indirectly, undoubtedly has implications for IR at the firm as well as sectoral level.

The changing role of the trade unions and workers' representation

Labour organizations such as the trade unions provide an additional potential source of labour protection. The strength and effectiveness of the trade unions, however, vary across industries and countries and over time. In India, trade unionism has a history of about 100 years, although only 4–5 per cent of the workforce in the non-agricultural sector (including the unorganized sector) is unionized (Shyam Sundar 2008). The All Indian Trade Unions Congress (AITUC) was formed in 1920 mainly to meet the requirement of the ILO that workers' delegates should be representatives of the largest organization (see Pandey 1967 for more detailed review). The legal incorporation of the Indian trade unions was established in 1926, much earlier than that in China.

The Indian trade unions are closely linked to political parties (Venkata Ratnam 2006; Shyam Sundar 2008), and some believe that Indian trade unionism is more associated with political than labour movements (Dufty 1965). As Dufty (1965: 42) noted, in the early days of unionism, the Indian trade unions were to some extent 'an arm of the liberalization movement'. Political parties allied with them because of 'their potential importance in the fight for independence' (Dufty 1965: 42). 'The Indian trade unions had considerable difficulty in gaining their legal positions' and had to form alliance with political parties and support pro-labour legislation to gain social and political recognition (Dufty 1965: 43). As such, 'their political strength has outweighed their industrial and economic strength' (Dufty 1965: 43).

Whilst party loyalties may have been loosened since the late 1990s, this has been accompanied by the unions' weakening ability to organize nationally (Bhattacherjee 2001; Candland 2007; Beale and Noronha 2009). In addition, union movements exhibit strong regional/municipal distinctiveness in part because of the variations in the political stance, policy regulations and economic and social performance of the state governments (e.g. Ramaswamy 1988; Bhattacherjee 2001; Kuruvilla and Erickson 2002; Beale and Noronha 2009). Nevertheless, the need to fight off proposed labour law changes that would have dismantled the job security enjoyed by a small segment of the labour force (i.e. those in the organized sector) in the early 2000s did bring the unions together for a short period of time in order to defend the rights of their members (Hensman 2010). As Kuruvilla (1996: 651) observed, 'the political orientation of trade unions has provided the labor movement with political influence far greater than their union membership alone would warrant. Labor is the swing vote in at least 30% of all parliamentary constituencies', despite the relatively low level of unionization. Union power is particularly strong in the public sector. The power of the unions is believed to have been the cause of a swelling and inefficient public sector and the slow and difficult process of rationalization and restructuring in the private sector (Venkata Ratnam 1993). For Candland (2007), while the public sector unions were able to resist privatization attempts, they have had to modify their demands in those sectors that have been liberalized (e.g. airlines, banks, telecommunications and financial services) in order to compete with the private firms for customers.

In China, whilst the ACFTU does not have to grapple with union rivalry problems, it has to operate under the leadership of the CCP, as noted earlier. The union–CCP tie dates back to the 1920s (the union was founded on 1 May 1925) when grassroots union organizations served as the Party member recruitment bases and provided vital support to the CCP by mobilizing workers (also see Zhu *et al.* 2011, for a history of the ACFTU). Although the relationship between the Party and the ACFTU has not always been smooth, attempts by the ACFTU to gain greater power and autonomy have been suppressed by the Party (Sheehan 1999). Similarly, attempts to form autonomous workers' unions are crushed, as was the case during the Tiananmen Square event in 1989 (Cooke 2012a).

The roles and responsibilities of the ACFTU are set out by a number of laws, namely the Trade Union Law (1950, 1992, amended 2001), the Labour Law (enacted 1995) and the Labour Contract Law (enacted 2008). According to the Trade Union Law (2001),

> the basic function and duty of the trade unions is to safeguard the legal rights and interests of the employees. While upholding the overall rights and interests of the whole nation, trade unions shall, at the same time, represent and safeguard the rights and interests of employees.
>
> (Article 6)

Local branches of the ACFTU are partly funded by the fiscal budget of the local governments, which oversee the union activities. The legal and structural position of the ACFTU means that its primary responsibility is the state whose interests are not necessarily aligned with that of the workers. Under the socialist system in which the state employer and the workers were perceived to share the same interests, the trade unions' main function was to organize social events, take care of workers' welfare, help management implement operational decisions, organize skill training, raise employees' morale and coordinate relations between management and workers (Verma and Yan 1995). The way the ACFTU is set up and operationalized has led to the questioning by international trade union organizations, labour movement activists and scholars, of the legitimacy of the ACFTU as a trade union (e.g. Taylor and Li 2007).

Since the mid-1990s, when SOEs shed millions of their workers, skill training and assisting laid-off workers to regain employment have been two major functions of the unions. With the growth of new ownership forms outside the state sector, and the concomitant social welfare reforms that were carried out in the state sector, the welfare role of the state has been diminishing. The once relatively harmonious management–labour relationship has been replaced with one that is characterized by conflicting interests and rising disputes. However, the role of the unions, or more specifically, the union officials' perception of their duties, has not changed in time to reflect the new reality. Union officials generally lack the resources and power, skills and legal knowledge to fulfil their collective bargaining role and to defend their members' rights (Warner and Ng 1999; Cooke 2012a). The union chairman's role at the workplace level is often assumed by factory directors or CCP chairmen. Union officials at the branch level are normally appointed by the local government and often rotate their positions in government departments as part of their political career development. Where a union function is established, membership level is high at over 90 per cent; notably in the state sector organizations (see National Bureau of Statistics of China 2010b). However, trade unions are considered ineffective in representing workers' interests against management prerogatives and at times side with the management (O'Leary 1998; Clarke 2005).

By contrast, the Indian trade unions have been relatively more proactive than the ACFTU in their attempts to unionize employees in the private sector, notably the new industries such as the IT and the BPO sectors. However, their efforts have been met with formidable resistance from both the employers, who want to be union-free in order to maximize their operational flexibility and efficiency, and the young professional employees, who have yet to develop their identification with the trade unions and turn to them for representation. As Noronha and D'Cruz's (2009) study of the unionization of call centre professional workers suggested, it was the political intervention at the high level, rather than the extreme working conditions endured by the workers, that has led to the formation of unions in the IT and BPO sector (see below for further discussion).

An inherent weakness of the top-down influence of unionism is the focus on the political strategy and wider issues at the high level at the expense of ignoring the grassroots representation needs. Unsatisfied workers eventually seek alternative mechanisms to represent their unmet needs. As Hammer's (2010) study revealed, residential communities where workers share similar working conditions and concerns have become venues for aggrieved workers to share information, voice concerns, provide mutual support and formulate strategies. These community-based unions may be loose in their form and fall short of developing into a larger social movement; nonetheless, their presence and potential growth as emerging actors in IR undoubtedly has implications for mainstream unionism, as was observed elsewhere (e.g. Heery and Frege 2006; Cooke and Wood 2011).

Collective bargaining

Collective bargaining in India takes a number of forms and occurs at different levels (see Venkata Ratnam 2009; Venkata Ratnam and Verma 2011 for more detailed discussion). Interestingly, despite strong political ties, there is a striking absence in the Indian IR law of 'provisions on recognition of a trade union as a collective bargaining agent' (Sen Gupta and Sett 2000: 145) at the national level, and only a few states have legal provisions for it (Venkata Ratnam 2009). The strong state intervention has inhibited the role of the trade union as an alternative and legitimate agent in collective bargaining and other IR issues (Sen Gupta and

Sett 2000). Nevertheless, Indian unions have had a long-standing involvement in collective bargaining. Through various means and forms, they have been able to achieve collective agreements often at the plant/enterprise level and sometimes at the industrial/national level (e.g. public sector firms). On some occasions, they did so through political ties and to pre-empt state intervention (Bhattacherjee 1987). According to the ILO (1997/8) statistics, less than 2 per cent of the Indian workers were covered by collective bargaining agreements.

For most of the socialist Chinese history, the trade unions did not have any role in collective bargaining, as employment terms and conditions were set unilaterally by the state employer. The notion of 'collective bargaining' was not introduced in China until the early 1990s, after the Trade Union Law (1992) authorized unions at the enterprise level to conclude collective contracts with the employer. The term 'collective consultation' instead of 'collective bargaining' is preferred by the state. It is believed that consultation is a more constructive approach than 'bargaining', as it conforms to the Chinese culture of non-confrontation and conflict avoidance. In 1994, the Provisions on Collective Contracts was issued by the then Ministry of Labour which provided detailed regulations to support the collective contract provision outlined in the Labour Law of China passed in 1994 (see Taylor *et al.* 2003 and Brown 2006 for more detailed discussion). Trade unions have been given the official role to represent workers for consultation with employers. This position of the unions has been reinforced and expanded in subsequent labour laws. According to Article 20 of the Trade Union Law (2001), a trade union shall represent employees in equal negotiation and signing a collective contract. Matters that can be concluded in a collective contract may include labour remuneration, working time, rest and vacations, occupational safety and health, professional training and insurance and welfare.

This tripartite consultation system in China is promoted by the government as an important mechanism for the government, trade unions and enterprises to strengthen social dialogue and cooperation in coordinating labour relations in response to the new dynamics of IR during the period of economic transformation. However, limited achievements have been made after a decade's implementation of the system. According to government statistics, the employment contract signing rate was less than 60 per cent in the mid-2000s, and private enterprises had an even lower rate at 30 per cent (cited in Qiao 2008). In spite of the legal requirement, many employers persistently refuse to sign contracts with their workers in order to avoid legal responsibility. Migrant workers in some areas also refuse to sign contracts with their employers in order to avoid paying social security insurance for which they must remain in the insuring city to benefit (Cooke 2012a), though the new Social Security Law goes some way to rectify this problem by making social security funds portable.

Workers' participation

India has a very long tradition of workers' participation in management, which dates back to 1918 (Mankidy 1995). Various schemes of workers' participation have been introduced by the government since 1947 in an attempt to achieve industrial democracy. Important examples of these include works committees (1947), joint management councils (1957), worker-directors (1970) and shop and joint councils (1975). The works committees and joint management councils took the form of a legal approach, whereas the shop and joint councils were promoted as a voluntary scheme. The worker-directors scheme was trialled in the public sector (e.g. the banking industry) with the hope of rolling it out more widely. More schemes of workers' participation were introduced in 1977, 1983 and 1985 (Venkata Ratnam 2009). However, none of these schemes have taken root and enterprises generally have shown little interest in them (see Mankidy 1995 and Venkata Ratnam 2009 for more detailed overviews). This is perhaps not surprising given the fact that these initiatives have been government led with the workers' interest at the heart of the schemes, at least in spirit. A common objection from the management of these schemes is that they represent sectional interests of the workers and not the enterprise as a whole (Venkata Ratnam 2009).

However, it has been noted that quality management initiatives, such as quality circles (QCs), total quality management (TQM) and suggestion schemes that require employee involvement (EI) have been widely adopted by Indian firms since the 1980s. These schemes do not require the involvement of the trade unions and the changing attitude towards unionism and IR is believed to have facilitated the propagation of the schemes (Mankidy 1995). It needs to be noted that productivity and the enhancement of competitiveness remain the primary motives of these schemes and therefore employers' vested interest lies at the very heart of the popular uptake. As Cooke and Saini's (2010b) study of HRM and innovation in 54 Indian firms shows, EI is the second most widely used initiative by the companies studied. This is implemented mainly in the form of suggestion schemes. Quality initiatives, such as QCs, professional circles, problem solving teams, lean initiatives, Kaizen, ISO 9000 series, TQM and total productivity management, are also commonly reported by firms that are innovation oriented. These are essentially forms of EI requiring employees to participate actively and contribute their ideas for business improvement. Firms use reward mechanisms to incentivize their employees (e.g. financial rewards, promotion and recognition when suggestions are adopted). Some even make it compulsory for professional employees to contribute ideas as part of their performance targets.

In China, the formal 'representative function' of the unions, according to the Labour Law, is supplemented by the trade union guided Workers' Representatives Congress (Workers Congress hereafter). It is an official mechanism of workers' participation, through the workers' representative, in enterprise decision making and management. Initially introduced in the late 1940s, the Workers Congress has been given an enhanced role since the 1980s as a result of the economic reform. Again, in reality, the role of the Workers Congress remains less than effective (Benson and Zhu 2000; Cooke 2005). Interestingly, an increasing number of private firms are setting up Workers Congress forums since the mid-2000s as evidence of legal compliance, although they fall short of recognizing the trade union. These Workers Congress forums serve as an extended HRM function in practice instead of playing an industrial democracy role on behalf of the workers.

Similar to Indian firms, quality management schemes have been adopted by Chinese firms since the 1980s for productivity enhancement. In fact, initiatives such as problem solving teams, suggestion schemes and innovation task forces have long been deployed by SOEs during the state-planned economy period, often instructed by the state employer and organized by the unions at the plant level (Cooke 2008a). Suggestion schemes are also increasingly used as part of the performance management system in Chinese firms to institutionalize employees' participation (Cooke 2012a).

The impact of globalization and HRM interventions on IR

Globalization and the economic policy pursued by the Indian and Chinese government have had profound impact on the economic structure and IR in both countries, as has been the case in other Asian countries (see Lee and Eyraud 2008). In other words, the new economy has brought new industries and new ways of managing IR at the firm level. Here, global integration has taken place at two levels: internationally and domestically (though the two are related and overlap). Internationally, this has been achieved in part by the export-oriented industries that are largely privately owned, such as India's BPO industry, employing young English-speaking university graduates, and China's manufacturing industry, staffed by young but lowly educated rural migrant workers. Domestically, this has taken the form of attracting foreign direct investment (FDI) into the country through the establishment of MNC subsidiaries or joint ventures with local firms (see Child and Rodrigues 2005).

In India, the rise of the IT-enabled BPO industry (see Kuruvilla and Ranganathan 2008 for an overview of the industry) presents opportunities as well as constraints for unions to organize workers in this sector, as noted earlier. Even when a union is established, the word 'association' instead of 'union' is to be used to avoid negative connotation of the union's past and to gain acceptance of employers (Noronha and D'Cruz 2009). A partnership approach and a combination of union and professional association function, i.e. a hybrid of servicing and organizing model, are adopted to attract members and address IR problems (see Noronha and D'Cruz 2009, for more detailed discussion). This development broadens the Indian IR system from the primarily manufacturing and public sector IR system in the organized sector to include the private and service sectors that are knowledge intensive, technology driven and high-value adding. The new 'consumer capitalism' ethos also calls for the trade unions to embrace a wider social agenda than their conventional sectional interests (Bhattacherjee and Ackers 2010). By contrast, the Chinese workers in the export-oriented manufacturing firms remain largely unorganized and unprotected, have little bargaining power and often work in sweatshop conditions (e.g. Chan 2001; Lee 2007; Pun and Smith 2007). Labour disputes often erupt abruptly when the tolerance level of the workers reaches its limit, and resolution mechanisms commonly express themselves in radical forms of protests, walk outs and violent struggles. The introduction of the new labour laws in 2008 does not seem to have led to the reduction of labour–capital conflicts, as evidenced by a string of strike actions in the foreign owned manufacturing plants (Cooke 2012a). Demands for pay rises and better working conditions have been the main reasons for the disputes (Wasserstrom 2010; Watts 2010; Hayter *et al.* 2011).

Another consequence of globalization has been the heightened differentiation in the labour market in both countries, with elite professionals whose skills are in great demand at the upper end and those unskilled and unprotected at the bottom end of the labour market. In order to attract, retain and motivate talented employees to enhance organizational competitiveness, Chinese and Indian firms have begun to show interest in Western-developed and MNC-imported HRM techniques. As discussed above, new management initiatives such as EI, TQM and suggestion schemes, performance management system and learning organization are introduced (also see other chapters in this book). The growing awareness, or rather belief, of employers of the positive effects of HRM on organizational performance, and the increasing level of professionalization of the management, have fuelled the adoption of HRM techniques to solicit management–employee cooperation, with or without the union's participation. However, we should be careful not to overstate the impact of globalization and relatedly the influence of foreign MNCs in the changes in IR experienced by India and China. National IR systems are deeply embedded in their societal context, where interests of social groups are 'ambiguous and context dependent', and require multiple disciplinary perspectives to make sense of (Williamson 1985 and Zeitlin 1987: 163 both cited in Bhattacherjee 2001: 245).

Conclusions

Globalization and the opening up of the Indian and Chinese economy in recent decades have led to some major changes in the labour market and IR system in both countries. These changes are rooted in, and therefore need to be understood from, a broader historical–institutional context of each of the two societies. For both countries, a major challenge to their current IR system has been the relatively large, and arguably increasing, proportion of workers engaging in informal employment, who are largely outside the scope of the formal IR system and are inadequately protected by labour regulations. This makes achieving decent work and adequate social security for these workers both an urgent task for the state and a mission near impossible. It is important to note that the enlarging segment of informal employment is partially an unintended consequence of the enforcement of laws in the formal sector. As Harriss-White (2010: 156) observed in the Indian context, which also aptly applies to the Chinese situation, 'both the state and the economy become socially regulated, with the degree of enforcement of regulative law defining the extent of the informal economy. Processes of selective enforcement likewise are socially embedded and "informalized" '.

Within the formal sector, the contraction of the state sector, the rise of a relatively young private sector, the emergence of high-tech driven new industries, and the growing force of young and well-educated employees who are highly ambitious and mobile, and the emergence of HRM initiatives all call into question the adequacy of traditional forms of workers' representation that have relied heavily on the direct intervention of the state (as employer) and the involvement of the trade unions which were closely associated with the political parties.

Compared with China, the Indian IR system remains more complex in part because of its 'persistent institutional heterogeneity' (Hammer 2010: 169), compounded by caste identity, regional political orientation and the nature of unionism. Meanwhile, as Bhattacherjee and Ackers (2010: 117) observed, employers' assault on unionism, and the rising popularity of the American business school model in Indian management education, have led to ebbing interest in traditional IR and 'an academic crisis of identity' which 'has forced Indian academic IR to redefine itself in relation to HRM and the new economy'.

In contrast, the Chinese IR system has been undergoing a period of transformation from its original unitarist approach governed mainly by administrative regulations, to a more pluralistic approach informed by an improving legislative framework that is underpinned by a political ideology of building a harmonious society. Trade unions have been instructed by the state to take on new roles in defending workers' rights, for instance, through the participation in collective bargaining and labour dispute resolutions. As Lee (2009) observed, the direct election of union leaders at the workplaces and their participation in collective bargaining have been associated with lower levels of inequality and disputes. Research and education on labour management relations have arguably received more recognition in the light of growing conflicts between management and labour in some sectors. All these signs suggest that 'the process of democratization and the institutionalization of labour relations in China' might be moving at a faster pace than some other developing countries in the region (Hayter *et al.* 2011).

Acknowledgement

This chapter draws heavily from F. L. Cooke (2012b), 'Employment relations in China and India', in M. Barry and A. Wilkinson (eds), *Edward Elgar handbook of comparative employment relations*, Cheltenham: Edward Elgar. We would like to acknowledge Edward Elgar for granting permissions to reuse the material.

5 Changing talent attraction and retention strategies

Introduction

Previous chapters (see Chapters 1 and 2) have explored the dynamism of the economic and social fabric of China and India in response to the challenges of marketization and globalization, reflected in significant institutional, legal and regulatory changes in both countries, driven by and coupled with major revisions of their approaches to human resource management. Subsequent chapters will discuss the applications of such specific HRM issues as performance management, rewards and career development strategies and programmes in these two contexts. In this chapter however, we focus on the crucial axis upon which both these macro and micro level HRM interventions revolve – namely, the attraction and retention of employee talent – in order to assure the continuing growth, productivity, profitability and sustainability of both their economies, and the public and private sector institutions which underpin them.

Talent management, encompassing the identification of the necessary numbers, skills, competencies and attitudes, of employees required to maximize present and future business opportunities; the ongoing development of national and firm level attraction techniques; and the design of effective employee retention programmes, is, of course, a major global workforce issue – the so-called 'war for talent' coined by the McKinsey company in 1997. Many authors (for example, Lewis and Heckman 2006; Nankervis *et al.* 2006; Collings and Mellahi 2009) suggest that talent management has often been equated with human resource management, although it is in reality only one (albeit important) component of the overall HRM 'recipe' (Sparrow and Budhwar 1997). It focuses primarily on nurturing the workforce 'stars' (managerial and/or professional/technical staff), with a distinctive elitist emphasis, and utilizes the broad repertoire of HRM functions (for example, specialist HR planning, job design, recruitment, rewards and career management) to achieve its aims, sometimes to the detriment of other employees. Cooke (2011: 252) provides a concise definition of talent management based on Lewis and Heckman (2006: 140) – namely, 'a collection of typical HRM practices, functions or activities' – but, for the purposes of differentiation with HRM as a whole, we prefer the following explanation from Stahl *et al.* (2007: 195) because of its clearer focus on the links between talent management and business imperatives, namely 'an emerging business strategy that enables an organization to identify, develop and redeploy key talented employees'. Rothwell and Kazanas (2004) cited in Cai and Klyushina (2009: 21), add its role in organizational transformation as 'the process of changing an organization, its employees (and) its stakeholders (by) using (specialist recruitment), planned and unplanned learning, in order to achieve and maintain a competitive advantage for the organization'. Recently, Scullion and Collings (2011: 6–7) have described *global* talent management as 'all organizational activities for the purpose of attracting, selecting, developing, and retaining the best employees in the most strategic roles … *on a global* scale' (our italics).

The sheer scope and speed of economic and social development in China and India, together with their esoteric contextual characteristics, provide particular difficulties in relation to talent management. As the President of Manpower (North America) cited in Downing *et al.* (2008: 1) explains,

> recruiting the right people, retaining the best staff and developing leaders of the future are difficult tasks in any market. For foreign (and local) companies operating in China, there is the added difficulty of understanding how to *adapt* talent management strategies to the country's unique business culture and values.

Cooke (2011: 251) concurs: 'the task of talent management … is performed in the context of a local labour market and historically-informed employment conditions and social relations that underpin much of the HRM policies and practices'. Indian observers echo similar dilemmas that 'the Indian economy is going through a period of unprecedented growth, while the supply of skills and talent is just not able to keep pace with this growth' (Anonymous 2010h: 1).

Whilst there are considerable similarities in China and India with respect to their economic and social development, together with their relatively recent resurgence as global players, their different historical, ideological, social and political heritages (see Chapters 1 and 2) provide them with diverse challenges with respect to both talent management issues and solutions. These are now explored, first in relation to China and then to India, concluding with a comparative evaluation of both countries' ability to adapt successfully to these important HRM challenges.

China's talent challenges

Informed observers generally agree that China's future economic growth is likely to be constrained by a serious shortage of technical and professional specialists, notably in information technology, financial services and accounting occupations, real estate and construction, legal and management consulting and in regional areas; as well as experienced senior managers with global mindsets (for example, Pan and Lou 2004; Downing *et al.* 2008; Gupta and Wang 2009; Rowley and Warner 2010a; Cooke 2008b, 2011a). As a specific example of the scope of talent shortages, Gupta and Wang (2009c: 179–80) suggest that changes to

Chinese accounting and auditing standards during 2006 demand more than 300,000 new qualified accountants, despite an annual supply of 25,000. These shortfalls are most pronounced in multinational companies operating in China, but are also present in many of the modernizing state owned enterprises and local private companies.

As evidence of the scope of this problem, a McKinsey & Company study (Farrell and Grant 2005) predicted that Chinese companies would require some 75,000 additional managers during the next decade; China Academy of Social Science researchers report that 25 million new jobs were created in 2010 alone (Sainsbury 2011: 34); Manpower research estimated that 40 per cent of employers in China could not fill senior management positions (Arkless 2007); and a later study not only confirmed these estimates, but further suggested that the problem was being compounded by extremely high attrition rates (more that 25 per cent higher than the global average) and associated replacement costs (between 300–2000 per cent of the departing managers' salary packages – Downing *et al.* 2008: 2). The latter authors did not miss the irony of this situation: 'the country with the biggest population is having such struggles identifying, attracting and hiring experienced executive candidates' (ibid.).

Some of these gaps may be attributed to the ageing of China's population, especially in contrast to India. As some recent UN data confirm, China's potential internal labour market will be adversely affected – 'the median age of an Indian is expected to increase from 23 in 2001 to just 29 in 2020, while in China it is expected to be 37' (Ganapathy 2011: C1) – with consequent effects on the latter's population (and labour market) growth. In addition, fertility rates are apparently declining in China – from 3.0 in the 1980s to 1.65 in 2009 (Ho 2011: C2) – at least partly as a result of the 'one child policy' (see later).

Apart from demographic issues and the gap between talent demand and supply, there are also significant challenges associated with the quality and expectations of the available labour markets. Despite the enormous growth in higher education institutions, and both formal and informal management programmes over the last decade supported by the national government – 4.79 million undergraduate and postgraduate students graduated in 2007 (1.68 million in management disciplines), together with the return of some 44,000 overseas-trained graduates (*China Statistical Yearbook 2008*, cited in Cooke 2011: 134) – many potential employers felt that there was 'a significant gap between what they seek and what Chinese graduates trained overseas (as well as home students) possess' (Cooke 2011). Deficiencies identified included a serious lack of actual work experience; limited knowledge of the European and American legal and administrative systems; an inability to deal with the financial aspects of mergers and acquisitions; inadequate English fluency and overall oral skills; a lack of leadership competencies (Downing *et al.* 2008; Hechet and Ruet 2009); undeveloped innovative and creative capacities; and, importantly, an absence of 'lateral thought and concept synthesis' (Anonymous 2007c: 2). Downing *et al.* (2008: 2) assert that less than 10 per cent of these overseas or home-grown Chinese graduates possess appropriate managerial skills. 'China's next generation of college graduates are not prepared for new ways of doing business' (ibid.), notably at the global level. In addition, there are constant reports of fake academic qualifications, testimonials and references, which are exacerbated by an absence of culturally-specific selection tests or background checking services (Downing *et al.* 2008: 9). Even at lower occupational levels, there are looming discrepancies between labour demand and supply. For example, some reports suggest that factories in China's manufacturing heartland are experiencing significant labour shortages, as rural workers employed in cities such as Guangdong have chosen to return to their villages on account of expensive accommodation and living costs, 'labour shortages estimated to be nearly a million workers' (Ho 2011: C2).

Although there is little doubt that finding the right candidates is a difficult task, made more problematic by the intense competition for talent between multinational companies, SOEs, private Chinese companies and prestigious government departments (for example, the Ministry of Finance, Ministry of Foreign Affairs and Trade), MNCs and some government departments are often fussy about those whom they choose to recruit. As Downing *et al.* (2008) report, only the top 20 per cent of available talent (from the diverse labour pools of non-Chinese expatriates, ethnic Chinese regional expatriates, mainland Chinese returnees and local graduates) are seriously considered for managerial roles (Downing *et al.* 2008: 8).

The apparent disconnect between employer expectations and perceived employee knowledge, competencies and skills has been attributed at least partly to the nature of Chinese secondary and tertiary pedagogy, with its heavily theoretical bias at the expense of more practical business applications or critical thinking. However, at vocational education level, there have been a number of recent encouraging developments which may redress some of these issues. The central government has, for example, reviewed the policy and regulatory components of the Chinese vocational training system, with respect to the links between pre-employment training, on-the-job training, re-employment and entrepreneurial training. The review's recommendations include the establishment of a vocational skills training system which focuses on three principles: extended coverage of trainees (especially in rural areas), multiple levels of training (as above), and a plethora of training providers. The new system will include vocational subsidies to employee groups under a Special Vocational Training Program; entrepreneur school cooperation; vocational skills assessment; and a national vocational classification code (ibid.). A recent OECD report praised many elements of these changes, but also noted some continuing challenges including inconsistent cooperation in such programmes by employers, variable school-based resources, relatively few training quality standards and 'insufficient' workforce planning systems (Kuczera and Field 2010: 5).

As well as these aspects of secondary, vocational and tertiary education in China, there are other identified actual or potential problems, including an 'expectation mentality' nurtured inadvertently by the 'one child policy' – the so-called 'little emperor syndrome' (Cooke 2008b; Cai and Klyushina 2009; Rowley and Warner 2010a; Rowley and Cooke 2010). It might also be argued that the latter characteristic may have been exacerbated by both the rapidity of China's economic expansion and the consequences of (global) 'Generation Y' attitudes towards work, careers and rewards. Certainly, like their counterparts in developed economies, China's new generation of graduates are highly techno-savvy, exceedingly well networked (*guānxì* 关系 revisited) – 'candidates are so closely networked that they alert each other so that they can use counter offers to their advantage' (Downing *et al.* 2008: 11) – and have been 'more socially and economically advantaged than previous generations (and have) significantly higher expectations' (Anonymous 2007c: 2).

This may also help to account for the significant job hopping which occurs in the larger Chinese cities and economic zones, especially from state owned enterprises to foreign multinational companies, the increasing dilution of loyalty from such employees (Cai and Klyushina 2009: 8), as well as the growing 'compensation creep'. As evidence of the latter trend, some research studies suggest that base salaries for Chinese professionals have increased by up to 33 per cent in recent years, and that around a third of skilled employees increased their salary packages by more than a half when moving from one multinational company to another (Downing *et al.* 2008: 6). In cities such as Beijing, Shanghai and Guangzhou salary rate rises reportedly rose annually by 7–9 per cent, and 7.5–10.6 per cent in some other economic zones (Downing *et al.* 2008: 7). However, as some recent research indicates 'only the people over 40 years care about benefits and need a stable income. The Chinese (applicants) below 35 years expect to be paid well, but have low needs for benefits' (Cai and Klyushina 2009: 39).

India's talent challenges

Parallel to the Chinese talent paradox, the Indian economy is also currently (and into the foreseeable future) facing significant talent shortages. Recent reports suggest that the Indian population will reach 1.6 billion by 2040, compared with China's likely 1.4 billion (Ganapathy 2011: C1), and the workforce is estimated variously to increase by 80–110 million (Anonymous 2010h: 59) or even 240 million young people (Ganapathy 2011: C2). Half of India's population is estimated to be under 35 years of age with 26 million babies born annually (Ganapathy 2011: C1), but recent Indian government data reveals that 126 million people between 13–35 are functionally illiterate (ibid.), in contrast to China's much older population, lower birth rate and higher literacy levels. An International Institute for Population Sciences expert, Professor P. Ariasamy, cautions that 'India will have the advantage of human capital, but the quality of human capital is a problem. Progress in literacy and education is good, but a little under half of the Indian states in the north are still lagging behind, and that is a concern for effective economic output' (Ganapathy 2011: C2), and he argues that this will only be addressed with the development of a further two thousand universities.

Whilst there is clear evidence of the transition from manufacturing towards the knowledge economy, exemplified best in India's high profile information technology sector, and more recently by extensive use of technology in clothing, jewellery and toy making companies reportedly halving their labour–capital ratios (Anonymous 2010h: 59), manufacturing is still an important segment of the Indian economy which provides an ongoing competitive opportunity with China:

> Labour is cheap in India: signage is painted by hand; bricks are piled nine-high on the crowns of construction workers; shops are more crowded with attendants than customers. As China's workforce becomes older, costlier and stroppier, some firms will look to exit the dragon. Only India has the numbers to match it.
> (ibid.)

This is an arguable prediction, given the plethora of restrictive Indian employment legislation and its strong industrial relations traditions (see Chapter 4), together with the relative absence of investor-friendly economic zones (unlike China), which may not prove as attractive to foreign multinational corporations. However, if accurate, a growth or simply the maintenance of present manufacturing job opportunities, combining extensive process automation with flexible labour conditions, may assist in the continuing employment of the huge unskilled or semi-skilled Indian labour market, especially in rural areas. As Gupta and Wang (2009c: 185) explain, '(the Indian job market) is today just as starkly divided between those with the skills sought by the new economy of call centers and software houses, and those ensnared in the old economy by a lack of skills'.

At the higher end of the talent spectrum, there are significant shortages in the information technology, banking, science and technology, retailing and government sectors, particularly in professional and senior management occupations. As in China, these shortages derive from both quantitative and qualitative origins. The growth in talent demand from local private companies, Indian and foreign multinational corporations and government departments is enormous and ongoing. As examples, the influential National Association of Software and Services Companies (NASSCOM) predicted a shortfall of half a million Indian IT professionals by 2010; Indian companies such as TCS, Infosys and Wipro have been growing their local workforces by 30–40 per cent annually; and 2003–08, IBM, Accenture, Microsoft, EDS, Capgemini, SAP, Oracle, GE and Cognizant have all massively increased their Indian professional workforces (Gupta and Wang 2009c: 182). The corresponding talent supply is made more difficult by the more active poaching of qualified and experienced Indian graduates by large US and European corporations such as Microsoft, Google, Hewlett Packard and IBM. As Davis *et al.* (2006: 281) explain:

> foreign firms can tap into India's well-educated, inexpensive, English-speaking manpower, as consulting companies like BCG and McKinsey or financial services like Citigroup (have) done. In the past, Indian manpower went abroad searching for jobs or training: today, foreign companies go to India to recruit talent, be it at the IIMs, the Institutes of Technology, or from their subsidiaries.
> (for example, Citibank, Proctor & Gamble, and Unilever)

Gupta and Wang (2009c: 182) concur, citing the experience of a head of human resources at a US motorcycle manufacturer thus, 'visiting any of the top tier (Indian) engineering institutions was like going to the beach after a tsunami. There was nobody left!' In response, many local Indian companies (like their Chinese counterparts) are actively recruiting talent from the diaspora who had previously relocated to the US, UK and Europe, with some success but with little real impact on the widening talent gap. There are, however, recent encouraging developments in this area, including the rekindling of nationalistic sentiments amongst some Non Resident Indians (NRIs) because of perceptions of the decline of Western economies following the global financial crisis and the associated resurgence of the Indian economy. Astute employers are using their global experiences for in-house mentoring roles (Ananthram 2011b).

Certainly, the advanced English language skills and knowledge of Western management styles and organizational systems possessed by many Indian graduates make them marginally more attractive than their Chinese counterparts. However, there are some similarities with respect to the perceived qualities and job expectations of the available Indian and Chinese talent. Despite their diverse educational systems, both Chinese and Indian graduates are seen to lack global competencies, 'the dynamics of the global markets' (Bassett *et al.* 2005: 3), managerial skills and experience and innovative capacities. As an example of the latter from the pharmaceutical sector, whilst India has talent with respect to 'process chemistry', it is apparently not as effective in the development of new drugs – 'Indian pharma companies need to sharpen their focus in this area' (Bassett *et al.* 2005: 2). Tymon *et al.* (2010b: 2) report that employers are keen to employ only 25 per cent of Indian graduates because of their perceived lack of the necessary training, language skills and cultural awareness.

There are also suggestions of cheating and bribery in some educational institutions. As an example, Anand (2011: 3) cites the case of a failing engineering student who:

> ... finally figured out the trick: writing his mobile number on the exam. That's what he did for the Theory of Computation exam, and shortly after, he says the examiner called him and offered to pass him and his friends if they paid 10,000 rupees each, about $250. He and four friends pulled together the money, and they all passed the test.

At the lower end of the job market, paradoxically, even call centres have problems attracting suitably skilled employees; '24/7 Customer Pvt. Ltd's increasing difficulty finding competent employees in India has forced the company to expand its search to the Philippines and Nicaragua. Most of its 8,000 employees are now based outside India' (ibid.: 2). Whilst this may (as in China) be merely fussiness on the part of the potential employers or the constant search for even cheaper labour, it may also reflect the nature of the talent market and/or the diversity of management approaches evident in 'modernizing and traditional organizations, and competing western and eastern influences, on dominant human resource practices' (ibid.: 12). On the positive side, some researchers (for example, Ananthram 2011b) note that Indian graduates tend to be more malleable and adaptive than their Western counterparts, facilitating a more effective cultural 'fit'.

There are also similar difficulties with respect to talent retention – considered by some researchers (Ananthram 2011b) to be the most crucial aspect of Indian talent management – because of the expectations of Generation Y graduates in India and China. As examples, Bhatnagar (2007a) attributes talent attrition (reported to be as high as 30–45 per cent annually – Tymon *et al.* 2010b: 2) in Indian companies to perceptions of inadequate human resource systems (especially poor communication or dissatisfaction with career paths), whilst others mention the lack of overall organizational support or intrinsic motivators and associated benefits and rewards (Sparrow and Budhwar 1997; Bassett *et al.* 2005; Rai 2005; Bhattacharya *et al.* 2008; Gupta and Wang 2009c; Tymon *et al.* 2010b) 'creating an environment that fosters a sense of pride in the organization and intrinsic rewards is germane for organizations seeking to create an employee value proposition that cannot be as easily copied by competitors as offering higher starting salaries or higher annual salary increases' (Tymon *et al.* 2010b: 42).

In addition, a looming problem is the current predominance of 30–35-year-olds in middle management positions who are unlikely to be able to progress into increasingly limited senior management careers, resulting in significant frustration, disillusionment and ultimately turnover. The themes of Indian employee commitment to their direct managers; pride in their companies' overriding values (including evidence of their corporate social responsibility focus); and positive perceptions of their companies' HRM practices, rather than merely their own remuneration and career development opportunities, are echoed by several observers (for example, Davis *et al.* 2006; Bhatnagar 2007a; Bhattacharya *et al.* 2008; Grant 2008; Cappelli *et al.* 2010). These authors provide a point of differentiation with respect to the apparent motivators of Indian versus Chinese talent. As Tymon *et al.* (2010: 36–7) encapsulate it, 'perceptions of career success (are) related negatively with intention to leave ... but not as great as satisfaction with the organization ... (and) employees are more likely to value their overall situation within an organization as opposed to stressing only their career success'. Based perhaps on the strength of traditional heritages, the centrality of religion in people's lives, or associated socio-cultural elements, Indian organizations and their managers appear to be infused with a more spiritual orientation than their Chinese counterparts. These aspects are discussed in more detail later in this chapter.

Convergent and divergent approaches to talent attraction and retention in India and China

Given the scope of the talent shortages in both India and China, it is intriguing to explore the manifold ways in which their companies have sought (and will need) to address the problem in coming decades. This section examines the spectrum of human resource management strategies and techniques available, and the similar and different approaches which fit effectively with the socio-cultural contexts of each country. The ongoing debate concerning the convergence or divergence of HRM practices within these contexts is used as a framework for these analyses (see, for example, Davis *et al.* 2006; Chatterjee and Nankervis 2007; Zhu *et al.* 2007, for further discussion). Research in both countries (e.g. Hui *et al.* 2004; Zhu *et al.* 2005; Rowley and Cooke 2010, for China/Sparrow and Budhwar 1997; Davis *et al.* 2006; Bhatnagar 2007a; Gupta and Wang 2009c; Tymon *et al.* 2010b, for India) reveals that both traditional and more contemporary characteristics influence talent attraction and retention in different ways, and that while there is demonstrable convergence of HRM practices towards Western-style approaches there are also considerable differences in their applications. This complexity is explained thus by Rowley and Warner (2010a: 488):

> (it is) contentious to assert that there exists or needs to be an indigenous Chinese theory of (HR) management … but an indigenous theory … may be neither a necessary nor a sufficient condition for an understanding of how national systems work.

More specifically, Cappelli *et al.* (2010: 85) assert that 'the unique Indian leadership approach derives from the India Way's emphasis on broad mission and purpose, and it builds on the stress on improvisation and adaptability'.

Whilst there has been considerable research on the defining characteristics of Indian and Chinese cultures and their impacts on labour markets, management systems and styles and ultimately HRM processes and practices (some of which have been discussed in earlier chapters, notably Chapters 2 and 3), it is sufficient here to suggest that both countries and their associated socio-cultural and workplace contexts are changing significantly in response to the pressures of globalization, economic restructuring, the demands and opportunities of technological change, educational developments and generational change (Hofstede 1991; Bu 1994; Child 1994; Budhwar and Debrah 2001; Hui *et al.* 2004; Cooke 2005; Björkman *et al.* 2008; Rowley and Cooke 2010; Cooke and Saini 2010a). It is also appropriate to note that the size and complexity of both countries ensures heterogeneity in cultural and human resource management practices between urban and rural environments and between coastal and inland regions. However, some generalizations are possible, as professionals, highly skilled technical specialists, and experienced senior managers (talent) are more often than not located in the burgeoning metropolises of India and China, in state owned enterprises, large private companies or foreign multinational corporations, and therefore subjected to similar changing social and cultural influences.

Thus, despite the pressures exerted on both Indian and Chinese talent from their pervasive exposure to the Internet; the so-called 'GenY factor'; the effects of the 'one child' policy in China; and the international experience of the Indian and Chinese diaspora; there are persistent (and sometimes conflicting) cultural and social legacies. As examples of these legacies, Davis *et al*. (2006: 11) maintain that:

> several 'traditional' characteristics of management in India remain in place – notions of authority and hierarchy; the role of familial networks, indigenous ethical-philosophical frameworks and community boundaries; the importance of continuity and stability in institutional and individual norms and practices; and finally, a general acceptance of ambiguity.

It might also be suggested that India's long affiliation with the United Kingdom, and more recently the United States, in particular shared linguistic and cultural understanding and generally harmonious post-imperial relationships, has facilitated the adaptability of Indian talent towards Western managerial and human resource management more effectively than their less connected Chinese counterparts.

However, Cooke's research in China indicates that such traditional values as, 'interpersonal relationships within a social hierarchical order' (2011b – Hofstede's 'high power distance'); collectivism (ibid.); Confucian learning principles, and a need for personal growth (ibid.); employee welfare; status and face-saving (*miànzi* 面子; *guānxì* 关系) and mutual reciprocity (old-style social networks) coexist with newer aspirations for individual recognition, financial rewards and benefits, career advancement and material possessions. She further suggests that younger Chinese professionals and managers appear less risk averse and are more receptive to traditional Western extrinsic motivators than their older colleagues (ibid. – see also Chapter 3). These findings are supported by a recent study of 30 senior managers in multinational companies in Qingdao which concluded that such employees are more prepared to accept performance related pay, are more comfortable with risk taking behaviours and the 'subjugation of traditional Confucian culture to material gain' (Ananthram 2011a: 5).

Strategic talent management

So how have these socio-cultural traditions together with contemporary global business realities been translated into human resource management applications, notably with respect to talent management, in India and China? In a recent interview with Brian Wilkerson, Wyatt Watson's Global Director for Talent (Anonymous 2008b: 22), the emerging global talent management issues were summarized as:

> workforce (HR) planning, involving predictive modelling
> linkages between talent remuneration and business metrics
> 'deep talent segregation', accompanied by 'a differentiation of strategies based on segments'
> the alignment of 'customer' and 'employment' branding
> talent retention as 'a 2-way value proposition.

Wilkerson also suggested that present talent management strategies need to be strengthened through more process, analysis and deeper discussion, and that talent management (TM) responsibilities should be devolved from HRM professionals to line managers or direct supervisors, alongside all other HR functions (in line with contemporary HRM theories). Given the complexity of a comprehensive TM strategy, involving the collection and analysis of talent demand and supply data, the design of effective talent attraction and retention policies; together with the development of associated recruitment, selection, rewards, career and succession plans, Downing *et al.* (2008) specify the need for employment branding, talent growth opportunities, work–family programmes, employee turnover planning and performance-based incentive schemes, (inter alia) it is likely that few line managers will possess the foresight, skills, interest or time to implement such strategies without the specialist assistance of HR managers, even in Western countries.

Many Chinese and Indian companies have abrogated such responsibilities by merely outsourcing their talent attraction activities:

> China's massive growth, coupled with huge talent shortfalls in certain sectors are imposing tremendous pressure on organizations operating in China. These challenges (have been) met by outsourcing part of, or the entire hiring process to a third-party to enjoy lower hiring costs, higher productivity, and business efficiency.
>
> (Downing *et al.* 2008: 17)

Conversely, there is considerable evidence of talent poaching amongst those companies, which are able to offer more competitive reward packages or career opportunities. However, there is limited but encouraging evidence from both India and China that at least some large companies, both local and foreign, are actively attempting to adopt a strategic approach to their crucial TM dilemmas (Warner and Goodall 2010: 1–11). As examples, the Cappelli *et al.* (2010: 57) survey of leading Indian company executives found that they were 'far more likely' than their American counterparts to adopt a strategic HRM approach, reflected in their unique relationships with their talented employees (see later). Their interviews with the CEOs of Reliance Industries (Mukesh Ambani) and Tata Consultancy Services (S. Ramadorai) revealed their commitment to TM – 'it's all human capital at the end of the day' (ibid.: 57) – and their associated HRM priorities (managing and developing talent, shaping employee attitudes, managing organizational culture and internationalization).

Similar rhetoric is evident from Mphasis (India) – 'we have to build *capability* and ensure our people are able to deliver faster, better and cheaper' (Prayag 2010: 1) – and associated findings from Mercer's 2010 Future of Talent Management Survey appear to support such statements. Thus the study found that two thirds of the Indian companies surveyed were in 'growth mode', accompanied by significant investments in leadership training (87 per cent), employee engagement (83 per cent) and workforce training (83 per cent) (ibid.). Or, as the CEO of Aditi Technologies (India) expressed it, 'last year (2009) was all about cost cutting. This year (2010) it's about retaining talent, especially learning and ensuring business success' (Prayag 2010: 1).

Cooke (2012a) evidences the findings of several Chinese researchers (Wei and Lau 2005; Zhu *et al.* 2005: Wang *et al.* 2007) whose empirical studies revealed high levels of alignment between HRM practices and organizational performance, especially with respect to their TM strategies, notably in private companies. Other authors cite the sophisticated strategies employed by foreign multinational corporations such Microsoft China, which 'grooms talent, rotates staff from (its) headquarters and creates a workplace environment which ensures that employees feel valued and are highly engaged in their work' (Anonymous 2007c: 2), including succession plans for technical and managerial staff. Cooke (2011b: 150) suggests, however, that there are few clear differences with respect to their strategic TM focus between organizational types, and overall, that 'MNCs are neither necessarily active disseminators of good (talent management) practices, nor are they passive recipients of host country constraints. Instead, they co-shape the environment and in some cases reinforce undesirable local practices'. There are also some sceptics such as Downing *et al.* (2008: 4) who suggest that 'the notion of proactively mapping out the market to determine the size of the talent pool and understanding the interest level of a company's employment brand is non-existent'. Differences between Indian and Chinese approaches to TM strategies may reflect the divergence between their cultural, ideological and social perspectives of employment relations, or, more particularly, their degrees of connection with Western human resource management styles and techniques.

Broad talent management concepts and approaches

In those Indian companies which have conscientiously adopted at least some of these theoretical TM strategies in response to the presented challenges, there is a plethora of traditional and more innovative techniques evidenced by several authors. However, there is an assumption behind all of them that the 'India Way' of management differs from both Western and other Asian models by means of the embedded relationship between business and national issues, and by its 'holistic engagement with employees' (Cappelli *et al.* 2010: 4). It is unclear whether these management foundations are the result of historical, social (e.g. the caste system), cultural and/or religious influences, although all of them have been put forward as causal factors (for example, Davis *et al.* 2006; Nankervis *et al.* 2006; Chatterjee and Nankervis 2007; Cappelli *et al.* 2010). Whilst these characteristics may be explained away as paternalistic management derived from Buddhist or Hindu principles of human relationships (for example, 'support, knowledge, recognition, empowerment and transformation', derived from the eleventh century mystic, *Gampopa* (Cappelli *et al.* 2010: 55)) and therefore comparable to the influences of Confucianism on Chinese working relationships, the period of communist rule has possibly diluted the practical effects of the latter, whilst they remain strong in Indian organizations and influence their chosen TM activities. Cappelli *et al.*'s interviews with Indian CEOs reveal that 'the melding of business and national leadership is *central* to the Indian

Way of doing business (and) many business leaders are deeply embedded in societal issues'(2010: 3) on the one hand, and on the other:

> firms (are) organic enterprises where sustainable employee morale and building company culture are treated as critical obligations and foundations of their success... people as assets to be developed, not costs to be reduced; as sources of creative ideas and pragmatic solutions; and ... creating ever-stronger capabilities in the workforce.
>
> (ibid.:4–5)

Other authors (c.g. Sparrow and Budhwar 1997; Tymon *et al.* 2010b) argue that such underpinning managerial assumptions inevitably demand transformational leadership styles (the so-called 'nurturant-task' leadership style) which seek employee commitment through managerial reciprocity. As most of this research was undertaken in Indian multinational or private companies, it may not be applicable either to government departments, small and medium size, or family companies. However, where present, these management philosophies positively link to strategic HRM theories, as well as effective TM through the conscious development of company culture, supportive leadership, employee commitment and engagement, rewards and retention systems.

There is little similar discussion in the contemporary literature with respect to the associated aspects of Chinese management, despite the contributions of Confucius (ethics and virtue), Mencius (harmony and benevolence), Xunzi (human relations), Sun Tzu (planning and organizing), Hanfeizi (leadership) or Mao Zedong (collective leadership and participative management) and his successors (Chatterjee and Nankervis 2003). The influence of 'socialism with Chinese characteristics', buttressed by the plethora of employment related legislation, seem not have been as effective in moulding management theory and practice as those features apparent in India.

The relevance of this discussion to TM lies both in the nature of leadership styles in Indian and Chinese organizations and in the expectations of the qualified and skilled employees whom they wish to attract and retain. Companies with transformational leaders who recognize and value links between their business and national interests are more likely to be attractive to applicants who share such principles as governance and corporate social responsibility, and if they also demonstrate holistic employee engagement practices, employee turnover rates will probably be lower than in companies where these characteristics are not present. This is certainly the theme of some India watchers (for example, Davis *et al.* 2006: Gupta and Wang 2009c; Anonymous 2010h; Cappelli *et al.* 2010; Tymon *et al.* 2010b); some of whom suggest that such companies and their leaders have focused on the development of positive work cultures, employment branding, employee commitment and engagement as their primary imperatives, based on their strong philosophical beliefs, to address talent shortages as part of their long-term staffing strategies. Cited company examples include the Pantaloon Retail and Intercontinental Hotels (India) Group, Infosys and Cisco Systems (Gupta and Wang 2009c); Reliance Industries, Dr. Reddy, Yes Bank, HCL Technologies, Tata Consulting Services and MindTree Consulting (Cappelli *et al.* 2010); Pfizer, GlaxcoSmithKline, Mayne Group, Zydus Cafila and Rantaxy (Bassett *et al.* 2005), amongst many others.

Whilst several authors (for example, Child 1994; Zhu *et al.* 2007; Rowley and Cooke 2010) have suggested that, 'there is little doubt, whatever happens, that "Chinese-ness" will remain a major characteristic, whether in managerial behaviour or in the more general context' (Rowley and Warner 2010a: 489), the links between 'Chinese-ness' and particular entrenched philosophies, leadership styles, or practices which might prove attractive to the required employee talent markets, are less well established in the associated literature. Similarly, the ability of these leaders to design and maintain positive work cultures, and subsequently to reduce employee turnover rates, are to date largely unreported, especially in the local private company and former state owned enterprise sectors. The company examples cited by China watchers are primarily from foreign multinational corporations – for example Microsoft China (Anonymous 2007c); Electrolux China and Atlas Copco (Cai and Klyushina 2009) – although a limited number of authors (e.g. Cooke 2011c) have explored local firms such as ZTE and Huawei (for further discussion, see also Chapter 7). However, almost all of these cases reflect a pragmatic rather than an underlying philosophical foundation for the chosen management and leadership styles. The following section of this chapter explores the associated HRM models and strategies which Indian and Chinese organizations use to attract employee talent, in both similar and different ways.

Employer branding, leadership, and the attraction and retention of talent

The theoretical literature on TM generally puts great emphasis on the importance of employer branding and charismatic leadership in attracting and retaining specialist staff, especially in the information technology, retailing, airline, consulting and high profile government sectors. Thus brands such as Microsoft, Google, IBM, Hewlett Packard, Wal-Mart, GE, Virgin, Watson Wyatt and McKinsey, amongst many other multinational companies, together with a handful of local government departments including those involved in foreign affairs, finance and scientific research, are sought after by qualified and creative applicants because of their innovative job and career opportunities, 'cutting edge' technology, generous employment conditions, extensive human resource development programmes, or simply because of the perceived magnetism of their CEOs. Whilst attraction may not always lead to long-term retention if any (or all) of these perceptions are misplaced, it is generally acknowledged that all competitive companies need to address their employment brand and leadership styles as priorities in talent attraction and retention.

Certainly, the above named multinational corporations aggressively use their well established global brands and word-of-mouth reputations as the primary means of attracting and retaining talent in both India and China, successfully appealing to the ambitions and desires of creative younger applicants. As examples, Microsoft has exported many of its US talent development programmes to its Chinese operations (special training for programme managers, knowledge transfer from its headquarters, and global employee rotation programmes called the Marco Polo Program and the Silk Road Scholar – Anonymous 2007c: 3); Atlas Copco uses a combination of job rotation, coaching, action and e-learning, self-directed-learning and in-house university qualifications, mentoring and coaching (Cai and Klyushina 2009: 50); Motorola provides localized management development programmes (ibid); and Electrolux employs succession planning, Intranet training, team-building schemes and mentoring techniques for such purposes (ibid.). A recent study of senior local managers (Ananthram 2011a) found that many Chinese organizations are adopting more objective Western HRM techniques for talent recruitment, selection and promotion, including national advertising, structured selection interviews, promotional criteria such as professionalism and competence, and selective rewards programmes, together with more traditional approaches such as network-based recruiting (*guānxì* 关系) and 'annual red packages' (ibid.: 10). Accordingly, it would be expected that competitive Indian and Chinese multinational corporations and local organizations (albeit with more limited resources) need to promote their brands, exhibit appropriate leadership styles, and provide similar levels of benefits and opportunities in order to attract the necessary talent.

There is growing evidence that Indian and Chinese companies are adopting some of these Western-style employment approaches as well as more culturally-based alternatives. Cappelli *et al.* (2010) explain that many of the larger Indian companies focus on investing in employees, empowerment and developing cultures that 'push employees to act in the interests of the organization' (2010: 70). Many foreign MNCs and large Indian companies have begun to adopt Western-style educational partnerships with overseas or local tertiary institutions such as the Indian institutes of management, institutes of technology and business schools to provide everything from short courses, in-house training programmes, accredited degree programmes, or even corporate universities. As examples, Pantaloon, Tata Consulting and MindTree Consulting conduct comprehensive 6–8 week induction and training programmes. In addition, Gupta and Wang (2009c: 193–5) suggest that Indian companies such as Cisco Systems and Infosys invest heavily in human resource development (notably leadership skills), citing as evidence Infosys' Global Education Centre. Pantaloon Retail, the Intercontinental Hotels Group, Dr. Reddy and Yes Bank's focus on 'nurturing the labor market ecosystem' (ibid.). Zydus Cadila provides customized and accredited qualifications in conjunction with the Indian Institute of Management (Ahmedabad); and Rantaxy Laboratories actively sources talent from the Indian diaspora (Bassett *et al.* 2005: 3). In similar vein, HCL Technologies, an Indian multinational corporation with 55,000 employees spread over 18 countries, has an unique mission statement – 'employees first, customer second' – which is reinforced by its above average salaries, employee empowerment opportunities, ongoing human resource development and 'collaborative management' (Cappelli *et al.* 2010: 54). Other companies have attempted to retain talent through such extreme measures as time-based employment contracts, reinforced by financial penalties for early departure or even the seizure of employees' passports (Ananthram 2011b); or conversely, by opening up job opportunities for younger employees by encouraging older employees to retire through Western-style voluntary retirement schemes.

The literature on local Chinese company approaches to talent attraction through such strategies is less available, although Cooke (2012a) provides some interesting insights. According to Lininger (2007), contrary to perceptions, financial rewards, career opportunities, the satisfaction of employees' needs for recognition and esteem and benefit packages (in that order), are strong determinants of employee retention. As illustrations of the use of above average financial rewards associated with the retention of managers and specialists in Chinese SOEs and private enterprises, Han Junliang (CEO of the former SOE, Sinovel Wind Group Co. Ltd) was paid 8.58 million Yuan, and Yang Yuanqing (CEO of Lenovo) became the highest paid Chinese executive in 2011, with an estimated 79 million Yuan (US$ 12 million) package, despite government limits of 2.8 million Yuan (Yue 2011). More than 120 CEOs of former SOEs and over a hundred private sector senior managers are reportedly paid more than a million Yuan, primarily in finance, IT, real estate, energy and pharmaceutical sectors (ibid.).

In addition, a small number of local Chinese companies have graduate management trainee programmes (for example, Huawei's University), whilst ZTE (amongst others) promotes its employee benefits, mentoring and career development opportunities and its training and development academy (Rowley and Cooke 2010: 269–70). Few studies report that the quality of company leadership or the nature of corporate cultures in local Chinese firms is a strong attractor of talent, despite traditional views which assert that 'Confucian philosophy gives mentoring an important role in social relationships in China ... relationships should be mutual and obligatory between senior and junior members of a group' (Cai and Klyushina 2009: 27). Generational value changes, together with the stronger bargaining position of young talented employees in a scarce Chinese labour market, may account for these apparent challenges to tradition. In an interesting example of cultural ambiguity, however, it is apparently common for Chinese candidates to 'say yes until the very end, so as not to upset the person who is interviewing them, and then turn down the opportunity' (Downing *et al.* 2008: 5), or, as with Western applicants, to play off competing hirers.

In contrast, several authors (e.g. Gupta and Wang 2009c; Cappelli *et al.* 2010) emphasize the greater importance of traditional company values and principles in attracting and retaining talent in local Indian companies. Evidencing the perceptions of senior Indian managers, such authors maintain that while rewards and benefits, and training and development opportunities, are important 'hygiene' factors in competing for quality staff with foreign multinationals, the real 'motivators' are more intangible, and are associated with India's cultural and social heritage. As Cappelli *et al.* (2010: 50) explain, 'employee commitment (is established) by creating a sense or reciprocity with the workforce, looking after their interests and those of their families, and implicitly asking employees to look after the firm's interests in return'. Gupta and Wang (2009c: 198) describe the phenomenon as 'emotional and intellectual bonding'. Combined with leadership styles that are values driven and strategically focused, it is claimed that the 'India Way' is founded on three main imperatives: strong cultures and employee commitment, extensive diversity management programmes and workforce planning closely integrated with ongoing performance management systems. As a result, Cappelli *et al.* (2010: 1) assert that:

> Almost without exception, Indian business leaders .... described the sources of competitive advantage as coming from deep inside the company, from new and better ideas, superior execution and the process of *jugaad* that gets things done ... positive attitudes and behaviors of employees.

(*'Jugaad'* is a Hindi word describing a particularly Indian approach to improvisation, flexibility and adaptability, involving iterative trial and error methods).

Some local approaches to talent management

Given the depth of the present and future talent shortages in both India and China, it is not surprising that multinationals, local companies and government departments have adopted a range of techniques for their attraction and retention, combining traditional with more modern approaches. Thus, together with the provision of competitive rewards and benefits packages, leadership development, continual learning and structured career development opportunities, coaching and mentoring, as well as the outsourcing of peripheral functions, many organizations have adapted their selection systems to access available technologies, and to more closely match the expectations and communication styles of new generation applicants. As examples, some companies in India and China employ applicant-friendly company websites, online screening and testing systems, and maintain comprehensive human resource management databases in order to access internal 'talent pool folklore factors' (Bassett *et al.* 2005: 3) as well as 'smart' business addresses and global relocation opportunities for external labour markets. With respect to the sourcing of different labour markets, Indian and Chinese companies have also ranged broadly, seeking talent from regional cities as well as from the major cities of Bangalore, Beijing, Guangzhou, Mumbai, New Delhi and Shanghai.

As discussed above, others have sought to lure skilled applicants from the diaspora (*hǎiguī* 海龟 or 'sea turtles' in Chinese) with varying degrees of success, or consciously seek a blend of expatriates and locals. Multinationals often use global career paths (for example, Motorola) as inducements for talent attraction and retention. Perhaps the most innovative approaches use employee referrals, mobile phone numbers, email and SMS to contact potential applicants, as described by Downing *et al.* (2008: 16):

> good firms reinvent themselves from 'blue-jacking' (SMS-ing) to social networking ... these new solutions allow you to reach out and get the attention of talent.

Conclusion

This chapter has explored the enormous TM challenges facing India and China, along with the rest of the world but on a larger scale given their predicted economic growth opportunities. Both countries have similar levels of shortages at professional and managerial levels, albeit for somewhat different reasons and in both similar and diverse industry sectors. There are also significant historical, ideological, social and political factors, together with the influences of generational changes, which mediate the relationships between talent demand and supply in India and China, and these have also been discussed in the chapter.

The problems with talent supply are both quantitative and qualitative, necessitating innovative human resource planning and management approaches (internal, external and global labour markets; new sourcing techniques) and the need to address the issues of applicant inexperience, undeveloped linguistic competencies and poor interpersonal and leadership skills through aggressive employer branding and a broad range of HRM programmes including rewards and benefits, human resource development and career and succession systems. The appropriate 'bundle' of HRM approaches is likely to differ in Indian and Chinese organizations, according to the relative influences of traditional legacies on talent attraction and retention aspects such as organizational culture, leadership styles and employee commitment. These may also differ between the various forms of organizations in the two countries – namely, local private companies, state owned enterprises, foreign or local multinational corporations.

The next chapter continues with the discussion of comparative HRM issues and practices associated with performance management, remuneration and career development in India and China.

6 Performance management, human resource development, rewards and remuneration systems

Introduction

The previous chapter examined the changing nature of broad talent management strategies and practices in China and India, suggesting that unexpectedly rapid economic growth in both countries has led to unpredicted shortages of qualified, skilled and experienced employees in both countries, notably in professional, technical and managerial occupations. These shortages have been exacerbated by exceptionally high employee turnover rates which are being partially addressed through comprehensive attraction and selection processes, but these are unlikely to be sufficient by themselves. This chapter discusses the human resource management (HRM) practices employed by organizations in China and India in order to ensure the continuing efficiency, effectiveness and productivity of their workforces, and ultimately to retain their best employees in their increasingly competitive labour markets – namely, performance management (PM), human resource development (HRD) and rewards and remuneration systems.

As discussed in earlier chapters, there is a continuing (and largely unresolved) debate in the literature concerning the convergence or divergence of Indian and Chinese HRM systems and practices with each other or with Western models (see for example, Nankervis *et al.* 2006; Chatterjee and Nankervis 2007; Warner 2009; Rowley and Cooke 2010). However, whilst some research indicates that elements of both Indian and Chinese cultures (see particularly Chapter 2) are likely to influence the nature of their approaches to PM, HRD and rewards and remuneration programmes, there is also a significant degree of convergence with Western traditions, especially in medium and larger firms, in foreign multinationals, and in their respective public sectors. Warner (2010a: 2064) described the latter as 'relative convergence', and suggested that in China, there is a strong capacity 'to synthesize what often appear to be competing, paradoxical, or even contradictory notions' (ibid.: 2054). Similar sentiments have been expressed about India (Raman *et al.* 2002; Bhatnagar 2008). Bjórkman *et al.*'s (2009: 195) study of 87 European owned firms in China and 83 in India also found that many 'blend global standardization with local responsiveness'. Warner (2009: 13) suggested, however, that 'full-blown HRM' is predominant in larger organizations, whether state owned enterprises, joint ventures, town–village enterprises or wholly owned foreign enterprises. Certainly this is evident in many of the larger global Chinese and Indian MNCs (for illustrations, see Chapter 7).

Even so, there is still debate as to how far HRM has been meaningfully adopted in China and India, as opposed to merely paying 'lip service' (see Warner 2010a). It is probably now accepted that in very large companies there is a reasonable degree of the adoption of Western-style HRM practices. As to the precise nature of the practices found, great caution must be adopted as much can be 'lost in translation'. Even where we can find a convincing degree of comparability, the implementation of foreign management practices is still filtered by indigenous cultural influences and values. The analysis of how successfully Chinese enterprises have adopted such practices also divides expert opinion. Some prefer universalist (convergence) interpretations, seeing more of a literal application of Western practices. Others stress the contingency (divergence) approach, taking for instance, a culturalist view. This chapter includes a number of empirical studies taking one approach or the other. The following section provides a broad summary of the current literature on PM, HRD, rewards and career management theory and practices in India and China.

Managing employee performance in China and India

Research by Huselid (1995), Delaney and Huselid (1996), Youndt *et al.* (1996), Becker and Gerhart (1996), CIPD (2001, 2005), Lawler (2005), Cheng *et al.* (2006), the Aberdeen Group (2007) and Chang (2007) all provide evidence that the alignment of PM systems and business strategies result in improved firm effectiveness. The CIPD study (2001: 7) concluded that

> more than thirty studies carried out in the UK and US since the early 1990s leave no room for doubt that there is a correlation between people management and (firm) performance, that the relationship is positive, and that it is cumulative – the more and the more effective the practices, the better the result.

Delaney and Huselid's (1996) earlier research supported such contentions but raised questions about how this occurs, and the Aberdeen Group study (2007) concluded that the solution to such successful linkages lies in aligning individual employee performance with overall firm objectives, a key component of PM theory. A 2006 study by the Institute for Corporate Productivity (Anonymous 2007d: 17) suggested that 'the coordination of multiple key (PMS) practices' is required for firm effectiveness, rather than a single PM practice (see also Guest *et al.* 2000).

This latter finding is supported to some extent by several Australian studies (for example, Nankervis and Penrose 1991; Nankervis and Leece 1997; Nankervis and Compton 2006). Thus, strategic HRM theory in Western countries is supported by an increasing quantum of research studies which agree that the linking of PM systems with business objectives and outcomes can contribute significantly to enhancing firm effectiveness. They further suggest that comprehensive PM systems embrace a host of other HRM processes, including (but not limited to) HR planning, job design, staffing, HRD, recognition and rewards schemes, retention, career development and termination.

Little research has been conducted on PM in local or multinational companies' (MNCs) subsidiaries operating in India and China, and even less on PM practices employed by local firms. The Chinese authorities have long been keen to emphasize indigenous cultural values so as not to be seen as taking up Western practices uncritically. A number of significant labour and personnel reforms were indeed successfully introduced in China in the 1980s and 1990s, which have assisted in the improvement of labour productivity in Chinese enterprises. Prior to this period, worker output was at a very low level and not competitive internationally. Under the command economy regime, managers were unable to dismiss surplus workers and labour flexibility was almost non-existent. Short term contracts were, however, introduced by a regulation (rather than a law) in 1986. A wider personnel reform also came about in 1992, known as the (*sān gǎigé* 三改革), the 'Three Reforms' legislation. It was introduced in the early 1990s in north-eastern China focusing on labour contracts, rewards systems and social insurance. The outcome of these changes was a move away from the old 'iron rice bowl' employment system towards a labour market emphasis. Consequent comprehensive labour laws set the scene for a more flexible labour market (see Chapters 3 and 4 for a detailed explanation of these legislative changes and their implications).

These legislative changes have all had important impacts on PM, HRD, rewards and remuneration systems and practices and HRM more generally. By the end of the 1990s, the reform programme was robustly institutionalized and PM was being implemented in large Chinese firms, in former SOEs that had been turned into joint stock companies, and in joint ventures and wholly owned foreign enterprises. This was a common occurrence as management innovations based on Western notions were usually to be found in these kinds of firms. Outside these types of enterprises, irrespective of ownership, it was still early days. However, in 1993 a performance appraisal committee of the Chinese Communist Party (CCP) was formed to assess civil servants, and it recommended that key performance criteria should include professional experience, managerial skills, work performance, efficiency and 'sound political views' (Rieger 2008: 14–15).

Since that time, some studies of PM systems in Chinese organizations have begun to emerge. A paper by Qiao *et al.* (2009) on 'high-performance work systems' in a Chinese context provided a theoretical framework as well as collecting a large amount of empirical data. The researchers argued that effective HR practices are positively linked to enhanced employee motivation and commitment. Another study by Zhang and Li (2009) linked high-performance work practices to firm performance, using evidence from the pharmaceutical industry in China. They found that the 'HRM index' (comprising high-performance work practices such as extensive training, participation, detailed job definition, results-oriented performance appraisal, internal career opportunities and profit sharing) was significantly correlated to the market performance of the firm.

Formal PM systems are now more widely seen in large Chinese local and foreign owned firms, although the extent of their practical implementation is still problematic. As one author notes:

> awareness of using the performance management system as a critical tool to drive business performance has grown very strongly in China in the past few years. We could see efforts were made to introduce new systems and process. Some of the organizations have experienced the benefits of using their system to enhance business results and retain talents while many of them are working hard to modify their implementations.
>
> (Mak 2003: 9)

The same researcher found some indications of the broad usage of PM systems (96 per cent, with nearly 80 per cent for all employees) amongst companies such as ABB (China), Beijing Havi Food Company Ltd., Shanghai General Motors and Cognis China; but with considerable dissatisfaction on account of a lack of employee participation in the process; weak links to promotions; and minimal feedback on performance (ibid.: 4). Forced ranking systems and subjective performance reviews are apparently commonplace.

We should, however, note that at this stage PM is only in its early days as an integrative HRM strategy in China, and it has only been found in a limited number of enterprises, mainly those open to Western influences. These were largely what might be classified as 'learning organizations' and were mostly found in major Chinese cities such as Beijing and Shanghai. As Li *et al.* (2009: 63) noted, 'firms with a high level of global-ness often have an open and transparent performance (management) system'. In an encouraging development, however, the Chinese government, through its State Owned Assets Supervision and Administration State Council, is using 'enterprise performance index systems' (Anonymous 2009b) to assess the effectiveness of PM systems in the former SOE sector. It has also encouraged the reform of associated vocational training, but this initiative has been somewhat stymied because of a lack of experienced trainers and outmoded teaching methods (Rieger 2008: 15).

Another example of PM is in firms described as exemplary:

> the China Super HR plants appear to operate differently than other facilities in China. Specifically, they are developing more skilled, higher-paid workers and are giving them the strategies and tools to improve. The impact from this effort, though, appears greater among Super HR JV/FEs ... Approximately 11 percent of the JV/FEs were Super HR, compared to 8 percent of private and 6 percent of state-owned plants.
>
> (Wellins *et al.* 2005:11)

A recent consultancy report on PM in China made the following observations:

1 Chinese firms have a highly structured approach to performance management, with 89 percent reporting that they had adopted a formal structure for their enterprise performance management systems.

2 In China, the dominant role of enterprise performance management is assessing performance. Other purposes such as aligning employee behaviour and improving operational efficiency are seen as less important. External reporting is seen as the least important role for performance measurement.
3 Generally Chinese firms appear to be making significant progress with their enterprise performance management systems. The balanced scorecard is particularly popular with 67 percent of firms reporting that they used this.
4 In spite of the progress made, however, firms still face significant challenges with their enterprise performance management systems. Less than half of the respondents attributed part of their companies' overall business performance to their enterprise performance management systems. This is particularly interesting as 59 percent of respondents claimed that they gained insight from their enterprise performance management systems and over 60 percent said that their enterprise performance management systems helped them make better strategic and operational decisions.
5 Despite the reported benefits of enterprise performance management, the fact that less than half of those surveyed attribute part of their overall business performance to their enterprise performance management systems suggest some shortcomings. Why don't a greater number of Chinese firms attribute more of their organisations' overall business performance to their enterprise performance management systems if they are delivering insight and enabling them to make better decisions?
6 A major factor is the confidence to act on information. Making decisions is all very well, but unless decisions are followed by action their impact will be negligible.
7 There are three reasons why Chinese firms might be hesitant to act on their enterprise performance management data. *First*, there are relatively few advocates for enterprise performance management in Chinese organizations. Less than a third of respondents report that their Chief Executives are advocates of enterprise performance management and advocates drop to less than 5 percent at the level of the employees. *Second*, there are clear concerns about how well enterprise performance management systems integrate with other organizational systems – especially those associated with risk management. *Third*, questions can be asked about whether Chinese firms are making best use of their performance data.

While many claim to be happy with the insights their performance data deliver, an over-whelming 73.2 percent of the respondents either have incomplete or partial understanding of cause and effect relationships in their companies. This is perhaps because 45.9 percent make no effort to visualize the links between their measures. So what should Chinese firms do to improve the impact and effectiveness of their enterprise performance management systems? For Chinese firms it appears that the primary issue concerns confidence to act on the data provided by the enterprise performance management system. Increasing levels of advocacy, enhancing integration and extracting more sophisticated insights from the data are crucial priorities'.

(Yaghi *et al.* 2008: 3–4)

In India, the situation is quite different on account of the pervasive influences of HRM strategies and practices from British colonialism (see Chapter 2) and, subsequently, other foreign multinationals. HRM theories and practices in India have replicated these exemplars for decades in both the public and private sectors. However, this by no means implies that most (or even a majority of) local and foreign private firms, or their public sector counterparts, have adopted the theory and/or practical applications of Western PM traditions. Indeed, research in several Western countries (for example, Nankervis and Leece 1997; CIPD 2001, 2005; Nankervis and Compton 2006; Aberdeen Group 2007) has revealed a significantly patchy implementation of PM principles even in these countries, and the links between PMS and firm effectiveness are far from assured (Becker and Huselid 1995; Cheng *et al.* 2006; Chang 2007).

There are, however, encouraging recent developments in India, spearheaded by the national government, which appear to reflect a change in emphasis towards the centrality of PM in assuring organizational productivity, efficiency and effectiveness. Whilst similar initiatives have been undertaken by the Chinese government (as briefly discussed earlier), because of China's longer road to HRM modernization and the more recent permeation of Western trends into both the public and private sectors, it may be argued that India is more highly developed in these areas. Certainly, the Indian government has in recent years been more proactive with respect to the implementation of integrated performance management systems under the 'new public management' (Anonymous 2009d) umbrella. In particular, the Centre for Good Governance (within the Department of Administrative Reforms and Public Grievances) has identified and promulgated the need for all Indian organizations, whether in the public or private sectors, to 'move from measurement of input usage for programs and appraisal of process compliance to assessment of outcomes and impacts through a well-designed system of performance management' (Anonymous 2009d: 1).

The Indian government has recently appointed an expert, Dr Prajapati Trivedi, a former World Bank economist, as its Chief Performance Officer to oversee a broad-ranging analysis of and formal report on performance monitoring and evaluation systems, with the public sector providing 'best practice' exemplars for all other industry sectors (Hicks 2010: 2). Annual reviews of 'best practice' HRM regularly include such firms as Infosys Technologies, Hindustan Unilever, ITC, ICICI Bank and Tata Steel as amongst those which have developed integrated PM in order to both make themselves more attractive to potential talent (see Chapter 5) and to ensure their continuing viability and competitiveness (Anonymous 2010c). Fewer studies have been conducted on Indian SMEs, but it is likely that the picture there is more random.

Nevertheless, the Indian government study mentioned above (Anonymous 2009d) revealed many interesting characteristics of former PM systems and made several useful recommendations with respect to future-oriented principles and practices. As examples, the study report criticized the prevalent 'rule-based' and 'process-regulation' foci of PM approaches; the lack of clarity and quantification of performance goals; an absence of two-way consultation and communication; inadequate feedback (and sometimes secrecy) about performance; and a distinct punitive rather than a developmental imbalance – PM 'rarely punish and never reward' (Anonymous 2009d: 5). Systemic issues included inflexibility in PM design, frequent (unrelated) employee transfers and a lack of conscious choice in work team membership (ibid.).

In response to these identified deficiencies, and ratified in recent legislation and associated regulations such as the Public Service Bill (2007), the Second Administrative Reforms Commission and the Sixth Central Pay Commission, a number of radical and quite precise recommendations concerning PMS in India were suggested. These included the establishment of performance-related incentives (PRIs), such as fixed and variable salary components and annual bonuses (up to 20 per cent for civil servants) to reward good performance; transparent approaches, interactive performance reviews and job specific performance appraisal formats; together with the signing of memoranda of understanding between the government and particular public sector agencies which 'specify (their overall performance) expectations and responsibilities' (Anonymous 2009d: 9). At least ten ministries, including the Department of Service and Technology, are reportedly implementing these reforms.

Other initiatives focused on delineating the rights of consumers in terms of service delivery criteria and complaints mechanisms, for example a Citizens' Charter which addresses service standards and consumer grievance processes, a Citizens' Report Card, a Community Service Card and Social Audits which encourage public scrutiny of public and private agency records, benchmarking systems which define service norms and 'align delivery capabilities with the expectations of citizens', and new service quality business processing systems (Anonymous 2009d: 13). Most of these programmes are funded from government sources, making them cost neutral for the participating organizations. Many have been a direct result of the Indian government's desire to protect consumers from 'irresponsible lending, predatory practices, and non-transparency' (Leonard 2010: 1), following the global financial crisis, as well as endemic local corruption especially in the banking sector. Whilst such reforms may be seen as over zealous or simply impractical within the entrenched Indian bureaucratic structure, they provide strong signals that the government is seriously attempting to address the deficiencies of both its own and the private sector's former PM systems through a series of interconnected HRM activities, including links to training and development, rewards and remuneration and career planning schemes. The following sections of the chapter explore these links in both China and India.

Human resource development in China and India

There are many definitions of HRD, but the following best encapsulates the discussion of HRD in this chapter – namely, 'the integrated use of training and development, career development and organization development to improve individual, group and organizational effectiveness' (American Society for Training and Development – cited in Zhao and Chen 2010: 91). As in many other countries, but perhaps with a heightened focus because of the growing talent shortages in China and India discussed in Chapter 5, there are indications at macro (government) and micro (firm) economic levels in both nations of more intensive strategies towards adding value to their human capital through continuous learning systems. For example, in the case of China, Cremer (in Warner and Goodall 2010: 71) explained that China's State Economic Commission 'came to appreciate that an army of managers was required with quite different capabilities and orientations from those who had worked under the previous planned economy'. This is supported by Zhao and Chen's (2010: 92) observation that 'human resource development has been given top priority by the (Chinese) government … HRD practices are the mechanisms aimed at the development of human capital, and many Chinese enterprises appear to have begun to understand the nature and relevance of human capital theory'.

However these initiatives are often tempered at the micro level by the contemporary realities of their broad labour markets, in particular diminished employee loyalty and high turnover rates, with employers consequently sometimes reluctant to invest in such programmes. Li and Sheldon (2010: 2066) explained these employers' dilemma thus: 'investment in transferable skills implies a heightened poaching threat … despite investments in training, employers cannot depend on Confucian values of loyalty and mutual obligations to inhibit employees from taking advantage of external labour market opportunities'. Zhao and Chen (2010: 95) suggest that this is a particular problem for the former SOEs, which have neither the resources nor the employer branding as potential employee retention levers.

These issues, and the innovative retention solutions adopted by some Chinese and Indian employers have been discussed in considerable detail in the previous chapter, but it is pertinent to note Warner's sanguine observation about the syncretic resilience of both countries' cultures in the face of such challenges – namely, their ability 'to synthesize what often appear to be competing, paradoxical, or even contradictory notions' (2010a: 2054) such as these. Tam and Chui (in Warner 2010a: 2067) suggest that in China Confucian values of 'life-long learning, constant renewal of one's knowledge, and paternalistic management style(s)' naturally reinforce the societal value of education as well as training and development as a component of employers' overall people management responsibilities. It may be argued similarly that the quest for knowledge underpinning Hinduism, Buddhism and Islam pervades Indian society even more strongly (see Chapter 2 for detailed discussion of these cultural issues).

At the macro level in China, successive governments have been proactive in supporting education, training and development at all levels with a mixture of legislative, regulatory, funding and promotional strategies. Goodall and Warner (2010: 15–20) highlight the historic legacies of the Zhou Dynasty (1046–1256) and Confucius (551–479BC), together with the later development of business-focused tertiary education programmes at Beijing and Tsinghua Universities, and subsequent international MBA programmes (for example, the joint venture China–Europe Management Institute, (later CEMI): the China Europe International Business School, CEIBS (Frohn 2010: 54); the growth of 62 MBA courses by 2000; and, presently, more than 90 MBAs throughout China), as key indicators of active government support for human capital development at the national level – 'the economic, political and social reforms after 1978 enabled the experiments of which new steps in management education forms a part, including the setting up of western style business schools and the diffusion of new widespread MBA (*gōngshāng guǎnlǐ shuòshì* 工商 管理 硕士) courses' (Goodall and Warner 2010: 1). Many foreign countries, including Canada, the US, UK, Japan and the EU have provided assistance to the government in these ventures, in cities such as Beijing, Chengdu, Shanghai and Tianjin. Even the British Open University became involved, partnering with the TV University in China (Warner 2011b: 399).

The ownership of these business schools is quite diverse, ranging from state owned (for example, Tsinghua University), joint ventures (CEIBS), or wholly foreign (Rutgers, State University of New York, Cheng Kong Graduate School of Business (Di Rollo 2010: 158)). There are now reportedly more than 1,400 dedicated business schools in China, and India has 1,600 such schools which graduate 150,000 students annually (Jenster 2010: 177). 'It is predicted that Chinese business schools will gradually move away from Western pedagogies and teaching materials towards China-specific theories and related training content' (Jenster 2010: 193). In addition, the corporate university concept has been broadly implemented in China by foreign MNCs such as Motorola (Beijing and Tianjin) and Ericsson (Beijing, Chongqing, Guangzhou and Hong Kong) since the 1990s (ibid.: 22), and replicated by local MNCs such as Haier (see Chapter 7) and Midea (Zhao and Shen 2010: 96). Most of these programmes have focused on the development of managerial competencies identified as deficient in many of the SOEs, local and foreign private firms – namely conceptual, diagnostic, analytical, problem solving, leadership, team building and people management skills (Child and Chen in Warner and Goodall 2010: 33; Frohn, in ibid.: 60; Chong, in ibid.: 109).

In spite of such programmes, however, employers in China often criticize their graduates' lack of business experience, inadequate knowledge of the Chinese and global business environments, or their lack of self-awareness (Di Rollo: 168). Goodall and Warner (2010: 137) reported on a particularly successful management development programme conducted at the Chinese firm COFCO, which focuses on strategic thinking and team leadership as a reinforcement of its learning culture imperative, and links this to career development – 'the training is linked to business strategy and business development … if you do not participate in the training you will be excluded from progression in the organization' (2010: 140). Zhu *et al.* (2010) proposed that effective managerial training and development programmes should concentrate on 'soft' rather than 'hard' management approaches, and 'internal' rather than 'external' cultures and structures – 'the soft-oriented management style, such as better communications, participation and provision of information, is more effective than the hard-oriented management restructuring of systems or structures. In addition, the effect of the internal-oriented clan structure is more profound than that of the external-oriented market culture' (Zhu *et al.* 2010: 457). These emphases are naturally reflective of culture-specific issues such as *guānxì* (关系) and collectivism, but also of generational characteristics, and the expectations of the new talent market, as discussed in the preceding chapter. As Rowley and Benson (in Nguyen *et al.* 2011: 1) suggested, 'training among countries seems to be associated with the stages of industry and economic development, cultural features, country institutions, or globalization'.

The legal framework underpinning education, training and development in China is quite extensive, commencing with the Strategic Declaration on the Education System promulgated by the Central Committee of the CCP and followed by the Compulsory Education Law (1986), the Vocational Education Law (1996), the Labour Reserve System (1996), the new Labour Law (2008) and other associated regulations including a vocational ability appraisal system and a vocational qualifications certification system (Nguyen *et al.* 2011: 11). However, there is a scarcity of qualified trainers and educational resources, leading to spasmodic and patchy coverage of training and development programmes in different industry sectors. As might be expected, FIEs (foreign invested enterprise) appear to conduct both more (and more sophisticated) training, whilst SOEs are more impoverished and tend to perceive training and development as a cost rather than a value-added investment in their human capital (Benson and Zhu 2000; Cooke 2005; Zhu 2005; Shen 2010; Nguyen *et al.* 2011).

Shen (2010: 339–40) explains that HRD programmes in small and medium enterprises are characterized by 'informality, emergence, non-bureaucratic cultures and an absence of sophisticated practices'. In a recent small study of SOEs and town and village enterprises (TVEs) in China, he found that employees were generally unsatisfied with their training and development opportunities, especially in relation to the (lack of) links to career development. The most satisfied employees were urban male managers aged between 40 and 50 years and with higher education qualifications, possibly because they are seen as those with the most future potential for their organizations. He concluded that HRD in these firms 'tends to be pragmatic and casual, and lacks long-term planning, strategic integration, commitment to employee development, and any consideration of what employees want' (Shen 2010: 349).

As mentioned earlier, India's HRD infrastructure has been in existence at both national and industry levels for considerably longer than in China on account of both its ancient scholarly traditions (see Chapter 2) and the legacies of British colonialism. As Gerhaeusser *et al.* (2010: 309) explain, 'India has established a very large, complex, and modern system of higher and professional education. It inherited the British model but developed an Indian style of its own … largely based on the practice of affiliation, which was started by the University of London'. It is a very diverse higher education system, with universities (central, state, deemed and private), institutes of national importance and colleges (ibid.: 310). Five Indian universities (namely, Hyderabad, Jadavpur, Jawarhal Nehru, Madras and Pune) are considered 'universities with potential for excellence' (ibid.), and the various Indian Institutes of Technology (IITs – Chennai, Delhi, Mumbai) and Indian Institutes of Management (IIMs – Ahmedabad, Bangalore, Kolkata) are well regarded globally as a consequence of their elitism (high quality academics, low and competitive student enrolments, secure funding and international linkages). A recent Asian Development Bank report concluded that 'India's higher education is better matched (than China's) to the needs of the country's economy' (Gerhaeusser *et al.* 2010: 330). However, despite these positive features, it discerned some potential weaknesses, including a significant imbalance between the arts/humanities and business education (in favour of the former); high graduate underemployment; inadequate quality assurance mechanisms; and a high degree of government control in institutional funding and operations (ibid.: 332).

Literacy levels in India are also noticeably lower than those in China. While Bhatnagar (2006: 417) suggested that 'the competitive edge (in India) will come from a company's ability to innovate, create and use the entrepreneurial energies of its people', he also mentioned a series of obstacles to employee learning in Indian firms, gleaned from the research of other authors. These include 'functional myopia' (or a 'silo mentality'), managerial 'command and control orientation(s)', a focus on short term operational issues, insularity and stasis (ibid.: 418). In another research study of the ITES (information technology enabled service) sector, he also found that 'while India does have a large talent pool, not all are "industry ready" … (whilst there is) plenty of supply at the entry level (call centre operators), there are huge gaps in the middle management and senior management levels' (Bhatnagar 2007a: 644). On the positive side, Raman *et al.* (2007: 698) pointed out there are 'over two million English-speaking graduates every year ... ready to work at up to 80 percent less salary than their western counterparts'. However, in recent years the competitive advantage afforded by these highly educated but relatively inexpensive call centre employees is gradually being eroded because of a reduction of contextual and skills training, a significant lack of career opportunities and rising wage levels and employee demands; together with objections from consumers in multinational firms concerned about the loss of local jobs. These aspects are discussed in more detail in the preceding chapter on talent management.

The broad HRD challenges facing Indian firms include a significant scarcity of technical and professional talent; the need to develop 'an appropriate training infrastructure for improving domain-specific knowledge', and subsequent employee retention strategies (Raman *et al.* 2007: 703). Other research studies (Anonymous 2009d: 37) have suggested that HRD customization requires 'well-designed value propositions', including a combination of training programmes (63 per cent respondents), rewards and recognition systems (73 per cent) and career development opportunities (59 per cent). In response to these challenges, many of the larger local private firms and multinational companies have designed and implemented innovative training and development programmes associated with their overall talent attraction and retention strategies. Thus, Hewitt's Best Employers' India (2007) Study found that the top 25 Indian firms consciously link their performance and competency assessment systems and loyalty programmes with education, mentoring and growth opportunities; and Wipro has retitled its HR department as a 'Talent Acquisition and Development Department' (Naquiri 2009: 90), reflecting its future-oriented imperatives. Bupharm, a local family owned Indian pharmaceutical company, classifies its employees into 'top talent; valued talent; talent under watch; and incompatible talent' (Anonymous 2010i: 12), and designs a variety of tailored development programmes accordingly, ranging from specialist executive coaching, job enrichment and 360-degree feedback to gradual employee attrition in the last category. Aviva Insurance Company India has a broad range of training, development and recognition programmes for different levels of employees rejoicing in such Bollywood-esque names as 'Head Start', 'Policy Hitters', 'Rockstar', 'Jewel Club' and 'Million Dollar Round Table' (Varkkey and Joy 2010: 111). Table 6.1 below illustrates the diverse and culturally esoteric development initiatives which Aviva uses to attract, maintain and retain its employees.

Other local firms, such as Infosys, Satyam Computer Services and Bharat Forge 'increase the supply of employable talent by training all new hires and

Table 6.1 HRD initiatives at Aviva India

A 'no-barriers', easy-to-approach executive management style makes the internal operations much more transparent, which in turn, fosters motivation of individuals.
A non-hierarchical inclusive organization.
A resilient leadership that is willing to travel the extra mile to ensure higher levels of employee engagement.
Talent management – focuses on 'vital many' and not 'significant few'.
Succession planning – scouting talent from within.
Meritocratic culture – driven only by performance.
Buddy scheme – an employee-friendly initiative for hand-holding new joinees into the organization.
Development opportunities in the best B schools of India (IIM, Ahmedabad) and abroad (INSEAD, Wharton and Centre for Creative Leadership).
Investment in our people through rigorous in-house programs like 'Managerial Excellence' and 'One Team One Dream'.
Innovative reward and recognition process – percolates to all functions and levels.
Communication channels – Global Climate Survey, Ideas4Aviva, Town Halls to keep the two-way communication.
Leaderful organization – a sustained effort to create leaders at all levels by institutionalizing the process of 360-degree feedback and coaching.
Friends to Colleagues (F2C) – a unique referral program that allows you to choose your colleague.
Allowing spouses to work as colleagues.
Unique wedding and marriage anniversary policy.
A very empowered and agile team – everyone is a CEO with freedom and accountability.
A very sensitive and robust diversity agenda that goes beyond the obvious.
Free cab facility for all commuters from NCR to the Head Office at Gurgaon.
Work–life balance – a five day week.
Gurukul – an in-house library.
Life skills session – unique learning platform.

Source: Adapted from B. Varkkey and R. Joy, 2010, 'Exhibit 8: Initiatives taken to make Aviva India a great place to work': 119.

strengthening the linkage with educational institutions' (Singh and Chaudhuri 2009: 10). Infosys and Satyam have close relationships with several Indian universities (Indian Institute of Science, Bangalore, Indian Institute of Technology, Chennai), and Bharat Forge conducts a bachelor's degree in manufacturing engineering with Birla ITS (Pilani) and Warwick University (UK). BASF focuses on the long-term attraction of potential young employees with its Kids' Lab and Service Express programmes (Singh and Chaudhuri 2009). In these cases, customized development programmes are the norm aimed at 'a no excuse culture, a measurement culture' (Raman *et al.* 2007: 706).

Foreign multinational companies such as Motorola India (Gurgaon) focus on personal development activities aimed at 'employee growth, happiness, involvement and high energy' (Srivastava and Bhatnagar 2008: 257), including company golf courses, aerobic centres, gyms and paid sabbaticals, replicating such US counterparts as Google, Microsoft and Hewlett Packard (Anonymous 2010c). Others search for future talent at Indian universities through studentship programmes and campus recruiting; implement extensive trainee induction systems; or provide a series of HRD activities such as job rotation, cross-functional projects, technical training and management development centres to meet the perceived needs of their aspirational talent (Bhatnagar 2008: 22) – 'the most powerful talent management practices are firm-specific and respond to an organization's unique business and human capital context' (ibid.: 21).

Despite these exemplary HRD initiatives in large local private and multinational firms and amongst specialist talent in India, it is unlikely that they are replicated in small and medium enterprises, in rural areas, or in industry sectors such as manufacturing (12 per cent growth (Gaba 2008: 3)) or agriculture (60 per cent growth (Gaba 2008: 3)) which still form a major component of the Indian economy. As in China, HRD in India is primarily a function of 'high-tech' industries, and highly educated and skilled technical and managerial professionals rather than semi-skilled or unskilled employees. However, in the latter cases, 'the process of skill development in the informal sector in developing countries is more important since formal training institutions do not have the capacity to train all those who want to acquire skills, and few of those who want to acquire skills have the means to afford formal training' (Gaba 2008: 2). Distance education is also becoming an important component of ongoing learning, especially in the healthcare, education and ICT sectors. Extensive government support for such activities in both countries is essentially restricted to leading edge firms and their scarce talent, not for general consumption.

Rewards and remuneration systems in China and India

Turning now to another theme in our chapter, we consider the extensive reform of rewards and remuneration models and systems in Chinese and Indian firms over the last few decades. In China, under the Maoist regime, the old adage was 'they pretended to pay us and we pretended to work'. Egalitarian pay structures were the norm. The system was based on the Soviet model, with a similar grading scale ('grade wage system' (Wang *et al.* 2009: 330)) as adapted to Chinese circumstances (Takahara 1992). Across China, broadly speaking, there were 8 grades for workers, 15 grades for technical personnel and 25 grades for administrative and managerial cadres. This was supplemented with 'high levels of subsidies for numerous expenditures including housing, education, medicine, transportation, staple foods … long-term disability, insurance, comprehensive medical coverage, winter heating fees, nursery schools for children etc.' (Wang *et al.* 2009: 330–1). This model was to be found widely in the state owned sector from the 1950s. When one of the authors of this book was conducting empirical research in Chinese enterprises in the 1980s and 1990s, much of which was conducted in SOEs and newly set up JVs (see Warner 1995) it was rare to find any reward systems other than the above multi-grade model. Since then, many aspects of remuneration have significantly changed.

As the market reforms impacted during the 1990s, efforts were made to motivate workers by paying them according to their actual performance. As De Cieri *et al.* (1998: 6) pointed out, 'the traditional compensation system became a major target of China's economic reforms. The first step in compensation reform involved the restructuring of SOEs into relatively independent business units and the development of links between compensation and enterprise performance. Consequently, the state-fixed wage system has been replaced by diversified wage packages with more emphasis on enterprise profitability and individual performance'. As an important component of wage packages, the bonus system was restored and further developed. In the SOEs, managers' salaries after 1984 were linked to enterprise performance (Rieger 2008: 11). The reform of remuneration systems has resulted in 'a shift from equal distribution to income polarization among employees working in different types of enterprises' (De Cieri *et al.* 1998: 6). It is hard to see whether this was an intended consequence of the reform programme but it is clear that Deng's pragmatism encouraged such differentials, indeed he is alleged to have said 'to get rich is beautiful'.

As a result of the economic reforms, China has thus seen one of the fastest increases in income inequality ever recorded in a single nation. Other transitional economies also saw rapid inequality rises but none have attained China's level of inequality so quickly. The Gini Coefficient, which measures income inequality, rose from around 0.25 under Mao to over 0.45 today. Such trends in China reflect fundamental shifts in the way labour is allocated as a factor of production and compensated for its efforts. It has moved in its transition from a 'socialist planned economy', with more or less fixed wage-scales and virtually no labour mobility to speak of, to a market-based system featuring a burgeoning non-state sector and a relatively competitive labour market. The results to date from the change in the remuneration model are in fact mixed under the 'rewards' heading, as many enterprises still pay group bonuses rather than individual ones. In a number of studies carried out by one of the co-authors of this book, individual-based rewards systems were not very common until recently (see Warner 1995). Where they are found, they are often associated with employees whose output can be easily measured, such as salespeople.

Wei and Rowley (2009: 494) suggested that reward systems in China have transformed from state administered, low-wage policies with flat structures towards enterprise administered, performance-based contracts with considerable diversity and flexibility in wage structures. The Labour Law (1995) was a key catalyst in this reform, allowing 'all firms, regardless of ownership, (to) have the freedom to set their wages' (Wang *et al.* 2009: 332). However, the Asian financial crisis in 1997 and the subsequent global financial crisis in 2008 have encouraged further significant changes in Chinese rewards and remuneration systems. As Wei and Rowley (2009: 494) noted, these economic crises 'did make organizations focus more on performance and be more market-orientated … to recruit and retain better performers'. There is also other evidence which suggests that high performing Chinese talent is both more receptive of and more motivated by a variety of rewards than their generational predecessors – 'of all the factors that make Chinese employees motivated, employee compensation and benefits packages always play a prevalent role' (Cai and Klyushina 2009: 80). The role of rewards and remuneration systems in the retention of skilled and scarce talent is discussed in more detail in Chapter 5. However, a recent study (Liu 2010) of the reward strategies of three major Chinese IT companies (Haier, Huawei and Lenovo) revealed their similarities and differences, and convergent approaches with Western models (see Table 6.2). The overall HRM 'architecture' in these three innovative companies, together with a comparison with three of their Indian competitors (Birla, Reliance and Tara) is discussed in considerable detail in the following chapter.

It is important to note here that, despite indications of moves towards convergence with Western-style remuneration models, there is still a range of mandatory employment conditions which must be provided to all employees. These include the so-called 'five plus one' benefits, legacies from the former centralized system but nevertheless consistent with Western employee protection mechanisms; namely unemployment and medical insurance, work-related injury insurance, maternity insurance, pensions and 'public accountability of funds for housing construction' (Lin *et al.* 2010: 291). In addition, many local and foreign private firms provide

Table 6.2 Reward strategies in Three Chinese MNCs

Component(s)	*Huawei*	*Haier*	*Lenovo*
Base pay	High	Median	Median
Long-term incentives	Stock options	Stock options	Share options (all performance-based)
Performance-related pay	Yes	Yes	Yes
Employee HRD	Customized	Variable	Customized
Employee recognition	Moderate	High	Moderate

Source: Adapted from Y. Liu, 2010,'Reward strategy in Chinese IT industry', *International Journal of Business and Management*, 5, 2: 119–20.

supplementary medical insurance, profit sharing schemes, flexitime, travel subsidies, career breaks, paid study leave and miscellaneous employee welfare projects (ibid.), which assist in talent retention. Some foreign firms, such as Atlas Copco (China) and Electrolux (China), have also recognized the (cost neutral) benefits of job 'title inflation' and structured employee recognition schemes for such purposes (Cai and Klyushina 2009: 80).

Yet, rewards and remuneration programmes are not determined simply by forces in the external environment. Instead, managers play a significant role in their adoption, modification and termination. However, there is little research on the contributions of line managers in pay for performance practices in the Chinese context. A recent study of line managers' perceptions of pay for performance and the key supports and barriers to their involvement in pay design and implementation was conducted in China's non-public sector knowledge intensive firms, and found that project intensification could be an important factor that impacts on line managers' understanding and responsibility in rewards systems and pay for performance (Rowley and Wei, 2010). Another study (Jaussaud and Liu 2011) reported that rewards might consist of fixed and variable parts, the latter including bonuses and allowances. However, variable elements were a higher share of total wages for Chinese firms compared with foreign owned ones. The determination of the variable pay was mostly based on individual characteristics and merit but also partly on collective performance.

Rewards and remuneration systems in India are more similar to those utilized in Western countries than in China, with a plethora of legislation prescribing wage and salary levels and overall employment conditions, although in reality such practices vary quite widely from state to state and between industry sectors. Certainly, it is in the interests of both the Indian government and employers, especially in the globally competitive information technology and low-cost manufacturing sectors, to maintain minimum wage levels whilst adhering as much as possible to the letter (if not always the spirit) of the relevant legislation. Undoubtedly, however, the law of labour supply and demand sometimes prevails over the laws of the land, albeit counter-balanced against the relative strength of sectoral unions. In the call centre sector, for example, high employee turnover rates – 'sixty percent of the Indian call centre workforce is estimated to have less than one year of tenure' (Thite and Russell 2010: 357) – have resulted in reforms to some employment conditions, including more flexible rosters, part-time options, limited career plans and more cooperative labour–management relations. Tymon *et al.* (2010a) also emphasized the relative importance of intrinsic (together with) extrinsic rewards on Indian talent attraction and retention (see also Chapter 5).

However, following the fallout from the global financial crisis, there has been serious debate in government, industry and trade union circles regarding the structure and outcomes of executive rewards systems in particular. The deputy chairman of India's planning commission, Montek Singh Ahluwalia, was reported as criticizing 'indecent CEO salaries', whilst Mohammed Amin, the General Secretary of the communist-affiliated union CITU, demanded that 'the government should bring a strict law to deal with this problem. Self-regulation is no remedy'

(Rai 2009: 1). Even the Reserve Bank of India became involved, promising to 'save Indian banking from flawed incentive compensation practices' (Anonymous 2010d: 1) by splitting remuneration packages into fixed and variable components, eliminating guaranteed bonuses and tying salaries to 'risk outcomes' (ibid.), although it cautioned that attracting and retaining talent would still require the design of attractive rewards systems. Other suggestions for improving process transparency, equitable outcomes and linkages between executive remuneration and firm effectiveness include shareholder advisory groups, 'say-on-pay' shareholder voting mechanisms, independent pay consultants, 'performance-vested share plans', industry peer group benchmarking and 'clawbacks' – 'the recoup of previously-earned incentive pay in the event of new information about (executive) performance' (Wise 2010: 4); the latter being perhaps the most controversial and problematic of all such suggestions.

In practical terms, the Indian Companies Bill (2009) revised earlier Companies Acts (1956, 1988) by aligning executive remuneration with firm financial performance, strengthening shareholder rights to approve executive pay packages, and encouraging regular salary reviews – 'executive compensation in India is considered (generally) to be well within sensible limits … in many cases, executive compensation is actually driven by profitability' (Rekhy 2009: 2). No such widespread debates have yet appeared in China, from either government or industry.

Overall HRM trends in China and India

It is not easy to discuss China and India with respect to the interconnected HRM aspects of PM, HRD and rewards and remuneration systems. In some ways they are similar in that they are both developing nations with high rates of economic growth. But their political histories differentiate the one from the other, and are reflected in both the relative stages of their HRM development and their characteristics. There is evidence of simultaneous convergence and divergence with Western-style models (and with each other), mediated by different political, historical, socio-cultural and legislative factors. There is further evidence of heterogeneous HRM applications in their diverse industry sectors and firm structures, but both demonstrate their shared capacity to blend indigenous with foreign approaches.

Despite its apparent conflict with socialist principles, PM (including performance-based pay) has now become common in large Chinese firms, joint ventures and wholly owned foreign enterprises (WOFEs), but less so in the former SOEs. This appears to be the result of conscious government productivity initiatives, exemplars from foreign multinationals and the changing attitudes of new generations of skilled Chinese employees and their managers. However, one should not assume that all enterprises in China have fully come to terms with PM – 'nearly all China plants claim to use performance management, a complex HR tool; however, the numbers don't necessarily bear this out, as there is little or no trending for any measures that typically align with use and degree of effectiveness of performance management' (Wellins *et al.* 2005: 9). On the other hand, from a more developed perspective, many Indian firms have utilized comprehensive PM systems for decades, but are now being encouraged by recent national government initiatives to move away from their compliance focus towards closer alignment with employee development and rewards systems, as well as to include a degree of stakeholder accountability. These aspects are not so evident yet in Chinese firms.

With respect to HRD, China has arguably gone further than India in providing legislative encouragement for education, training and development, and has been more effective in the dissemination of such activities across its various industry sectors and firm structures. This has been the result of both ideological and more pragmatic (for example, labour shortages, talent demands) imperatives. Both countries, however, have historic learning traditions derived from Confucianism, Hinduism, Islam and Buddhism (see Chapter 2 for further discussion of these influences), apart from their contemporary political challenges and opportunities. India has a highly developed legislative framework for determining wage and salary entitlements, together with an adversarial industrial relations system based on its colonial heritage. These factors have ensured that employment conditions in Indian organizations are regulated and that employees are strongly protected, whilst the Chinese economic reforms have led to less equality, if greater productivity, under such conditions. In India there is recent evidence, following the global economic crisis, that the foundations of executive pay systems are being challenged, with government support for various reforms under consideration. These issues have not been raised in China to any great extent.

Conclusion

From the above, we can come to a number of limited conclusions. It is not easy to compare China and India in any straightforward way, as the differences between their two historical experiences are both complex and subtle. A number of studies have tried to make a comparison between their economies, mostly at the macroeconomic level, but there is as yet much less research comparing management, let alone their HRM, systems.

It is obviously hard to generalize about HRM systems. As far as leading enterprises are concerned, great progress has been made with respect to PM, HRD and rewards and remuneration systems. But there is still a long way to go yet in terms of these practices becoming common across the whole gamut of enterprises in China and India. It is too early to say whether HRM practices as understood in the West have been fully implemented in Indian and Chinese enterprises, but it is sufficient to suggest that they will continue to transform, representing both emic and etic characteristics.

7 The dynamic human resource management architecture of Chinese and Indian global organizations

Introduction

This chapter presents two sets of current case examples from China and India to help explain the dynamic restructuring of industry in both countries, and the associated changes in the human resource management (HRM) 'architecture'. These specific cases illustrate, in our view, the 'best practice' HRM systems, processes and practices, reflecting the globalization experiences of these multinational corporations (MNCs) and their eclectic incorporation of Western and local approaches in all the countries of their operation. They cannot, however, be claimed to represent HRM practices in all, or even most, organizations in China and India. Given their various stages of development, there appear to be as many differences as similarities in the HRM systems between state owned, domestic private, wholly foreign owned, joint venture and multinational enterprises in both countries, as discussed throughout this book.

The chapter begins with a brief explanation of the HRM 'architecture' concept, followed by discussion of each of the companies' operations and HRM systems, and concludes with a comparison of their approaches and implications for other Chinese and Indian organizations. The Chinese companies we use as pragmatic examples include Haier, Huawei and Lenovo, and will be compared and contrasted with Indian counterparts Birla, Reliance and Tata.

The HRM architecture

The term 'HRM architecture' is now common amongst both researchers and professionals across the world as an umbrella framework which assists in the analysis of the relationships between business strategies and HRM processes and practices, and which thus reflects the horizontal and vertical alignment components of strategic human resource management theory. The concept of HRM architecture was first developed by Lepak and Snell (1999: 32), who defined it as 'the alignment of different employment modes, employment relationships, HR configurations and criteria for competitive advantage'. Using a combination of resource-based, human capital and transaction cost economic theories, analyses of an organization's HRM architecture can reveal the underlying causes of its success or failure.

As the authors explain, 'the ability to manage the HR architecture itself may actually become a core capability that other firms find difficult to replicate' (Lepak and Snell 1999: 45).

Accordingly, we use this framework broadly in the following sections of this chapter to analyze the links between business and HRM strategies and processes in the six chosen Chinese and Indian companies. The particular companies were chosen for their global prominence, innovative business strategies, benchmark HR processes and promotion of explicit links between business systems and HRM architecture. We suggest that these choices are pragmatically (if not statistically) representative of the majority of Chinese and Indian MNCs. Accordingly they have clear credibility in our view, and are worthy of particular examination of what we consider to be the 'flagships of best practice' in both countries.

Three Chinese companies

All of the Chinese companies were developed from the old state owned enterprise (SOE) structures, with 'iron rice bowl' employment systems (discussed in earlier chapters) as a result of Deng Xiaoping's post-1978 economic reforms. They represent the HRM architecture of a bygone age but one which has not totally disappeared from the Chinese scene and lingers on as a residual factor. Even so, as will be seen from the company histories presented below, each was the outcome of entrepreneurial individuals coming forward and turning around an old inefficient management structure, transforming the firms into dynamic market-related enterprises (see, for example, Warner 2009a). There are a number of key stages in their transformation, including shedding the SOE status, adopting a new corporate structure and setting up joint ventures. Each company has become a global player in its respective markets in recent years, and all employ very large production and HR departments, both within China and overseas. They have set up production line activities across the globe, including in the United States. Other similarities include their conscious incorporation of specialist research and development (R&D) activities; extensive human resource development programmes; and sales revenues that now run into billions of US dollars, so they are currently major players on the international scene. They are all profitable companies and are recognized as models for aspiring Chinese entrepreneurs. For example, the latest Chinese Top100 List of electronics and IT companies ranked Huawei, Legend Holding Ltd. (Lenovo) and Haier (in that order) as the first three companies (Nacsa 2011). Thus, they all also represent a move up the 'value-added chain' for Chinese businesses, transforming them into world-class high-end global players.

A number of important aspects of Chinese companies should be noted. First, that the Chinese business system is characterized by the 'enduring role of government' (Cooke 2011c: 3) and relationships between companies and other social institutions; and second, that HR practices in overseas Chinese subsidiaries 'may differ from those in their parent company in China' (ibid.). In addition, as Teagarden and Cai (2009: 80) pointed out, 'the success of China's largest multinationals provides one model for growth and expansion: Learn from others first and then leverage that knowledge to build talent from within'. As some of the following cases illustrate, global Chinese companies often face more difficulties than their Indian counterparts for a variety of reasons, including political barriers, technological and financial limitations, negative perceptions (especially concerning HRM practices) and management styles, as well as perceptions of ethical, intellectual property and CSR (corporate social responsibility) deficits (Cooke 2011c: 6). Thus, they tend to prefer greenfield operations, joint ventures or direct acquisitions in their international expansion. Brief histories of the three chosen companies are followed by a discussion of the characteristics of their organizational structures, business strategies and cascading HRM systems, processes and practices.

Case Study 1: Haier

Haier, perhaps the best known Chinese company internationally, has been in operation for over a quarter of a century, and is the world's number one brand in refrigeration, laundry equipment and wine coolers. Based in Qingdao, in Shandong province on the eastern seaboard, its story goes back even earlier to when it was a small refrigerator factory in the 1920s. On the assumption of power by the Chinese Communist Party in 1949, the company was turned into a SOE. By the time of the economic reforms after 1978, the company was heavily indebted and in a very poor state, producing a mere 80 refrigerators a month. The local government sought the help of an up-and-coming young local manager, Zhang Ruimin, who was appointed managing director in 1984. At that time, it had total assets of US$ 300,000, sales revenues of US$ 178,000, 600 employees and a net loss of US$ 178,000 (Lin 2005: 3). Keen to take advantage of Western and Japanese management innovations, Zhang set out to revive the company. As a result, the Qingdao Refrigeration Company was set up in 1984 and it soon established joint ventures with foreign companies including Liebherr from Germany. Since then it has developed a set of horizontal business alliances in areas such as electroplating to make microwaves, air conditioners and freezers. Under Zhang's leadership, by 2003 Haier had total assets of US$ 2 billion, sales revenues of US$ 9.7 billion, 30,000 employees and a US$ 100 million profit (Lin 2005: 4). Subsequently, it has become one of China's Top 100 IT companies, and has diversified into white goods and telecommunications products, with more than 240 subsidiaries across the world, 30 design centres, and now over 50,000 global employees (Lin 2005; Haier 2009).

The Haier brand is now more or less recognized globally, the name coming from the Chinese transliteration of Liebherr (namely Li-bo-hai-er taking up the last two syllables), if not yet a prestige brand. It is probably better known in Asia than globally but is growing in its prominence in the international marketplace. Moving onto the international stage, it opened production lines in Indonesia in 1996, in the Philippines and Malaysia in 1997 and eventually it opened a production plant in Camden, South Carolina (US) in 2000. It also has factories in India and Iran (Peng and Meyer 2011). It launched a global brand building strategy under the slogan 'Create resources, world-wide prestige'. It is regarded as a great 'success story' all round – for both Chinese management and the wider economy in China. The brand is characterized by its product design, quality and reliability and will no doubt become more visible in Western high streets in the coming years. Haier's annual sales revenue for 2011 was US$ 23 billion.

Haier's broad business vision – 'creating resources and worldwide prestige' (Haier 2009) – embraces innovation, a strong customer focus, 'fashion and personalization', with conscious concerns for its environmental impact. Its strengths lie in its technological capabilities, corporate culture, global integration, spirit of innovation, effective management control system (OEC – 'O stands for Overall; E stands for Everyone, Everything and Everyday; C stands for Control and Clear' – Lin 2005: 3; also Ou-Yang 2003) and high quality service, but threats also exist with respect to its global competitors and the image of Chinese manufacturers abroad. In his characteristic style, Zhang Ruimin declared his 'corporate wolf' metaphor in response to these challenges: 'wolves have come. If Haier wants to survive, it must transform into a wolf itself. In this way, it can dance with other wolves' (Haier 2009: 29). This rhetoric underlies Haier's HRM architecture as well, 'a holistic system, aligning every HR activity from recruitment to performance management to the company's business strategy – a relentless focus on growth, quality and innovation' (Xin and Pucik 2006: 2). It is already a topical case study which is now taught and discussed in many business schools and MBA programmes across the world.

Haier HRM vision and goals

Haier has a set of specific HRM goals, which give strong priority to what it calls 'excellence'. Its vision is set out as follows: 'Promotion is based upon excellence, not appearance'. They present it as 'Haier's Rule of HR Development' (Haier 2009). Operational details include the following:

> During our HR development, we insist on innovation of notion, innovation of system. We keep creating a kind of environment of fair, just and straightforward, and build up a set of mechanisms to develop personnel potentialities. Therefore, while we [present] our enterprise's objectives, we can offer each individual a developing space to realize his (sic) own value.

It is broken down into four major points:

1. 'Each individual is a talent, and promotion is based upon excellence, not appearance'. This is an ambitious goal but it is not clear how precisely it will be carried out
2. 'Who is incumbent who shall be inspected'. This implies that noone is able to escape scrutiny with respect to their performance
3. 'Usually more deeply [the] dolphin dives, [the] more highly it jumps'. This is a reference to expecting a high level of motivation from employees
4. Using an 'Elimination Quota'. This is aimed at laying-off the percentage of poorly performing staff on a regular basis.

The Elimination Quota is based upon the so-called 3E cards, which daily record the job quantity, product defects, use of materials, condition of equipment, safety, work attitudes and discipline of workers. These are then collected by managers, wages calculated accordingly, and posted on bulletin boards. Employees are subsequently divided into the best, the good and the trial workers. The latter are subject to future dismissal (Ou-Yang 2003: 4).

While some of the expressions of these goals are rhetorical (or merely corporate jargon) and perhaps something is lost in translation, they appear to actively guide the development of HRM systems and processes, albeit in the unitarist traditions of Japanese or US companies, and seem to be 'sincerely' felt by the senior managers of Haier throughout the world. They inform all its HRM architecture, attempting to develop 'fair, effective and efficient recruitment processes, training programs, performance appraisal, payment mechanisms, and promotion systems, which match the objectives of Haier's global branding strategy' (Haier 2009: 47).

On the negative side, critics suggest that Haier's approach to HRM represents a revised form of 'scientific management', that its workers are often overworked, and that the 'Elimination Quota' system in particular is inequitable (Anonymous 2011b). Almost certainly, it would be untenable in many pluralist industrial relations contexts, although not entirely unknown in a number of Western MNCs. In similar vein, whilst 'the foundation of Haier's HRM strategy is rigorous performance management' (Teagarden and Cai 2009: 74), there are also queries about the propriety of some of its performance and career management practices, in particular its '6S footprints', 'smiling face' charts and 'race-track' career development framework. The first practice requires below average performers to stand on a set of footprints on the factory floor daily and explain their reasons for under-performance, and is somewhat reminiscent of Cultural Revolution rituals. 'Smiling face' charts perform similar functions, with red (excellent), green (average) and yellow (below average) variations. Given the mixed messages implied here for Western employees, Haier switched to 'stuffed brown bears' (positive performance) and 'pink pigs' (under-performance) in the United States as reinforcement mechanisms. The 'race-track' model of career development is based on backing winners and eliminating losers. Few of these practices would be 'politically correct' in pluralist industrial relations systems, however, suggesting that Haier may need to invent different approaches if it intends to expand into these countries in future. Whether this HR approach is effective is very hard to judge objectively and there is no hard evidence to decide one way or the other.

Case Study 2: Huawei

The next company we consider is Huawei, which is more technologically sophisticated than Haier, in the sense of producing more complex products and systems. It was established in 1987, when it was set up in the Shenzen Special Economic Zone (SEZ), as a sales agent for a Hong Kong company producing private branch exchange [PBX] switches. From the 1990s onwards, Huawei has embarked on an independent research and exploitation of these technologies, mainly targeting hotels and small enterprises. In 1992, it moved into rural digital switching solutions. By 1995, it had generated sales of 1.5 billion Yuan, mainly derived from the rural sector.

It moved into the metropolitan areas of China in 1998 and launched wireless GSM solutions, and then established a R&D centre in Bangalore (India) in 1999, and another in the following year in Stockholm. By this time it was generating a hundred million US dollars from international markets in revenue, increasing to US$ 552 million by 2002. In 2003, Huawei established a joint venture with 3Com based on enterprise data networking solutions, and it set up another joint venture with Siemens in 2004, with the result that its international contract orders surpassed domestic sales for the first time in the following year. Subsequently, it has established various R&D joint venture operations with global partners such as Motorola, Symantec and Global Marine. By 2008, it was recognized by *Business Week* as one of the most influential global companies, and in 2009, it ranked number two in the global share of radio access equipment. In more recent years, it has moved into cloud-based mobile telephony ('Vision' and 'Blaze' mobile phones in China and the UK respectively (Browning 2011; Shen 2011)).

Today, Huawei (often translated as 'China can' or 'splendid act' – Anonymous 2011g) continues to go from strength to strength. Huawei's annual sales revenue for 2011 was US$ 32 billion. A recent annual report (Huawei 2011) makes impressive reading; revenues were 185 billion Yuan (US$ 27.4 billion), having grown at an average rate of 29 per cent in the past four years; and profits were up by 56 per cent. The Chinese multinational overtook both Nokia and Siemens and is catching up on Ericsson (Anonymous 2011g). It currently has eight regional headquarters, more than 70 global branches (US, Europe, Middle East and North Africa), more than 110,000 employees (Anonymous 2011g) and six R&D centres (Silicon Valley, Dallas, Bangalore, Stockholm, Moscow and Shenzhen – 'the tower of a thousand engineers' – Huawei 2011; Anonymous 2011g). Huawei is expanding rapidly into Russia and Africa, with nearly 3,000 African employees (Cooke 2011c: 14).

Several governments, including the US and India, have had anxieties about its security status, however, as it has allegedly strong links to the Chinese government and army, including receiving loans from Chinese banks (Anonymous 2011g). It has been disbarred from several important contracts as a consequence. The chief executive, Ren Zhengfei, is rumoured to have had a role in the Chinese military and the chairperson, Sun Yafang, is said to have worked for the Ministry of State Security. According to *The Economist* (23 April 2011: 69), its new openness and transparency in reporting are to be welcomed but it is likely to continue to have problems.

The company's 'secret weapon' is arguably its competitive pricing, being able to offer products at around 30 per cent lower price than its competitors. According to a recent report, it has been at the heels of Cisco, its main rival in networking for the Internet. This company is a now a renowned 'brand leader' in China, and even beyond, and has a global range of operations. Its slogan is '[to] enrich life through communication' and its mission is '[t]o focus on our customers' market challenges and needs by providing excellent communication network solutions and services in order to consistently create maximum value for customers' (Huawei 2011). Its company 'spirit' incorporates a sense of responsibility, innovation, devotion, teamwork, 'hardworking, selfless, self-discipline, and skilful' (Huawei 2011), heavily weighted towards the loyalty and commitment of its employees. There is no objective way of assessing the effectiveness of this policy, however. It has, nonetheless, grown into a very large global enterprise. The company has 95,000 employees across the world, no mean achievement by any standards. It operates across four areas, namely telecom network infrastructure, applications and software, professional services and devices.

This makes it a major player in the global industry. Its sales revenue in 2009 exceeded 149.1 billion Yuan (US$ 21.8 billion). This was a year on year increase of 19 per cent with a net profit of 18.3 Yuan (US$ 2.7 billion). Today, it has partnerships with 45 of the top 50 global telecom operators. It grew very fast by setting up 3G networks in China as well as expanding in the mobile market in India. Huawei is ranked second in global markets in the share of radio access equipment and delivered the world's first LTE/EPC network. It was also the first to supply end-to-end 100G solutions from routers to transmission systems. Its employees today hold 148 leadership positions in 123 industry standards organizations globally. It offered 18,000 standards proposals and a total of 42,543 patent applications in 2010 (Huawei 2011). With respect to its corporate governance, the main board has nine members, with overall responsibility to manage and oversee the operations of the company. It has a supervisory board under Chinese company law, consisting of five members who are elected by shareholders. It has a matrix structure under the executive management team (EMT) that consists of strategy and marketing, R&D, business units, market units, delivery supporting platform and functional units.

Echoing the imagery of Haier's CEO, Huawei's CEO, Ren Zhengfei, described his global business strategy thus: 'if MNCs were elephants, Huawei was a mouse in comparison and because it was no fight match for an elephant, it had to have a wolf spirit, a keen nose, a strong competitive instinct and a spirit of cooperation and sacrifice' (Huawei 2011: 3). This 'wolf culture' strategy led in 2007 to some questionable HRM practices which harmed the companies' global image (see later). It leads the observer to question whether the company took advice on this matter from a sound PR advisor.

Huawei's HRM structure, vision and processes

Huawei has moved away from a centralized model to a more decentralized HRM structure, allowing its subsidiaries and employees to have more decision making power and to relate resources more responsibly to consumer needs. Its HR and Administration Department incorporates separate HR and IT divisions, together with associated administration and legal divisions (Huawei 2011). This step appears to be appropriate to the extension of activities to the global marketplace.

Its HRM slogan is 'internationalisation through localisation' (Cooke 2011c: 22), and it promotes its HRM vision thus:

> dedicated and passionate employees are Huawei's most valuable asset. In recognition of their contributions, Huawei has established policies to ensure that employees are given growth opportunities and competitive remuneration ... We attach high importance to employees' mental and physical health. By providing a complete Employee Health Security System, a wide range of leisure activities, and open communication channels, Huawei makes every effort to facilitate staff recognition and ensure employees' personal growth is realized alongside Huawei's success.
>
> (Huawei company newspaper 2011).

Its Code of Conduct follows:

> Huawei has a Huawei Business Code of Conduct, which ensures that all our employees hold themselves to high standards of ethical behavior.
>
> *Working Environment*
>
> We understand that our employees' working environment is crucial in ensuring their overall job satisfaction.
>
> *Training*
>
> At Huawei, we are committed to building a learning organization, and established Huawei University to facilitate a variety of training programs for both customers and employees.
>
> *Career Path*
>
> Huawei offers a Dual Career Development Path for all our employees, which comprises of [sic] a managerial path and a technical/professional path.
>
> *Compensation*
>
> Here at Huawei, we not only comply with local legislation on employees' minimum wages, but also offer highly competitive compensation packages.
>
> *Mentorship Program*
>
> Huawei has established an effective mentorship program which serves to help new employees adapt to Huawei.
>
> *Employees' Club*
>
> Huawei understands the importance of the well-being of our employees.
>
> *Diversity*
>
> Huawei is currently established in more than 100 countries and continues to localise its operations worldwide.

Feedback

> Employees are also welcome to bring their opinions and suggestions to the company's attention through various channels, beginning with their immediate manager.
>
> (Huawei website 2011)

This explicit statement of its HR goals is clearly expressed and articulated. With respect to specific HRM processes, Huawei has sophisticated staffing, human resource development (HRD), performance management and rewards systems, developed in consultation with global consulting companies such as IBM, the Hay Group and FhG (Teagarden and Cai 2009: 75). Its HRD programme encompasses both technical and management training, together with opportunities for self-learning (Huawei School Online), coaching and tutoring, and it has an 'employee training ladder' linked to its career development system (Huawei 2011). Company-wide communication involves a plethora of techniques, including business information sharing meetings, an 'open door' policy, an HR-BRIDGE mailbox and a bulletin board system. Huawei Technologies (a subsidiary of Huawei) is one China's best known telecommunications companies, employing over 60,000 people across China and worldwide. The company's headquarters in Shenzhen has the feel of a university campus, similar to the Googleplex in California's Silicon Valley, and is widely seen as the place to be for young and ambitious men and women 'hungry for success'.

Cooke (2011c: 23), however, suggests that Huawei's HRM system faces a number of serious challenges, including growing wage levels, employee retention, a 'lack of identification from local (non-Chinese) employees with the employer', an imbalance between employee development and cost-effective deployment and a relative absence of diversity management policies. There is no doubt more than a grain of truth to this criticism. Over the last few years, two more serious events have shown Huawei in a less positive light. In October 2007, the company pressured about 7,000 long serving employees to resign and rejoin on short term contracts so that it would not be bound by the unlimited contract provisions of the Labour Contract Law (Liu 2007; Anonymous 2011b). The move was condemned by the local government and trade unions who stated that Huawei would be bound by the terms of the new law regardless. Others claimed that this action was 'an irresponsible act which not only undermines the company's image, it hurts the hearts of the employees, thereby reducing the cohesion of the enterprise and competitiveness' (Meng and Jianmin 2009: 1). There is no doubt that the Chinese government would have been embarrassed by these steps, given its active encouragement of its new labour legislation in contrast to the common practices of some multinational organizations. Recently, there have been suggestions in Guangdong Province that Huawei's 'new' contracts might be considered invalid by the regulatory authorities especially if contested by its adversely affected employees (Hong 2011: 1).

Then, on 6 March 2008, a Huawei employee jumped to his death from the third floor of the company cafeteria. He was the sixth Huawei employee to have committed suicide or die in mysterious circumstances in the previous two years (Anonymous 2011b). In addition, the company's 'mattress culture' (managers sleeping on mattresses in their offices because of their long working hours) has been criticized for its adverse effects on their health (ibid.). These issues have cast a shadow over Huawei's reputation. There is little doubt that there is considerable pressure on employees to perform and this may have both intended and unintended consequences. Ren Zhengfei has a stated policy of weeding out five per cent of the worst performing employees. Within the company, employees have been told by managers that in practice only one to two per cent of the worst performing employees are laid-off, but that is small comfort to one employee, who summed up his feelings as follows, 'I still feel like somebody is cracking a whip behind me'(Anonymous 2011b). As in the Haier case, the rhetoric of an innovative HRM architecture may be tempered by the legacy of a paternalistic and somewhat punitive managerial culture.

Case Study 3: Lenovo

Lenovo was originally derived from a Chinese SOE called 'Legend' in the 1980s. In 1984 its founding chairman, Liu Chuanzi, with ten like-minded colleagues set up the New Technology Development Company, funded by the Chinese Academy of Sciences (Warner 1999). The company was part of a study of China's high-tech revolution in computing hardware and software and related products, carried out by one of the present authors, who had visited a wide sample of such companies over the years. The study explored the HRM systems of both large and small firms in Beijing's 'Electronics Valley' during the late 1990s. Legend was very active in the development of Chinese character (CC) recognition systems and its CC card received the highest national science technology progress award in 1988. In the same year, it set up its subsidiary in Hong Kong. In 1990, it launched its first PC and became a producer of branded computer products in its own right. In 1994 Legend was listed on the Hong Kong stock exchange. In 1996, it became the market share leader in China but this time through the 'Ledger' brand laptop. It also signed an intellectual property agreement with Microsoft. Legend became the top PC vendor in the Asia Pacific region and one of the top 10 world's best managed PC vendors (*China Daily* 2011). It changed its name to Lenovo in 2003, combining 'Le' from Legend and 'novo' to reflect its innovation focus (ibid.). In 2005, Lenovo completed its acquisition of IBM's personal computing division and in 2006 introduced the first dual core IBM ThinkPad notebook PC. It has developed research centres in Beijing, Shanghai and Shenzhen (Jobsearch China 2011). Lenovo's annual sales revenue for 2011 was US$ 21 billion.

Liu Chuanzi is chairman of the board of the Lenovo Group and is rated one of the top worldwide business leaders by *Business Week*, *Forbes* and *Time* magazines. Although he had retired in 2008, he returned in 2009 following a remarkable US$ 97 million loss. The Group's executive headquarters are now in Research Triangle Park, North Carolina. In 2009, it was the fourth largest seller of PCs in the world with a market share of over 10 per cent; in China about one in three PCs sold come from its production lines. It has reported annual sales of over US$ 15 billion per year. It also has a PC joint venture with the Japanese company, NEC. By 2011 China had become the 'world's biggest personal computer market, spearheaded by the Lenovo Group' (Fletcher and Feng 2011).

Its vision is expressed as 'proactively building a talent pipeline, leadership development, building a strong employer brand' (ibid.), and, as at March 2010, it had more than 22,000 employees globally. Its 2009–10 annual report explains its business model as 'built on innovation, operational efficiency and customer satisfaction, as well as a focus on investment in emerging markets' (Lenovo 2010a: 1). It also embraces high performance work culture principles, including effective global teamwork and collaboration, customer responsiveness, rapid decision making, accountability for outcomes and measuring 'what is important' (Anonymous 2007e: 2). Prima facie, it looks like it should work well but it is very hard to assess objectively.

Lenovo's HRM goals and processes

The company has ambitious aims with respect to world-class performance. Its HR goals are expressed in the following terms:

> Lenovo is dedicated to building the world's most innovative personal computers. We are creating a culture where people achieve their highest potential and deliver extraordinary results. No matter how large we grow, we will pursue innovative, creative people; relationships that are respectful; leaders who inspire, and meaningful work.
>
> (Lenovo website in 2011)

Teagarden and Cai (2009: 74) asserted that Lenovo focuses on 'creating space to develop employees, upgrading their value, and improving their working and living quality ... consequently employees subordinate their individual pursuit to Lenovo's long-term development'. In pursuit of these admirable goals, it renamed its 'personnel department' as a 'human resource department' as early as 1995, and, as one of the present authors has personally observed, the HRM function is taken most seriously; it has very professional staff, and is responsible for a plethora of integrated HRM processes. It was the first Chinese major company to appear to offer a credibly modern HRM architecture (Warner 1999). However, Chen (2006: 5) observed that Chinese employees were often regarded as 'candles' which 'burnt until the end', but that Jiang Beilin (vice president of Lenovo's HR department) considered them as 'storage batteries' instead, meaning that his company treats them as human capital which can be 'recharged and re-utilized' (Chen 2006: 40), not a term a Western HR professional would normally employ.

According to managerial informants, the corporate priority is 'talent management'. A new scheme called the Mobility Plan has been implemented at the international level. The purpose of the plan is to give managers an opportunity to work overseas to gain international experience in order to be able to lead at a global level – 'we have very focused development programs in which our top talents take up short and medium term assignments in other countries' (Gina Qiao, VP Human Resources (Anonymous 2007c: 1)). It is not aimed at Chinese managers in principle but, in reality, has mainly involved sending Chinese managers to the US for development (Cooke 2010b). It also conducts an associated Accelerated Leadership Program for Hi-Potentials in ASEAN (ALPHA) which combines talent mapping with individual development plans, coaching and mentoring schemes (Selvaretnam 2011: 2). Lenovo has also developed its own 'university'; conducts staged programmes which integrate induction, general technical, professional and managerial training (Chen 2006: 44); and presents a 'Women in Lenovo Leader ship (WILL)' course (Anonymous 2009d). With respect to the latter, Cooke (2010b: 614) notes that:

> The HR directors from Lenovo (US) are well aware of the challenge they face in transferring their US-developed diversity management programme to other branches across different countries and cultures. How to accommodate the diversity of the global workforce and leverage it to enhance the performance of the firm on the one hand, and how to develop a strong corporate culture that all employees will identify with on the other hand is their main HR concern, and a solution has yet to be found.

With respect to other components of the HRM architecture – notably performance management, rewards systems and retirement benefits – Lenovo is a market leader in China, and globally. Its performance management process is well structured; based on target setting, employee guidance to reach these targets, regular performance reviews and associated bonus pay. The rewards system incorporates 'salary, bonus and welfare, and bonus' based entirely on the employees' position rather than their qualifications. Lenovo's retirement policy is unique in that it mimics similar Western programmes with a defined contribution plan, consisting of both the company and employees' supplements, and related to years of service and the company's performance. Lenovo has also developed sophisticated CSR, data privacy, employee complaint processes and environmental and health programmes, together with associated internal committees (audit, compensation, strategy and governance committees (Lenovo 2010b: 5)). Despite these admirable developments, company practice to some degree damaged its social contract with its employees in January 2009 by retrenching 11 per cent of its workforce (2,500 jobs) and reducing executive rewards by 30–50 per cent in the face of a significant financial loss (Wang 2009: 1).

In the HRM architecture of all three companies one can see the hand of in-house HR professionals and possibly also those of outside consultants (Teagarden and Cai 2009: 75). All three of them place a value on building a culture in which individuals can enjoy personal growth within an organizational context consonant with the goals of the business. They may be said to be 'at the cutting edge', although they are not exempt from criticism, as discussed earlier. A particular concern for all three companies, and one not as pressing for their Indian counterparts, is that none of them have clear management leadership transitions. It appears that at least one of these companies (Huawei) is attempting to become a family business (Shengiun 2011).

Three Indian companies

The companies discussed here are all well established global corporations comprising multiple integrated businesses, but, unlike their Chinese counterparts, they remain family owned, together with charismatic CEOs. All of them have encountered serious business problems connected with family issues but have survived them to grow exponentially. Whilst their managerial and HRM architecture superficially resembles that of Haier, Huawei and Lenovo, their socio-cultural and historical contexts ensure that 'the Indian management mindscape continues to be influenced by the residual traces of ancient wisdom as it faces the complexities of global realities' (Chatterjee 2007: 92). The outcome is the pervasiveness of values and traditions in moulding and reinforcing management and HRM styles and processes, in contrast to the more contemporary and less traditional visions of the Chinese CEOs who have been more directly influenced by Western management and HRM approaches.

In particular, the influences of Vedantic philosophy ('human nature has a capacity for self transformation and attaining the spiritual high ground while facing the realities of day to day challenges' Chatterjee 2007: 92); Guna (spiritual orientation); and a focus on interpersonal relations (*Sradha* – upward respect, *Sneha* – downward affection and *Bandhan* – bonding) underpin the contemporary Indian management and HRM architecture (see Chapter 2 for more detailed discussion of these cultural influences). It may also be suggested that the Chinese companies discussed adapted their business and HRM strategies from external (largely Western) exemplars whilst the chosen Indian companies derived theirs from within their own society's traditions and values, blending them where appropriate with global components.

Case Study 1: The Aditya Birlas Group

The Aditya Birlas (AB) Group has been a continuously family owned conglomerate for more than a century, since it was established by G.D. Birla in the early 1900s. The founding father developed industrial operations in sectors such as textiles (Eastern Spinning Mills, Calcutta), energy (Hindustan Gas), chemicals (Indo–Gulf Fertilisers & Chemicals Ltd), engineering goods and the manufacture of viscous staple fibre (Grasim) (Maps of India 2011). G.D. Birla, a confidante and supporter of Mahatma Gandhi (who was assassinated at Birla House in January 1948), is acclaimed as

> a great visionary who himself set out a bold, uncharted path that proved that Indian businessmen are second to none when it comes to creativity and adventure … his vision was to help build a new India, an India free from fear, free from want and free from exploitation.
>
> (Prime Minister Manmohan Singh, in Aditya Birla 2011: 1)

Reflecting these values, and in common with the other two Indian companies considered in this chapter, the AB Group established and maintains a strong CSR imperative under the umbrella of the Centre for Community Initiatives and Rural Development (Aditya Birla 2011), 'a value-based, caring corporate citizen' (Som 2010: 560), and later on, the AB. India Research Centre at London Business School (London Business School 2011). His son, Aditya Vikram Birla (1944–95), is given credit for building the company into what has been described as 'one of the most diversified and profitable global business empires in Indian history' (Parashar and Salwan 2005: 1). Certainly, it is the third largest Indian conglomerate (Som 2010: 549), with an impressive collection of business achievements – the only Indian producer of linen, world's largest producer of viscous staple fibre, largest refiner of palm oil, third largest producer of insulators and the sixth largest producer of carbon black (Som 2010: 550) – and operations throughout India, and in Indonesia, the Philippines, Thailand, Malaysia, Egypt and Australia. In an expansion to other parts of the world, the AB Group has more recently acquired Canada's aluminium roller manufacturer, Novelis, for US$ 6 billion, together with the world's largest carbon black producer, US Columbian Chemicals, for more than US$ 875 million (Hiscock 2011: 1), both under the stewardship of G.D. Birla's grandson, Kumar Mangalam Birla (known as 'Mr Birla'), the current group chairman. The company's vision is expressed as 'to be a premium global conglomerate with a clear focus on each business', and its mission as 'to deliver superior value to our customers, shareholders, employees, and society at large', and its values include integrity ('honesty in every action'), commitment ('doing whatever it takes to deliver as promised'), passion ('a missionary zeal arising out of an emotional engagement with work'), seamlessness ('thinking and working together across functional silos, hierarchical levels, business lines and geographies'), and speed ('one step ahead always') (Som 2010: 551). All of these values are symbolized in the corporate logo which reflects Aditya as the 'Rising Sun'.

The Western-educated Mr Birla presides over a conglomerate which now includes textiles, cement, tea, aluminium, fertilisers, shipping, carbon black, palm oil refining, chemicals, mining and the manufacture of viscous staple fibre (Maps of India 2011). Combining the company's traditional values with more innovative practices derived undoubtedly from his Western experience, he has been responsible for significant restructuring of the organization's structures and HRM architecture. Thus, he has attempted to emulate the ex-CEO of GE Capital, Jack Welch's approaches by creating divisional and product-focused organizational structures, with the overall aim of transforming the AB Group from 'a paternalistic to a professional culture' (Som 2010: 555). In pursuit of his goal, the AB Management Corporation (ABMCL) – 'the nerve system of the group' – was established to integrate the activities of all conglomerate businesses, together with the creation of Active Centres of Excellence in order to 'think like a company and not like a group' (ibid.), or as the current CEO asserts, 'we are not a family-run business' (Som 2010: 558). HR directors were consciously included in the ABMCL as a business partner. In tandem, he set up the so-called Birla Management Centre to 'institutionalise the sharing of best practices' (Som 2010: 556).

The prior culture of this Marwari (or *babu*) business has been transformed from a hierarchical, command and control style towards consultation, empowerment and delegation.

The Aditya Birla Group's HRM systems and processes

The present CEO has initiated dramatic and comprehensive changes to the HRM architecture of Aditya Birla Group which reflect the company values discussed above. Thus, he has deconstructed some traditional HR practices such as lifelong employment, family-based staffing and primarily internal recruitment, and introduced state-of-the-art systems, whilst simultaneously attempting to retain the crucial bonds between the company and its employees. Thus, one of his first activities was to introduce a compulsory retirement policy which resulted in the loss of more than three hundred executive managers in a single day; subsequently hired external replacements; and focused selection processes on merit rather than compliance criteria (Som 2010: 557).

In pursuit of his aim of changing the company from 'a paternalistic, centralized, decision-making system to a decentralized, consensus-based process' (Som 2010: 558), in 2002 he established a talent pool of two hundred potential 'fast track' managers who were then mentored through structured career plans, trained a hundred specialist internal job analysts, evaluated more than five thousand jobs, developed clear and distinct job bands and subjected all senior managers to 360-degree performance reviews (Som 2010: 559–60). In addition, routine business school recruiting was initiated, teamwork became an integral part of most jobs, healthcare and children's education facilities were established, a AB. Group Management Trainee Scheme was set up, and an annual global organizational health survey was instituted (Som 2010: 560). Many of these new HR systems had their origins in his Western business education and from his fascination with Jack Welch, but all were then comparatively unknown in Indian organizations. They also challenged the traditions and expectations of the AB Group, and certainly upset some older employees, but appear to have been incorporated relatively seamlessly into the fabric of the company. As the HR director explained, 'we never thought of changing the core of the company … its values, the respect for individuals, empowering people, being in innovation, and the emotional connect that the employees have with Aditya Birla' (Som 2010: 560). However, the company acknowledges that it faces several ongoing challenges including the 'globalization' conundrum, i.e. 'being global in attitude without letting go of the company's roots' (Som 2010: 561), maintaining its pivotal 'moral contract between the employees and the organization' (ibid.), and strengthening its customer service orientation.

The AB Group has so far been successful in juggling its financial, operational, human resource and community responsibilities, but like its (earlier) Chinese and (subsequent) Indian counterparts, its future will be determined by its capacity to continue to make effective strategic choices with respect to its markets, competitors, global structures, culture and the role of the HR architecture in contributing to these choices (Som 2007: 824).

Case Study 2: The Reliance Group

Founded by Dhirubhai Ambani (1932–2002) in 1958 as a small trading company, the Reliance Group is similar in its history and family ownership to both Aditya Birla and Tata (see later), although its exponential business growth was challenged by a bitter succession dispute in June 2005 caused by conflict between sons Mukesh and Anil Ambani which eventually led to a separation in their management responsibilities (Kazmi 2008: 1573; Dance with Shadows 2011). Until then, Reliance had surged into the Indian marketplace, with business interests in textiles, polyester fibre, plastics, petrochemicals, petrol refining, oil and gas exploration, dairy foods, retailing (Kazmi 2008: 1573; Reliance Group 2011).

Like the other two Indian companies discussed in this chapter, Reliance is a global conglomerate which has a strategy of 'sustained backward vertical integration' (Kazmi 2008: 1573), which is dynamic and has moved away from 'an organic growth model to a mix of organic and aggressive acquisitions-led models of growth aimed at a mix of local and international expansion into sunrise industries' (ibid.). Accordingly, Reliance has impressive business credentials: the world's third largest single-location oil refinery (Jamnagar, Gujarat) and the first export-oriented refinery (Reliance Petroleum (Kazmi 2008)); the world's largest polyester yarn and fibre producer and among the top five petrochemical producers (I love India 2011). Mukesh Ambani was considered 'the richest man in the world' in 2007 (Dixit 2008: 1), and his brother Anil (CEO of Reliance ADA Group) was ranked sixth on the 2010 *Forbes* List of India's billionaires, and in control of the second largest local mobile telephone firm (Anonymous 2011e). He established the Dhirubhai Ambani University in Bhopal which focuses on ICT research, primarily based around Madhya Pradesh state (Live India 2011) .

Reliance Industries Ltd had an aggregated worth of approximately US$ 125 billion in 2008, around a hundred direct and many more affiliated companies, more than 80,000 global employees, and was structured as 'several hundred investment companies, satellite companies and trusts' (Kazmi 2008: 1573). Other observers noted that its corporate structure conforms to the characteristics of an Indian 'business group' – 'a set of firms which, though legally independent, are bound together by a constellation of formal and informal ties and are accustomed to taking coordinated action' (Khanna and Rivkin 2001; Kedia *et al.* 2006: 559). It is listed on the Indian Stock Exchange, 'its share prices influence the movement of the Indian stock market' (Bhasin 2010: 153), and it is considered to be committed to corporate governance; although the auditors reported potential issues with its strong family share ownership (51 per cent), and the age of its senior managers (half of the Board is over 70 (ibid.)).

Whilst the founding father of Reliance Industries was generally respected for his foresight and business acumen, in particular 'global benchmarking, intense cost-consciousness and determined pursuit of goals' (Kazmi 2008: 1574), he was also suspected of 'bending government rules, manipulating the stock markets, and taking advantage of loopholes in the laws' (Kazmi 2008: 1574), undoubtedly like other commercial counterparts at the time. His sons have variously been accused of other flaws, including claims of corruption in mobile telephone sales, greed and the ad hoc and aggressive downsizing of employees in Reliance Group following the 2008 global financial crisis (Dixit 2008). The resolution of the harmful succession dispute in 2005, brokered by their mother, was a clear split in the company between Mukesh and Anil – the former kept Reliance Industries Ltd and the Indian Petrochemicals Corporation, whilst Anil received Reliance Energy, Reliance Infocomm and Reliance Capital (Kripalani 2005: 1).

The Reliance Group's HRM philosophies and systems

Despite their differences, the corporate philosophy and culture reflect the traditions and values of its founding father, and are similar to those discussed in the two other Indian companies in this chapter. The enshrined values include a global focus, state-of-the-art technologies, value chain integration, international competitiveness, financial conservatism, efficient project management and leadership excellence – expressed as 'think big, think fast, think ahead. Ideas are no-one's monopoly' (Kazmi 2008: 1575). With respect to leadership styles, Dhirubhai Ambani's principles included competitiveness, trust, 'love', 'by example' and loyalty – 'this in turn creates loyalty of the entire team; and the loyalty is not to an individual, the loyalty is to the mission and to the vision … and then becomes a common mission and vision' (ibid.). This perhaps represents a halfway house between old-fashioned paternalism and state-of-the-art HRM.

The Reliance Group has developed a comprehensive yet pragmatic HRM architecture cascading from its corporate vision, mission and values. Despite the unrest associated with its forced redundancies in response to the global financial crisis (see earlier), it has built a complex set of global HRM systems, similarly to Aditya Birla and Tata. Thus, it focuses on constantly up-skilling managers, poaching qualified staff from its local and global competitors, offering above-market reward packages (including stock options), and providing them with ongoing training and development opportunities (project management, marketing, communication, manufacturing, finances and administration (Kazmi 2008: 1576)). In addition, it provides significant educational and healthcare support to its employees, together with environmental and community welfare programmes within its local and global contexts (ibid.). Like the other two Indian companies discussed in this chapter, Reliance assumes a proactive stance as a good corporate citizen. As Gerhaeusser *et al.* explain, it is 'a leader in providing health care, education, infrastructure, and clean drinking water for their enterprises and in securing production safety and good health for all employees. Reliance also provides special assistance for ant natural disasters. The Dhirubhai Ambani Foundation provides scholarships for hundreds of students every year … Moreover, Dhirubhai created hospitals and medical research centers, such as the Sri Hurkisondas Nurrotumdas Hospital and Research Centre, a charitable hospital' (2010: 403).

Case Study 3: The Tata Group

The Tata Group is India's largest private sector conglomerate, with nearly one hundred associated companies (28 of which are publicly listed), revenue exceeding US$ 30 billion (more than 3 per cent of India's GDP, and 57 per cent of which is obtained internationally (Grainger and Chatterjee 2008: 229; Tata Group 2010)), and seven major business interests: ICT, engineering, materials, services, energy, consumer products and chemicals (Goldstein 2008: 6; Tata Group 2010). It operates in more than 60 countries, and employs approximately 400,000 people globally (Gerhaeusser *et al.* 2010). Founded in the 1870s by Jamsetji Nusserwanji Tata, a Parsi from the strongly religious Zoroastrian community, Tata is distinguished from other large Indian companies by its innovative business practices, both locally and globally. For example, Tata was the first private Indian company to establish a steel mill, a power utility, a luxury hotel chain (Taj hotels) and the national airline (Air India) (Goldstein 2008: 7). It established the Taj Mahal Palace Hotel in 1902; followed by Tata Steel (1907), Tata Power (1910), Tata Airlines (1932), Tata Consulting Services (1968) and Tata Motors (1998) (Gerhaeusser *et al.* 2010; Tata Group 2010).

Its corporate structure is complex, with Tata Sons and Tata Industries as the 'promoter companies' (Goldstein 2008: 12) for a plethora of subsidiary companies, the chief of which are Tata Steel, Tata Motors, Tata Consulting Services (TCS), Tata Power and Titan (Tata Group 2010). With respect to its global expansion, Tata's business history began in 1907 with the establishment of Tata Limited (London) in 1907, followed by its association with Daimler Benz (1950s), Tata Precision Industries (Singapore, 1972), Tata African Holdings (1994), the acquisition of Tetley Tea (UK) by Tata Tea in 2000 (53 per cent of the global packaged tea market) and finally, the takeover of the Anglo-Dutch steel company, Corus, by Tata Steel in 2007 (Grainger and Chatterjee 2008: 229; Goldstein 2008: 29). In the latter case, the concerns of Corus' European union – 'Corus workers are nervous. The boys were asking if we would have to wear safety turbans now' (Goldstein 2008: 29) – were relatively easily assuaged with reassurances by the new owners. Some of their concerns might have been reduced by the realization that almost two-thirds of the equity in Tata Sons is held by philanthropic trusts, including the Sir Ratan Tata Trust (1918), the Sir Dorabji Tata Trust (1932), the MK Tata Trust (1958), the Tata Social Welfare and Tata Education Trust (1990) and that the current CEO, Ratan Tata, owns less than one per cent of group shares (Gerhaeusser *et al.* 2010; Anonymous 2011d: 1). In addition, he is considered 'a natural gentleman who lives austerely, litters his conversation with references to "dignity" and "duty" and is happiest when talking about his pet dogs' (Anonymous 2011c: 1).

Tata's corporate vision, called the 'Tata Commitment', is expressed as 'striving for leadership and global competitiveness in the business sectors in which we operate' (Tata Group 2010), and its heavily promoted values include integrity, understanding, excellence, unity and responsibility (Goldstein 2008: 14). These values are pervasive throughout Tata's HRM systems and policies, together with a strong emphasis on innovation and CSR. Innovation is associated with its products and services, and CSR is enshrined through both the corporate equity structures as discussed above and enormous social funds. The two are blended in the company's concept of 'frugal innovation' – a conscious effort to develop new products for poor people, such as small benevolent trusts and the Nano or 'people's car'. More recently, Tata has 'focused on converting deserts into fertile land and developing new medicines to counteract or eliminate epidemics' (Gerhaeusser *et al.* 2010: 398).

This blend of social values and corporate entrepreneurship is arguably the crux of Tata's success – 'Tata's culture of probity has helped to insulate it from India's endemic corruption' (Anonymous 2011c: 3). It is also its potential Achilles heel. To date, there have been no scandals and very little media criticism of the sincerity of the Tata family business philosophy, unlike its Indian or Chinese counterparts, and is a positive factor in its global image as a progressive company. However, Ratan Tata's decision to restructure and streamline the company in 1991 – 'we are in more businesses than we should have been ... we need to define our businesses more articulately and remain focused rather than diffused ... more aggressive ... more market driven ... customer satisfaction' (Sen 2009: 32) – caused ripples amongst more traditional stakeholders.

Another factor buttressing its image is its sheer size and conscious global diversification, which would allow the insulation of any future problems to a single Tata business. However, so confident was Ratan Tata of the integrity of his own and his group's behaviours, that he recently took the rare action of publicly attacking one of his competitors, Mukesh Ambani (CEO, Reliance Industries, discussed earlier) for his extravagant lifestyle (Anonymous 2011d). Future threats to Tata may lie in its diversification strategy, a lack of central control planning (Goldstein 2008: 8), its relative senior management parochialism, and generational issues associated with CEO succession. The latter issue appears to have now been resolved with the appointment of Cyrus Mistry, former director of Forbes & Co, as Tata's new chairman from late 2012 (*The Times of India* 2011).

The Tata Group's HRM philosophies and systems

Tata's HRM vision is stated simply as 'what comes from the people goes back to the people many times over' (Tata Group 2010), and is underwritten by a plethora of principles, processes and practices. The company has adopted all of the requirements of the ILO (International Labour Organization) Declaration of Fundamental Principles and Rights at Work, including freedom of association, compliance with local labour legislation and minimum employment conditions (Goldstein 2008: 18). However, since the early 1900s, it had implemented many other employee initiatives, including the eight hour day (1912), free medical aid (1915), company-supported children's school fees (1917), leave with pay (1920), maternity benefits (1928) and a retiring gratuity (1937) (Gerhaeusser *et al.* 2010; Tata internal documents 2011). It has a well developed HRM architecture, with comprehensive programmes for all HRM processes. While these differ across industry sectors and in its global subsidiaries, these include modern staffing techniques;

extensive HRD, performance management and reward programmes, together with gender equity systems. A high priority is given to talent management, incorporating an Executive Selection Scheme (ESS) which is designed to fast track talented managerial aspirants through intensive training in association with prestigious higher education institutions such as the International Institute of Management (IIM) Ahmedabad (Scribd 2011). This initiative is supported by a series of complementary HRM activities, including hiring new recruits directly from the top global business schools and offering competitive salaries (Krishnan 2005: 218), providing internal training through Tata Administrative Services (TAS) and, recently, a China Management Training Programme which recruits potential managers from top Chinese business schools such as the CIEBS in Shanghai and Tsinghua University in Beijing (Srivastava 2011: 1). Interestingly, the criteria for acceptance into the latter require dual Chinese and Indian language fluency, knowledge of the Tata business and willingness to relocate within China. This demarche may be unique to this particular corporation.

Particular Tata companies offer different retention incentives, but, as an example, TCS promotes the choice of working in over 170 offices across 40 countries, together with more esoteric options such as paternity leave for the adoption of a girl child and discounts on group parties (Grainger and Chatterjee 2008: 100). As the latter authors suggest, Tata is 'very successful in distributing the cost of their in-house HRD by developing managers across different countries, businesses and functions ... strong micro-level management mindsets attuned to the group vision and ambitions' (ibid.: 231). Unlike many of its rivals, Tata has also consciously addressed the issue of gender equity at several levels, with reflections of both paternalism and US Affirmative Action principles. As an example, Tata Motors has established a Grihini Social Welfare Society which looks after the needs of female dependents of its employees (scribd 2011). At a different level, Tata has recently established a Second Career Internship Programme (SCIP) for Women in Mumbai and Pune aimed at qualified professional women with a CPA or CFA qualification and four years' experience, who have taken a career break and who wish to re-engage with industry (TMI 2009: 4).

Summary and conclusion

Generalizing about the six companies discussed raises a number of problems, including their different sizes, technologies, industry sectors and diverse country cultures. We have chosen a number of high-tech companies in both China and India, each of which employ a large number of people locally and globally. Their management and organizational structures, as well as HRM architectures are, in our opinion, very much influenced by these respective variables. However, all the companies are well known globally, and are led by charismatic leaders. With respect to the Indian corporations, Gerhaeusser *et al.* (2010: 386) pointed out that the CEOs of Birla and Reliance are included in the 2008 *Forbes* list of the top ten global billionaires.

Many scholars believe that global MNCs resemble each other in many ways, since they have common characteristics as organizations employing large numbers of employees. Size in the latter sense becomes a determining variable. We know from the findings of the Aston research (Hage 2002) that these entities have a great deal in common with other firms which are smaller. Size is correlated positively with formalization and standardization and is in turn negatively correlated with centralization (ibid.). A good number of the measures used by the Aston researchers relate to personnel/HR matters. The implication is that large organizations are able to function effectively because of the formal and standard procedures used to manage people. As global MNCs, these companies may have rather similar HR architectures because of the large number of employees which they have on their payroll. Some would argue that it follows from the organizational logic of large firms, given that there is also a relatively common technological context. Others would stress cross-cultural variables, when looking for significant differences. They would emphasize that these are not overly large corporations, but Chinese and Indian ones. Whatever the internal logic relating to the characteristics of these firms, they often resemble each other in the managerial and HR practices, in that they either copy each other in many respects and/or take the advice of international consultants who often offer a ready made template. In this sense we can talk about a relative degree of convergence (see Warner 2002).

On the other hand, what is often more interesting about organizations is the way that they are differentiated from each other because of their adaptation to their specific environments and here 'the devil is in the details'. So, although all the six organizations look superficially similar, they are in reality quite distinctive. For example, Haier, Huawei and Lenovo have all been relatively recently transformed from former state owned organizations to private companies, whilst Birla, Reliance and Tata are family owned corporations with considerably longer histories and generally cohesive management succession plans. All of the companies have charismatic leaders with well articulated missions, visions and business strategies which inform their HRM architectures, but it is evident that the traditional values of the three Indian companies are more observably entrenched than in their Chinese counterparts. As Gerhaeusser *et al.* (2010: 387–8) have suggested, these Indian companies 'rather than focusing solely on generating personal income, aim to create wealth for the country and society … set large goals … develop values for their enterprises. (Their) codes of conduct universally address integrity, honesty, trust, equality, responsibility, understanding excellence, and unity'. Other Indian corporations such as Wipro, Hindustan Computer Limited (HCL) Technologies, Mahindra & Mahindra Limited and Hero Group also display such contextual characteristics.

It will be seen from the preceding accounts that there are very interesting variations in the HRM architecture of the respective country cultures and organizations involved. We are aware that there are many limitations in the case study approach, but we would argue that the differences may be as important as the similarities. Such variations relate both to the preceding and current HRM traditions, structures and processes to be found in the respective countries. Each country has experienced a somewhat different path of development, both quantitatively and qualitatively.

Another major factor is that globalization is proceeding apace and at some stage many large MNCs eventually employ more people overseas than in their home country. This is a characteristic which will no doubt increase over time and is likely to have very important long-term consequences for the HRM architecture. As a result of this, they may have to adapt to these international environments, such that a higher degree of localization, in both managerial and HRM terms, occurs. They may then appear to be less 'Chinese' or 'Indian' as it were, and to take on the characteristics of the specific locale. If they make acquisitions of companies, as in the case of Lenovo's acquisition of the IBM PC (US) division and more recently of Medion (Germany) in a similar market, Tata's purchase of Tetley Tea (UK), Huawei's close collaboration with Siemens (Germany), or Birla's acquisition of Novelis (Canada), they may or may not take on the specific 'national' characteristics of this firm. It is useful to have what looks like an American brand here, as was the case with Haier setting up a production base in the US.

The HRM architecture of these global firms may look to the outsider as very much of a synthesis, whether generated by the internal logic of organizational processes and/or by external influences, either models recommended by international consulting firms and so on. Again, the devil of course is in the details, as ever. The Chinese firms we have used as case studies very quickly began to seek advice from foreign consultants as they expanded their operations both in the home market as well as overseas. A virtue of joint ventures was to be able to tap not only the technology of the partners but also their management and organizational models, notwithstanding their HRM practices. Many of these JVs are very US-based but a good number are also Japanese or European. One would expect a high degree of isomorphism, but the result of this has in fact been to create more HR heterogeneity than less. By contrast, the cited Indian companies appear to have more effectively blended global with local values and practices in all locations, even when seeking advice from Western management and HRM consulting companies. Gerhaeusser *et al.*, for example, concluded that most of the Indian global companies which they examined have utilized similar HRM approaches, including comprehensive 'employee training, improved performance, and promotion opportunities … world-class training methods and curriculum arrangements, and they hire professors from world-renowned business schools to deliver courses' (2010: 393).

One's assessment of these relative tendencies is of course, in the last analysis, possibly relative and even subjective. Thus, although relatively common HR goals are promoted on their websites, there is considerable differentiation, especially when looking at specific joint ventures and subsidiaries, and in different national contexts. Some of the companies even had investments in each other's countries. For example, Huawei has recently set up sites in India. There is thus no simple template of HRM architecture which can be easily implemented.

There are also contrasts between the HRM architectures on account of global firms operating across a wide range of country cultures, environments and markets. What is particularly interesting about the case studies presented, is that they originate from countries which are less developed and with lower levels of GDP per capita than those to which they have expanded in the more developed economies and markets, not only distributing products and services but also setting up production plants. It will thus be clear that there are increasingly large variations in the specific details of the HRM architecture, both within these companies and between them, and cross-nationally. The HRM architectures may become increasingly differentiated in their job design, talent attraction and retention, performance management and reward structures over time. Following this train of thought, it is reasonable to propose a relative degree of 'divergence' rather than 'convergence' in HRM architecture, at the end of the day. At first it might appear that these companies display a high degree of similarity, but closer examination will show that there is considerable differentiation which might have been expected from their unique characteristics. Not only is the environment changing within the home country, whether China or India, but also in the specific contexts within which they operate. Thus, we may conclude that there is a 'double dynamic' at play, each one reinforcing the other as they develop over time.

8 Towards new models of human resource management

Introduction

A number of authors (e.g. Heery and Frege 2006: 602; Delbridge and Keenoy 2011; Thompson 2011) have pointed out that studies on HRM have often focused on the organizational level, implicitly assuming the firm 'as a strategic actor' in its labour deployment. There is an increasing range of actors whose role in shaping industrial relations has largely escaped the attention of researchers (Heery and Frege 2006). These include the state institutions as well as private agencies such as management consultants and employment agencies. According to Heery and Frege (2006: 602), these institutions 'promote isomorphism in employer practice, even in societies with flexible, lightly regulated labour markets, and weak employers' associations'. There is therefore a need, as some authors have argued, to situate the discussion of HRM practices in a broad context (e.g. Kim and Wright 2010) and from a political economy perspective (e.g. Boxall and Macky 2009), rather than a strategic perspective that focuses narrowly within the organization, as a more insightful approach to make sense of the constraints and choices facing organizations.

Indeed, to understand what HRM practices are in place, and why, in the Chinese and Indian context, we need to adopt a broad analytical framework that enables us to assess what factors are at play and how institutional actors interact with each other to shape the environment in which firms operate and individuals make their living. It is precisely with this in mind that we have explored, in previous chapters of this book, the development of the HRM and industrial relations systems in China and India within their dynamic economic, political, industrial, social and cultural environments. We also examined challenges and opportunities facing the two nations and provided a series of illustrative case studies from both countries which reflect the amalgam of domestic and international influences on HRM principles and practices in some of their most successful multinational corporations. This concluding chapter addresses the major underlying questions posed throughout this book – namely, is there evidence of identifiable 'new' models of HRM in China and India, how are these new models similar to or different from each other; and what (if anything) do these models add to extant global HRM models and practices? We do so by contemplating a range of broad institutional and cultural factors from a comparative perspective between China and India, and what may exist in Western countries. We acknowledge the limitation of a broad brush approach in branding 'Western countries' as one category while practices may vary significantly across developed nations.

The chapter comprises four sections. The first outlines some of the major similarities and differences in the institutional context and the role of the institutional actors and HRM practices in India and China. It also identifies aspects of HRM that may converge with or diverge from Western-style systems. This is followed by an overview of the main contextual challenges facing HRM in China and India. The third section provides a brief consideration of comparative HRM theoretical frameworks. The fourth section discusses theoretical and practical HRM issues within new conceptual frameworks for China and India.

Institutional context and the role of institutional actors in India and China

China and India have often been considered together as two major resurgent economic powers in Asia. Their cultural similarities have also captured much attention in contrast to the vast differences that exist between the two nations in their political and economic systems and social traditions. Table 8.1 summarizes some of the major similarities and differences in the institutional environment of the two nations, and the role of their respective institutional actors in shaping HRM practices in broad terms.

India has had over 60 years of independence and a multi-party democratic political system. This political pluralism influences the way the industrial relations system operates, including unionism and workers participation. By contrast, the tight grip on power by the Chinese Communist Party and its unrivalled 60 year reign (as a result of the suppression of other political parties) has meant that state intervention via its control of various institutional actors (e.g. trade unions, employers associations, professional associations and business schools) remains a defining feature in China's economic development. As noted in previous chapters and below, the state owned sector still consists of a large (albeit shrinking) proportion of the economy.

Decades of democracy in India, however, have not led to a more equal society as one might have expected, as the strong social hierarchy influenced by the centuries-old caste system has proven to be a much more powerful and enduring fabric in structuring social relationships than the fragile rhetoric of democracy that is of a more recent fashion. In comparison, China is a relatively more egalitarian society that has been influenced by Confucianism and Socialism, particularly during the state-planned economy period, although much less so in recent years as the process of marketization deepens. The Chinese one-party state did much to address gender inequality in the state-planned period, an achievement that has been eroded in the ensuing marketizing economy (Cooke 2010a).

Compared with China, India has a much larger informal (also known as unorganized) sector that is non-unionized. The education level of females still lags significantly behind that of males in India. The concentration of women in the informal sector, in part as a result of their lower level of human capital, further dampens the prospect of achieving a higher level of gender equality and social development. Nevertheless, a higher proportion of Indian women than their counterparts in Western countries and China have made their way to senior leadership positions in corporations and in politics (e.g. Cooke 2010a; Hill 2011).

The role of the state has been crucial in the rapid economic development of East and Southeast Asian countries in recent decades (e.g. Johnson 1987; Öniş 1991; Zhu 2004). This has been characterized by a strong commitment to growth, productivity, competitiveness and the privatization of property and market, in the absence of a commitment to social equality and welfare. It has also been marked by a relatively high level of state intervention in the process of marketization via various state agencies, often managed by elite bureaucrats (Öniş 1991). The economic transformation of China since the 1980s shared many of these characteristics (Cooke 2011d). So did India since the early 1990s to a lesser extent.

In China, the state plays a hands-on role in crafting its policies and incentives to encourage convergent HRM practices and to raise professional standards through a range of means and via various institutional actors (see Cooke 2011d, for more detailed discussion). This top-down approach, however, does not guarantee success even in a one-party state like China as a result of the deepening marketization and decentralization of administrative power. Tensions may arise between the state and local agencies, and amongst the local institutional actors, in the process of implementing state driven regulations and initiatives. As such, state intervention takes place at both macro and micro levels, often in subtle rather than coercive ways in reality, through an intricate web of institutional networks and social relations of compromise and cooperation (Cooke 2011d). The Indian government, by contrast, plays a much less direct role and individual states have their legal and operational autonomy. This has in part led to a more dynamic, if at times more chaotic, liberalization process and more complicated legal environment, notably the labour regulations within which businesses operate.

Compared with India, both employers' associations and HR professional associations are less developed in China. Controlled by the state, their activities are sanctioned and need to be aligned with national objectives and interests. Like the trade unions, they serve as the conduits for the implementation of state initiatives in human resource management and development (see Cooke 2011d). Civil associations, such as independent non-government organizations (NGOs), as emerging actors in employment relations (e.g. Heery and Frege 2006; Cooke and Wood 2011) are severely constrained in their scope and operations (e.g. Lee and Shen 2008; Cooke 2012a). By contrast, democratic India has a much more established and active NGO sector which consists of both international and domestic organizations. These organizations have a long tradition of worker organizing, for example, organizing women in the informal sector, where mainstream organizing bodies fail to reach or make an impact.

HR consultancy firms and business schools are two relatively new institutional actors in shaping HRM practices and developing HR talent. The HR consultancy industry is more developed in India than China in part because of the latter's constraints on how foreign firms can operate in the country (see Chapter 3). Similarly, business schools in China are mostly state owned and an integral part of the state owned universities, the curricula of which are sanctioned by the Ministry of Education (see Warner and Goodall 2010; Cooke 2011d). The restriction of the participation by foreign educators in the Chinese education market constrains the dissemination of foreign HRM practices in China. By contrast, Indian business schools are mostly privately owned and emerged in the late 1980s and 1990s to take advantage of the rapidly expanding market and in response to the huge corporate demands for management talent. Independent, relatively small in size and highly market oriented, Indian business schools appear to have a strong influence from American business schools and management theories. Indian students and corporations appear to be more enthusiastic than their Chinese counterparts in adopting Western-style HRM initiatives. However, are these institutional forces and the wave of globalization sufficient to bring the HRM practices in India and China closer to those prescribed in the West? We look at this issue next.

In spite of critiques of the notion of HRM and its plethora of initiatives (e.g. Legge1995, 2005; Alvesson and Willmott 2002; Thompson 2011), a range of techniques have been promoted by HR researchers, professional associations and consultants. These include, amongst others, emotional intelligence and empowerment in leadership, 360-degree performance appraisal, coaching and mentoring, total rewards, diversity management and work–life balance (see Table 8.2). It is believed that strategic implementation of these schemes will lead to enhanced individual competence and commitment which will in turn lead to improved organizational performance and ultimately competitiveness.

In previous chapters, we have reviewed a number of studies on HRM in the Indian and Chinese context. A common conclusion from these studies seem to be that strategic HRM does lead to enhanced organizational performance, thus pointing to the universality of certain HRM practices such as extensive training and development and supportive leadership. However, studies have also revealed that few Chinese and Indian firms have adopted these HR initiatives strategically for the benefit of the employees as well as the organization.

For example, Cooke and Saini's (2010b) study of 54 Indian firms, that investigated the role of HRM in supporting an innovation-oriented business strategy, revealed a mismatch between the HRM practices adopted by the firms and those desired by the employees. Sample firms have typically adopted a short term performance-oriented HR strategy that was largely organizational goal driven and control oriented. In pursuing greater efficiency, employee involvement has primarily been implemented in the form of suggestion schemes to benefit the company rather than the employees. There is little real empowerment of employees, or participation by them in decision making.

Similarly, Cooke and Saini's (2010a) study of 24 firms of different ownership forms in a number of industries in India revealed that the majority of the case study organizations have not adopted a strategic approach to diversity management. Some of them saw diversity as already embedded in the society; others were

Table 8.1 Institutional context and the role of institutional actors in China and India

Role of institutions and actors	*India*	*China*
Political system	Multi-party democracy	One-party reign since 1949, with other small parties in a consultation role that does not challenge the leadership of the Chinese Communist Party
Current political ideology	Empowerment, inclusion and social development	Building a harmonious society through better social relationships and social development
Labour market	Small organized sector Large unorganized sector mostly unregulated Increasing level of workforce education Worsening skill shortage alongside excessive labour surplus	Urban workers versus rural migrant workers Formal versus informal employment Increasing level of workforce education Worsening skill shortage alongside excessive labour surplus
Gender issues	Relatively low proportion of female participation, especially in organized sector Low level of female unionization Gender organizing highly active in the informal sector	High level of female participation in full time employment through strong state intervention during the planned state economic period High level of union membership in unionized firms close to that of men
Societal culture	Collectivism, paternalism, strong social hierarchy influenced by the caste system	Collectivism, paternalism, egalitarianism influenced by Confucianism and Socialism
Level of integration of the IR system	Decentralized because of variations in federal states' IR laws and other interventions, industrial and sectoral-based IR systems	Relatively centralized and homogenous within industry, sector and ownership forms, but is diverging across ownership forms, industry and regions

State/local government	Enacting labour laws Arbiter of labour conflicts Promoting initiatives to achieve peaceful employment relations and protect labour Holding tripartite meetings with social partners annually A large but shrinking state sector since the 1990s	Enacting labour laws Suppression of non-ACFTU-led labour organizations and movements Promoting initiatives to achieve harmonious employment relations Promoting nationwide human resource management and development initiatives A large but shrinking state sector since the 1980s
Trade unions	Multiple unions highly active in the political arena Multiple unions, both independent and party-affiliated Inter-union rivalry exist Union strength once high but has been in decline since the 1980s Changing attitudes of unions in the wake of economic priority and global competition Unionism rivalled by professional associations and difficult to take roots in new industries (e.g. IT and BPO)	Single union under the control of the Communist Party Welfare role in the state sector Weak in the private sector Largely ineffective in defending workers' rights and interests
Collective bargaining/negotiation	No legal specification on the trade union's role in collective bargaining Scope of bargaining is constrained by law (Industrial Disputes Act 1947) Collective bargaining and mutual consultation on a voluntary basis are encouraged by the government to resolve disputes Bargaining at national and industrial level (e.g. public sector) and plant level (e.g. private firms)	The notion of collective bargaining/negotiation was introduced to the Chinese ER in the early 1990s Recognized by laws and promoted by the government Wage level is the main issue of collective negotiation Bargaining mainly at workplace level but is encouraged by the government to take place at regional level (for multi-establishment firms)

Continued

Table 8.1 Continued

Role of institutions and actors	*India*	*China*
Workers participation	Workers Representative Congress, legal requirement but not effectively implemented Quality management schemes (e.g. suggestions schemes, problem solving teams) promoted by employers since the 1980s	Legal and voluntary initiatives historically promoted by the government, with limited uptake Quality management schemes (e.g. suggestions schemes, problem solving teams) promoted by employers since the 1980s, more widely adopted
Labour laws	Extensive and complicated	Becoming more comprehensive
Labour dispute resolution mechanism	In place but not effective	In place but not effective
Employers' associations	Independent and relatively more established and stronger compared with those in China	Emerging but are controlled by the state
HR professional associations	Developing, more active in organizing seminars and training workshops to develop HR professional competence	Weak, not so active and under the guidance of the state
HR consultancy industry	Growing strength	Emerging
Foreign owned MNCs	Disseminating imported HRM practices Adaptation of local HRM practices	Disseminating HRM practices Adaptation of local HRM practices
Chinese/Indian-owned global firms	Truly global firms led by private entrepreneurship	Dominated by large state owned/connected firms
Business schools	Mostly independent and privately owned, hence relatively small sized, more market-oriented, with strong American influence	Mostly state owned and controlled as part of the universities which are usually large undertakings
Role of the business schools in management development	Extensive EMBA/MBA education	From cadres management education to EMBA education, with curriculum controlled by the state
HR function in organizations	Largely administrative with little strategic input	Largely administrative with little strategic input

Source: Adapted and expanded from F. L. Cooke, 2012b, 'Employment selections in China and India'.

sceptical of the notion of diversity management. Instead, the majority of managers from these organizations took a pragmatic and 'problem solving' approach to managing their workforce diversity. The findings of the study suggest that we cannot simplistically promote diversity management 'as part of strategic HRM without taking into account the institutional environment and cultural preference for the highly context-specific HR issues such as diversity' (Cooke and Saini 2010a: 496).

In the Chinese context, Cooke and Huang's (2011) study of four Chinese IT firms acquired by US-owned firms revealed their lack of enthusiasm for 360-degree performance appraisals in these fast growing high-tech firms. Chinese managers commonly felt uneasy about giving their staff detailed behavioural feedback and were uncomfortable about being evaluated by their subordinates. The lack of skills to conduct appraisals for development purposes, and the preference of staff for reward-oriented performance appraisal, meant that the Chinese managers have opted for the simple and home-grown methods to conduct performance reviews of their subordinates.

The findings of poor uptake of strategic HRM initiatives by Indian and Chinese firms are perhaps not surprising given that similar criticisms have been levelled against their counterparts in Western countries such as the UK and the US. These findings do, however, reveal the distance between what is prescribed in the HRM rhetoric and what is happening in reality, as summarized in Table 8.2. They are indicative of what organizations need to do if they wish to enhance their competitiveness.

Two points are worth noting here. One is that whilst general HR competence may be relatively underdeveloped in China and India compared with that of developed countries, some of the HR techniques recently promoted in the HRM literature may have long been practised in China and India. For example, good leaders are expected to demonstrate their care to their subordinates and to extend support to solve their personal and family problems, in order to win trust and reciprocal obedience. This in some ways reflects the notion of emotional intelligence promoted in the Western leadership literature. The other point is that, as noted in previous chapters, the cultural values exhibited in Indian and Chinese societies may actually be more conducive to the adoption of HRM techniques to enhance organizational performance. For instance, Chen *et al.*'s (2011: 3393) study of knowledge management in Chinese firms revealed that 'collectivist but not individualistic values promote open-minded discussion of views which results in knowledge sharing'.

In the rest of the chapter, we will further discuss key challenges to, and implications for, HRM in the two countries by contemplating a broad range of factors at the societal and industrial level as well as choices at the organizational level.

Challenges facing HRM in China and India

Over the past century, the domination of the West in economic activities was achieved through massive investments in technological capabilities, innovations

Table 8.2 Convergence or divergence? A comparison of Western promoted approaches to HRM and Indian and Chinese practices

HRM dimensions	*Western promoted approach*	*Indian and Chinese approach*
Leadership	Emotional intelligence Empowerment	Emotional intelligence long existed through developing relationship with subordinates and understanding their family problems and help provide solutions Limited evidence of empowerment
Performance management	360-degree feedback Development-oriented performance appraisal (prospective)	Reward-oriented performance appraisal (retrospective)
Training and development	Extensive training, coaching and mentoring, career planning, succession planning	Limited existence of training and development system Uneven training and development practices concentrated on a small proportion of highly marketable talent
Reward	Total rewards (financial reward, welfare benefits and personal growth opportunities, with an increasing emphasis on the latter)	Financial rewards remains the major motivational factor, followed by career development and promotion opportunities Workplace welfare provision is the cultural norm and to be expected
Equal opportunities and diversity management	Individual rights (social justice perspective) Celebration and utilization of individual differences as part of talent management (strategic HRM perspective)	Equal opportunities regulations in place but not effectively enforced Diversity needs seen as an 'issue' to be managed Emerging awareness of the concept Little understanding of the concept in China, even less practising it
Work–life balance	Employee well-being	Worsening work intensification and declining employee well-being, limited work–life balance initiatives and poor uptake
Employer–employee relationship	Relational contracting/high performance work practices to enhance organizational commitment and engagement	From job-for-life and reciprocal relationship towards transactional relationship emphasizing on individual rewards (material and intrinsic)

in production alliances, marketing effectiveness and greater efficiencies in distribution systems. During the 1970s and 1980s, a divergent approach to Western supremacy adopted by Japan saw economies of scale through the development of global products and logistical innovation. As Chinese and Indian companies emerge as leaders in global production and services respectively, a necessary shift in human resource management imperatives becomes urgent. Chinese economic life is still highly influenced by state owned enterprises and in India, traditional family-dominated business houses continue to play an enduring role.

Despite these distinctive differences, China and India have seen the development of a large number of companies leveraging global talent. The macroeconomic changes brought about by the corporate governance systems of these global companies, as well as the declining role of trade unions and the adoption of globally compatible employment practices, are having profound influences. The stakeholder-oriented corporate Japanese perspective provided an alternative to the shareholder-based US and European models in the 1970s and 1980s. With the recognition of the importance of the knowledge dominated economy, the primacy of human capital management became imperative to rising global companies from China and India. The 2011 list of the top 500 companies included 61 Chinese and 8 Indian companies, with Beijing being the location of the largest number of global corporations in the world (41 companies – *Fortune* 2011b). Interestingly, it was noted recently that the growth and international expansion of such companies and the evolution of HRM in the region are two sides of the same phenomenon (Yeung, Warner and Rowley 2008: 2).

However, global expansion has not yet undermined the two countries as sources of inexpensive labour for foreign MNCs, though there is emerging evidence that the sharp rises in wage cost in the developed eastern coastal regions in China has weakened these regions' attraction to foreign investors as well as domestic investors. In addition, local Chinese and Indian organizations are demonstrating considerable resilience and innovation, and alternative learning methods. As pointed out in a recent report:

> Developing countries are becoming hotbeds of business innovation in much the same way as Japan did from the 1950s onwards. They are coming up with new products and new services that are dramatically cheaper than their Western equivalents: $3000 cars, $300 computers and $30 mobile phones that provide nationwide services for just 2 cents a minute.
>
> (*The Economist* 2010: 3)

The emergence of indigenous Chinese and Indian companies as global leaders, an increased presence of traditional Western MNCs in both countries, together with the imperatives of new business models to serve new markets, are demanding innovative approaches to employee recruitment, retention and development. China and, to a lesser extent, India have reprioritized the role of education. The relatively recent reform of employment legislation in China (see Chapters 3 and 4) has, on the one hand, enabled considerable flexibility in employee conditions and management for global organizations. However, on the other hand, a number of high profile industrial disruptions and disputes by workers in MNCs in both China and India imply a degree of counter-balance in their employer–employee relationships.

Earlier chapters have considered the implications of an estimated 130 million 'floating population' of Chinese migrant workers who had formerly contributed to the rise of China by their willingness to relocate wherever economic demands pulled them. However, the unlimited supply of such human resources is fast approaching its end in China:

> Workers are becoming harder to find and to keep. The country's villages still contain perhaps 70 million potential migrants. Other rural folk might be willing to work closer to home in the growing number of factories moving inland. But the supply of strong backs and nimble fingers is not infinite, even in China.
>
> (*The Economist* 2010: 7)

Cities and towns in China, where workers looking desperately for employment milled outside factories a decade ago, now have equally desperate worker shortages. It is therefore becoming clear that the unlimited supply of workers that fuelled China's dazzling economic growth outpacing its peer, India, is likely to be unsustainable over the coming decades. As discussed in Chapter 5, similar if different difficulties also bedevil India's dreams of building global advantage in key service industries. However, China faces a potentially more serious labour supply problem than India on account of the latter's previously discussed 'demographic dividend' (see Chapter 1). China's former heritage of a large workforce supporting a smaller number of non-working children and the elderly is set to change dramatically. This is because the population is living longer, marrying later and, of course, the consequences of the 'one child' policy (see Chapter 1). India, however, will continue to benefit from the age structure of its population. These developments will have serious implications for export competitiveness in general, and for human resource management in the manufacturing sector in particular.

In addition, social and organizational cultures in China and India are under significant pressure to change. For example, traditions of unconditional loyalty and obedience to leaders (see Chapter 2) are likely to have diminished within both Chinese and Indian global corporations (see Chapter 7), despite persistent cultural traditions. Interestingly, Clause 49 of the Chinese Constitution requires all adults to take care of their parents, and Clause 183 of the Chinese Constitution imposes a penalty of up to five years in prison for failing to care for elderly parents. Obviously, the impact of these demographic shifts on human resource policies and practices in all types of organizations in China is likely to be significant, especially given the macroeconomic pressures of chronic labour shortages and increased healthcare costs for an ageing population.

It is, however, in the area of knowledge-based organizations and large scale innovations where a synergy is emerging as the cognitive orientations of managers from China and India have shared a common heritage over centuries, as discussed in Chapter 2. As a recent study asserted:

> when faced by that unknown future, managers use their cognitive frameworks, gained from past experience, their habits of mind, and/or their tacitly or explicitly learned 'cultures' to frame, understand, and then act upon the challenges they confront. The implication is, of course, that different people use a different 'how' to comprehend and act in their managerial environments.
>
> (Kase, Slocum and Zhang 2011: 3)

This challenge of 'how' managers can act responsibly to the emerging issues of building and sustaining future-oriented organizations inevitably needs to be anchored in the values and belief systems of the two societies. As discussed in previous chapters, these values and belief systems espouse both openness to the ideas of others and adherence to earlier cultural traditions. Thus, Chinese traditions have embraced both Buddhism and Confucianism.

The continuing success of Chinese and Indian leaders in global organizations will require the easing of many of the rigidities which underpinned their cultural traditions. Many scholars suggest that this process needs to begin with the educational system and its pedagogies. As the noted observer of Chinese society, Lucien Pye, suggested:

> The paradoxical combination of achievement and dependency was central to the traditional Chinese socialization practices, which sought to teach the child early that disciplined conformity to the wishes of others was the best way to security, and that being "different" was dangerous. The result was a positive acceptance of dependency. The combination of achievement and dependency dictated an implicit goal of the traditional Chinese socialization process, which was to strive to resolve achievement needs by diligently carrying out the assigned role within the family, and hence by being properly dependent.
>
> (Pye 2000: 250)

Moulding of achievement, creativity and dependency into character can also be traced back to the Indian heritage, as discussed in Chapter 2. Just how the global interface impacts on personal and social lives and a reorientation of values becomes noticeable is the subject of considerable attention by anthropologists (D'Mello and Eriksen 2005). New corporate contexts in China and India are creating new social and cultural frameworks for their employees. The dependency relationships discussed above are transforming into creative and achievement-oriented associations. However, our understanding of the impact of globalization on micro or organizational level (see Figure 8.1) cultural reforms is limited, in the absence of scholarly research in this area (Parry 1999). It is important to examine national and organizational culture not only as a constant (or residual) variable, as is often the case in HRM literature, but also as a dependent (or intervening) variable; in order to examine how the attitudes, values and social relations change according to the extent of globalization. The Figure illustrates the complexity of convergent and divergent forces at several levels on the adoption of HRM strategies and systems in multinational companies in China and India, and suggests a range of cross-verging ideas which inform their contemporary HRM practices.

Figure 8.1 attempts to summarize the key ideas contributing to the cross-verging themes of this book. It comprises cascading macro, meso and micro level components, representing global, local and institutional influences. The macro level includes the dynamics of the interaction between the convergent forces of globalization and the divergent forces of localism. Four key waves of the global tide are identified:, the rise of the market ideology; the influences of global regulatory regimes (e.g. World Trade Organization, Organization for Economic Cooperation and Development); the rise of local MNCs; and the critical demand for global talent management associated with the knowledge economy. These macro forces of convergence are interpreted and contextualized through a variety of traditional local filters including 'holism', 'virtue' and the 'common good'; emphases in both China and India on harmony and wisdom; and the complementarity of intuition, logic and rationality within the context of Chinese and Indian demographic uniqueness and their dynamic national contexts.

As discussed in Chapter 2, this interaction requires managers in China and India to seek synergies between the primarily 'deductive' processes of Western management and their own 'inductive' emphases. As an example of the complexity and circularity of this phenomenon, the highly successful Indian civil service over the past century was essentially derived from the British civil service system, which was itself drawn from the Chinese 'mandarin' system. The Figure captures this 'inductive–deductive' synergy.

The meso level imperatives tune the balancing of the global–local conundrum and challenge the global ambitions of innovation seeking multinational companies. The relative intensity of global, regional and local emphases (namely, the superimposition of informal 'family' structures, represented in China by *guānxì*, over more formal structures, and ancient traditions in both countries of learning, mentoring and 'apprenticeship') in turn shape their business strategies, organizational structures and systems, in particular those associated with human resource management.

These traditions, structures and systems assist in the formulation of such 'cross-verging' practices as corporate adaptability (*jugaad* in Hindi), integrated job rotation programmes designed to broaden employee horizons, innovative human resource development initiatives, reward systems and indigenous 'work–life' balance imperatives (see Chapter 7). In addition, many Indian and Chinese managers emphasize the notions of a 'network of nests' as their primary focus (rather than individual employees); and constant training and feedback in order to allow local staff to develop their careers into the global arena. The importance of familism or a high degree of culture-based relationships act as proxy to the more rational legal and formal systems.

This book argues that, in spite of the many differences between China and India, there is a convergence of cultural syllogism in terms of this 'network of nests'.

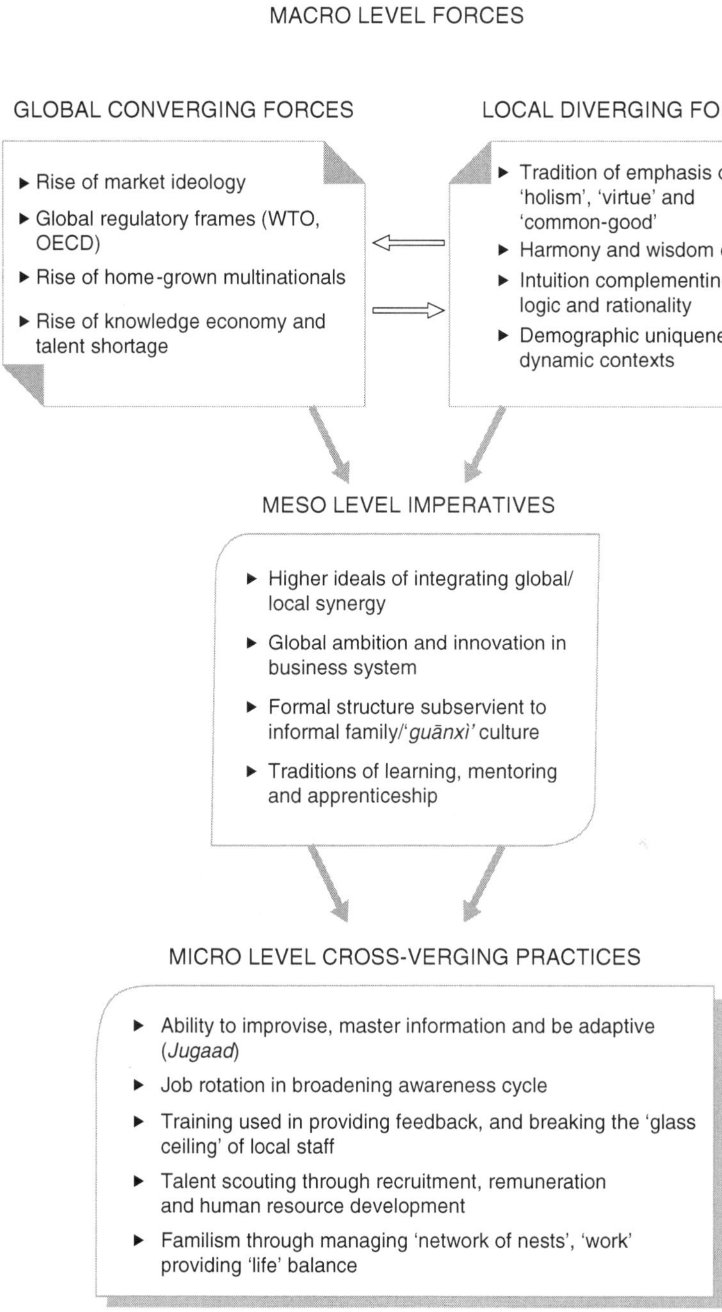

Figure 8.1 Cross-verging HRM ideas from China and India.

Thus, focusing on collective rather than individual behaviour in human resource management strategies and practices remains largely non-negotiable in Chinese and Indian HRM models.

Figure 8.1 also recognizes the human resource enrichment potential of culturally-coded knowledge within the interaction of global and local forces. This paradigm attempts to capture the transformative role of HRM in complex societies such as India and China, by not only rejecting 'converging' or 'universalistic' models, but also by questioning the 'diverging' or 'relativist' perspectives of stereotypical national contexts. Such macro–meso–micro level understanding allows managers to recognize the limits of Western frameworks and to improvise new ways of energizing and managing their human resources.

From an economic to a multidimensional paradigm: HRM in transition

The resurgence of the Chinese economy commenced with a steady inflow of FDI (foreign direct investment), initially to leverage a large pool of low-cost human resources. Economic growth was the primary objective in the early 1980s. This initial goal has now widened to include social, political, global and strategic dimensions. The success of the state owned or state sponsored organizations has resulted in a multidimensionality of paradigms. As discussed in Chapter 1, the Indian economic pathway has been totally different, where deregulation and liberalization has led to unprecedented dynamism from the private sector. This empowerment of the private sector has unleashed ripples of change in many other important social and cultural dimensions, notably education and the enhancement of human resource capabilities. The ascendancy of China and India as global leaders can only be achieved through perspectives which encompass social, educational and cultural domains. The educational infrastructure in particular, will require transformation. In addition to producing the largest number of technically trained graduates, emphases in all disciplines including the humanities and the arts is necessary. While the improvement in literacy rates and the increasing proportion of those receiving higher education in China has been a major achievement, India has yet to follow the same route.

Global outsourcing and large scale off-shoring of Western backroom services to India, and manufacturing in China, has in many ways changed the nature of both blue and white collar, as well as their managerial, workforces. Both countries have learned very rapidly through their collaborations with Western MNC, albeit in different ways. For example, large Indian software companies have expanded overseas and climbed the value chain on the shoulders of their pool of technical specialists with English language skills. In contrast, Chinese software firms focused on their expertise domestically by working with mostly US and European MNCs. They have tended to be more ambivalent with respect to global expansion in this industry sector. In essence, the learning and mobilization of human resources in the internationalization process have followed divergent paths in the two countries. Indian IT companies, for example, entered China initially by serving Western MNCs, but have now gained sufficient confidence in its culture and language to experiment with domestic Chinese companies. However, the number of Chinese employees in Indian companies is still relatively marginal.

It is interesting to note how Indian software companies have complemented their human resource deficiencies by acquisitions over the past decade. Their need to move up the value chain and to augment a lack of local human resource expertise has prompted a shift in strategy. Leading Indian companies have focused on acquiring Western firms mainly to gain access to new HRM skills and as a catalyst for greater market penetration. In contrast, the emergence of human resource capabilities in the software outsourcing industry in China was developed modestly, and primarily through their domestic operations on behalf of Western MNCs first, and later internationally with Japanese companies. As Niosi and Tschang (2009: 283) explain:

> The size of the Japanese economy, and its attraction for Chinese firms that want to sell services offshore, illustrates a similarity to the USA-India situation in its early days. Chinese firms were initially called on to do lower value work for Japanese clients. Many Chinese firms seek to imitate the success of Neusoft, a firm that achieved the strongest export performance by servicing the Japanese market.

In spite of these divergent approaches, a commonality of purpose adopted by both countries is noteworthy. There is a strong recognition of the role of tradition in the development of their companies. As discussed in Chapter 2, the Confucian concept of knowledge and the traditional reverence of learning in India are paramount underpinning values. The Sino-Indian consensus in tradition suggests that knowledge and action exist in a symbiotic relationship – ‘knowledge, in its genuine and earnest aspect, is action; and action, in its intelligent and discriminating aspect, is knowledge’ (Eliade 1992: 18). Success in the software industry requires both knowledge and action in both developing and managing global networks. The industry has demonstrated significant collaboration in learning and development through joint ventures and cooperative training arrangements.

Asian tradition considers knowledge creation as a continuous self-transcending process where spirit and wisdom unfold as competencies grow. Human resource management in the knowledge-based economy may find this Sino-Indian holistic paradigm more appealing than other models. Leveraging the capabilities and knowledge base of a large cadre of managers, and creating opportunities for them, cannot be achieved by organizations that lack passion or soul. One of the most significant contributions of Sino-Indian HRM, therefore, is to stimulate a holistic and spiritual connection between employees and their organizations.

Implications for specific HRM processes and practices

The staggering scale of employment challenges in India and China presents a real dilemma for human resource managers and scholars. As the nature of work in all industry sectors changes rapidly, the gap between industry labour demand and the supply from educational institutions is widening. In both countries, the quantity and quality of required graduates (see Chapters 1 and 5) is proving inadequate, and is revealing deficiencies in the their educational systems. India's 'demographic dividend' promises an additional million young workers every month for the next 20 years (Sabharwal 2011). It is argued that this huge number of job seekers will also be affected by dynamic geographic, sectoral and skills variations over this period. In the latter case, the German or South Korean models of vocational skills-based training, coupled with multi-skilling within articulated development systems, may provide a more effective approach.

The large scale, low-cost manufacturing strategy which has underpinned China's economic growth will inevitably transition in different directions in the near future. The micro level managerial implications of these changes in both indigenous and global Chinese organizations will be profound. In India, these likely challenges are becoming gradually understood. The 2010 Indian budget, for example, allocated 500 crore rupees (US$ 110 million) for the national government's Skills Development Fund, which aims to sponsor job related training for 550 million job seekers by 2022. Foreign MNCs are also actively participating in this endeavour. Toyota, for example, has established a technical training institute at Bidadi, near Bangalore, where three year residential courses are offered to prospective employees. On completion of the programme, successful graduates are offered employment at the Toyota joint venture called the Toyota Kirloskar Motor Pvt. Ltd.

The critical skills shortages accompany a rise in wage and salary costs, as well as retention problems in a number of industry sectors. India's wage and salary costs are forecast to rise by 13 per cent, and China's by 9 per cent, by 2012. In response, several US companies have considered relocating their manufacturing plants away from China. Conversely, both Chinese and Indian MNCs have sought to recruit global rather than domestic talent. As examples, Beijing Automotive Group (BAIC), a state owned car maker, organized a 'recruitment fair' in Germany in 2011 in order to attract German engineers; Reliance Retail, one of India's most powerful businesses, recruited the former CEO of Walmart China as its Chief Operating Officer; and four Chinese financial organizations joined the annual student placement fair at the Indian Institute of Management (Calcutta) in order to recruit MBA graduates, alongside a crowded list of top 100 Western MNCs.

New HRM frameworks emerging from China and India

In their book entitled *The Quest for Global Dominance*, Gupta, Govindarajan and Wang (2008) argued that China and India have introduced four 'game changing' realities in global business. These are, first, the rise of mega-markets for all types of products and services; second, the opportunity of significant reductions in cost structures; third, a new platform for global technology and innovation; and, finally, the emergence of 'fearsome global competitors' from the two countries. Their argument is based on a number of factors, including that the cost of production workers is a fraction of that in developed countries. Earlier chapters of this book have demonstrated that these cost differences are ephemeral, with likely spiralling wages especially in urban areas in China and India. The maintenance of cost advantages can be argued as more an HRM challenge than the tapping of socioeconomic endowments. A new managerial paradigm is also needed to ensure the dominance of the two countries' global technology platform, as well as excellence in innovation. As Gupta and Wang (2009c: 201) pointed out:

> which side of the balance sheet people belong to depends very much on how effective a company is at recruiting the right talent, nurturing it, and keeping it dedicated to building the company rather than moving on to its competitors. Given the scarcity of professional talent, this task is particularly challenging in China and India.

The model at Figure 8.2 represents an emerging HRM framework for China and India based upon the factors discussed earlier in this chapter, and throughout the book.

The framework highlights the human resource management foundations of China and India. These include the three variables of 'traditional foundations', 'foundations of corporate culture' and 'globally convergent forces', which are mediated by three indigenous and exogenous variables (see also Table 8.3), leading to an 'emerging HRM focus'. The three 'foundation' forces extend the generic cross-vergence model presented earlier in this chapter (Figure 8.1). The 'traditional foundations' are very real and shape the spirit of work organizations. 'Foundations of corporate culture' demonstrate conflicting belief systems, including the struggle

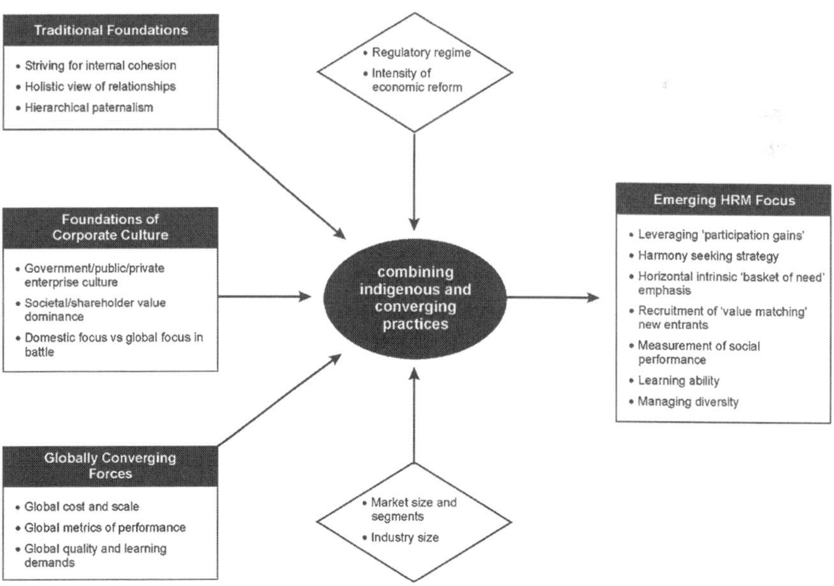

Figure 8.2 An emerging HRM framework for China and India.

Table 8.3 A classification framework for HRM systems in Chinese and Indian organizations

	Old	*New*
Indigenous	1	2
Exogenous	3	4

between 'old' and 'new' values and beliefs. The third variable highlights the global ideas that are forcing their way into Indian and Chinese organizations. For example, Tata in India is an organization in which traditions, the changing dynamics of managerial culture, and global perspectives coexist in its managerial mindsets. Such combinations of values and perspectives also permeate companies such as Huawei, Lenovo and Reliance (see Chapter 7).

The dynamics of stable cultural traditions, changing work cultures and the inescapable forces of global convergence are three critical elements of the model, triggering a re-assessment of Western HRM models within the diverse contexts of China and India. The macro level regulatory regime and the velocity of economic reform determine how rapidly alternative indigenous HRM models will evolve. This evolution, however, shows distinctly divergent characteristics. Recruitment systems which display shared employer–employee values, intrinsic rewards, learning and ongoing development opportunities, are more likely to be important in attracting and retaining talent in all organizational types in China and India. Considerations about the rights of employees in these new models will likely be characterized by 'hierarchical paternalism', where harmony is still an important factor.

Lessons from recent decades of human resource management in China and India demonstrate that culture, employee commitment, confidence and continual learning are important characteristics of HRM models, reflecting traditional values such as mutual trust, discipline, loyalty and the importance of family. Two recent articles explore the model discussed above. The first highlights the 'five things' that the US can learn from China. These include ambition, education, valuing and caring for the elderly, thrift and a future orientation (Powell 2009). The second article explored the remarkable 'export' of Indian CEOs to foreign MNCs (Power 2011). It contends that the multinational context and human resource shortages may provide an ideal training ground for global leaders. Using finite human resources in an innovative and adaptable way, paying particular attention to the lower end customers, and doing more than just making money, are some of the managerial traits of the 'India Way'. As Power (2011: 94) suggested, 'the only groups that scored as high on inner strength as Indian CEOs were Catholic nuns and monks'.

Paradoxically, the model presented above may be of greater relevance to India and China than to other countries. This is because many Chinese companies and their managers lack an understanding of the managerial ethos of Indian managers. Equally, Indian managers may lack a deep knowledge of the Chinese precepts which inform their managerial cultures. However, when these deficiencies are addressed, new and more innovative HRM frameworks might emerge, in contrast to those promoted by their Western counterparts.

As a counterpoint to the above more complex models, we present a useful classification framework built upon the above discussion and within which all types of organizations in China and India might be located. It comprises four quadrants as below, using two vertical (indigenous and exogenous) and two horizontal (old and new) axes (see Table 8.3).

Quadrant 1 includes 'old indigenous' HRM practices (for example, the former SOEs in China, and the state authorities in India); quadrant 2 represents 'new indigenous' approaches (reformed Chinese SOEs with local characteristics and upgraded Indian organizations); quadrant 3 combines 'old exogenous' systems (local firms influenced by Soviet Union or colonial models); and finally 'new exogenous' practices, representing innovative domestic and global companies. Some of the companies discussed throughout this book may blend features of both 2 and 4.

Conclusion

This chapter reflects on the major themes addressed throughout this book, with a view to identifying the likely characteristics of a 'new' HRM model for organizations and their stakeholders in China and India. It begins with a consideration of the broad societal contexts in both countries which mould and define their HRM systems and practices, including domestic, regional and global factors; together with the plethora of 'actors' (governments, unions, owners, shareholders, HR professionals, employees, education systems) which have associated interests. There is evidence, on the one hand, of similarities between China and India with respect to the influence of traditional cultural values on contemporary management, leadership and HRM practices; whilst, on the other hand, India's heritage of political pluralism is in stark contrast to China's unitarist political system. In addition, government influences on Chinese organizations are more pervasive than in their Indian counterparts.

The effects of these influences include shared emphases on the central role of paternalistic and ethical leaders, the importance of knowledge management, ongoing employee learning and development and an encouragement of innovation together with, conversely, a complex and entrenched adversarial industrial relations framework in India, which contrasts with the tightly-controlled Chinese system. We suggest that Western-style HRM practices such as emotional intelligence, employee empowerment, 360-degree performance reviews, coaching and mentoring and reward-oriented performance management techniques have parallels in both Chinese and Indian traditions.

The models presented in the chapter are intended to assist in the identification of characteristics which might constitute a new model of HRM in China and India. They are not intended to be prescriptive. However, we contend that contemporary Western HRM models are unable to incorporate the diversity of HRM systems and practices experienced in the myriad of organizational types, within the complex and dynamic socio-cultural contexts of China and India. Thus, we propose a new analytical framework, incorporating a series of independent and mediating variables (Figure 8.2), leading to 'an emerging HRM focus', which may be used to classify particular HRM models in diverse organizational types. We suggest that, rather than a single HRM model, there will inevitably be multiple variations, including relative convergence and divergence with Western-style frameworks; based upon government principles and imperatives, organizational types, the degree of exposure to regional and global HRM strategies and practices and the balance between traditional and more contemporary values. In addition, given the geopolitical importance of China and India, it is highly likely that Western HRM will be progressively influenced by such new models.

Bibliography

Aberdeen Group (2007), *Enhancing operational results with employee performance management*, June, UK.

Aditya Birla (2011), *Let's reach for the sun*, Aditya Birla Management Corporation Pty. Ltd.

Agrawal N. M., Khatri N. and Srinivasan R. (2011), 'Managing growth: Human resource management challenges facing the Indian software industry', *Journal of World Business*, doi:10.1016/j.jwb.2011.04.002.

Aiyar S. S. A. (2009), 'It's goodbye Chindia and hello Chimerica', *The Times of India*, 19 April: 1–4.

Akhtar S., Ding D. Z. and Ge G. L. (2008), 'Strategic HRM practices and their impact on company performance in Chinese enterprises', *Human Resource Management*, 47, 1: 15–32.

All India State Government Employees Federation (2003), 'Public employees & workers cannot forego their right to strike', Internet source: http://www.tradeunionindia.org/miscellaneous/public_rights.htm, accessed on 5 September 2009.

Alvesson M. and Willmott H. (2002), 'Identity regulation as organizational control: Producing the appropriate individual', *Journal of Management Studies*, 39, 5: 619–44.

Anand G. (2011), 'India graduates millions, but too few are fit to hire', *The Wall Street Journal*, April 5: 1–7, www.online.wsj.com/article, accessed 11 April 2011.

Ananthram S. (2008), 'Drivers of globalization in the Indian and Chinese services industry: An empirical insight', in P. Verma, P. B. Bhasharas and P. M. Madhani (eds), *Globalization: Opportunities and challenges*, Delhi: Wisdom Publishing Company, 3–17.

Ananthram S. (2011a), 'Talent management philosophies and practices in the Chinese multinational companies', paper presented at the 12th Society for Global Business and Economic Development Conference, July, Singapore.

Ananthram S. (2011b), personal discussion on recent Indian research.

Anonymous (2007a), 'Chindia – Should India and China merge?', *Issues Paper*, Australian Chamber of Commerce and Industry, March: 1–6.

Anonymous (2007b), 'The Chindia Effect: What it means for US companies', *Perspective*, NY: J. P. MorganChase and Company, www.chase.com/ccpmweb/commercial/document/ChindiaWhitePaper.pdf, accessed 17 June 2010.

Anonymous (2007c), *Multinational companies in China: Finding and keeping talent*, US: SHRM.

Anonymous (2007d), 'No silver bullet for performance management', *Training and Development*, 61, 2: 16–17.

Anonymous (2007e), 'Lenovo Asia-Pacific', *hrm Asia*, 1 March, www.hrmasia.com/site-search/china-case-study-lenovo-asia-pacific/32874, accessed 27 April 2011.

Anonymous (2008a), *Chindia: The emerging and merging of two Asian giants*, New York: Bank of New York Mellon.

Anonymous (2008b), 'Talent management in question: An interview with Brian Wilkerson, Wyatt Watson's Global Director for Talent', *WatsonWyatt*, Fall: 19–22.

Anonymous (2009a), 'The more the merrier: India and China are creating millions of entrepreneurs', *The Economist*, 12 March, www.economist.com/node/13216067, accessed 1 June 2011.

Anonymous (2009b), *2008–9 Annual Report on the performance management of China's enterprises*, China CCM, June 10, www.prlog.org/10254428-20082009-Annual-Report-on-the-performance-management, accessed 14 December 2010.

Anonymous (2009c), 'Global economic crisis hits China HR', *hrSpectrum*, www.ilr.cornell.edu/cahrs/hrspectrum/May09, accessed 14 December 2010: 1–4.

Anonymous (2009d), 'Innovations: Training for success in emerging markets', *Strategic Directions*, 23, 9: 36–8.

Anonymous (2010a), 'The world turned upside down', *The Economist*, 17 April: 6.

Anonymous (2010b), 'Honda's ad for new workers triggers renewed discontent as strike enters 5th day at China factory', www.news.xinhuanet.com/english2010/china, accessed 17 June 2010.

Anonymous (2010c), 'Socialist workers: Is China's labour market at a turning point?', *The Economist*, 10 June: 7.

Anonymous (2010d), 'India's surprising economic miracle: The country's state may be weak but its private companies are strong', *The Economist*, 30 September: 1–3, www.economist.com/node/17147648, accessed 11 October 2010.

Anonymous (2010e), 'Contest of the century: China and India', *The Economist*, 21–27 August: 9–10.

Anonymous (2010f), 'A Himalayan rivalry', *The Economist*, 21 August: 17–20.

Anonymous (2010g), 'The next China', *The Economist*, 29 August, www.economist.com/node/16693397, accessed 29 August 2011.

Anonymous (2010h), 'Economic focus: The Himalayas of hiring', *The Economist*, 7 August: 59.

Anonymous (2010i), 'Talent management is Bupharm's prescription for success', *HRM International Digest*, 18, 1: 11–3.

Anonymous (2010j), 'The 10 best companies to work for in India', *Rediff.com*, 29 January, www.business.rediff.com/2010/jan/29, accessed 31 January 2011.

Anonymous (2010k), 'Making management pay: Reining in excessive risk at India's banks', www.knowledge.wharton.upenn.edu/india/article.cfm?, accessed 31 January 2011: 1–5.

Anonymous (2011a), 'The service elevator: Can poor countries leapfrog manufacturing and grow rich on services?', *The Economist*, 19 May.

Anonymous (2011b), 'Is corporate "wolf culture" devouring China's overworked employees?', *China Labour Bulletin*, www.clb.hk/hr/node/100253, accessed 2 May 2011.

Anonymous (2011c), 'The Tata Group: Out of India', *The Economist*, 3 March, www.economist.com/node/18285497, accessed 25 May 2011.

Anonymous (2011d), 'Ratan Tata slams Mukesh Ambani, Corus, JLR management', *Indian Express*, 22 May, www.bx.businessweek.com/tata-group/view, accessed 25 May 2011.

Anonymous (2011e), 'Reliance "examined" over 2G scam', *Emirates 24/7*, www.emirates247.com/news/world/reliance-examined-over-2g-scam, accessed 25 May 2011.

Anonymous (2011f), 'Education in India: Past, present and the future – Ideas, policies and initiatives', www.education-in-India/Reliance'sforayintoeducation.mht, accessed 15 May 2011.

Anonymous (2011g), 'The long march of the invisible Mr. Ren: China's technology star needs to shine more openly', *The Economist*, 2 June.

Appelbaum E. and Batt R. (1994), *The new American workplace*, Ithaca, NY: ILR Press.

Arkless D. (2007), 'The China talent paradox', *China–Britain Business Review*, June: 14–15.

Bao Y. J., Olson B., Parayitam S. and Zhao S. M. (2011), 'The effects of psychological contract violation on Chinese executives', *International Journal of Human Resource Management*, 22, 16: 3373–92.

Baruch Y., Budhwar P. and Khatri N. (2007), 'Brain drain: Inclination to stay abroad after studies', *Journal of World Business*, 42, 1: 99–112.

Basham A. L. (2007), *The illustrated cultural history of India*, Oxford: Oxford University Press.

Bassett P., Buxton C., Pathami R. and Sharan M. (2005), 'Talent management is key to India's Pharma future', *Korn/Ferry International*, www.kornferryasia.com, accessed 19 June 2011.

Beale D. and Noronha E. (2009), 'Indian public sector trade unionism in context: Gujarat and West Bengal compared', unpublished working paper presented in the Fairness at Work Seminar Series at Manchester Business School, University of Manchester, UK.

Becker B. E. and Gerhart B. (1996), 'The impact of human resource management on organizational performance: Progress and prospects', *Academy of Management Journal*, 39, 4: 779–801.

Benson J. and Zhu Y. (2000), 'A case study analysis of human resource management in China's manufacturing industry', *China Industrial Economy*, 4, 1: 62–5.

Bhasin M. L. (2010), 'Corporate governance disclosure practices: The portrait of a developing country', *International Journal of Business and Management*, 5, 4: 150–68.

Bhatnagar J. (2006), 'Measuring organizational learning capital in Indian managers and establishing firm performance linkage: An empirical analysis', *The Learning Organisation*, 13, 5: 416–33.

Bhatnagar J. (2007a), 'Talent management strategy of employee engagement in Indian ITES employees: Key to retention', *Employee Relations*, 29, 6: 640–63.

Bhatnagar J. (2007b), 'Predictors of organizational commitment in India: Strategic HR roles, organizational learning capability and psychological empowerment', *International Journal of Human Resource Management*, 18, 10: 1782–811.

Bhatnagar J. (2008), 'Managing capital for talent engagement and pipeline development', *Industrial and Commercial Training*, 40, 1: 19–28.

Bhattacharya S., Sen S. and Korschun D. (2008), 'Using corporate social responsibility to win the war for talent', *MIT Sloan Management Review*, 49, 2: 37–44.

Bhattacherjee D. (1987), 'Union-type effects on bargaining outcomes in Indian manufacturing', *British Journal of Industrial Relations*, 25, 2: 247–66.

Bhattacherjee D. (2001), 'The evolution of Indian industrial relations: A comparative perspective', *Industrial Relations Journal*, 32, 3: 244–63.

Bhattacherjee D. (2010), 'Book Review of Candland C. (2007), *Labour, Democratization and Development in India and Pakistan*', *British Journal of Industrial Relations*, 48, 1: 215–18.

Bhattacherjee D. and Ackers P. (2010), 'Introduction: Employment relations in India: Old narratives and new perspectives', *Industrial Relations Journal*, 41, 2: 104–21.

Bisogno S. (2007), 'Speeding Up the Auto Industry', *Beijing Review*, 15 March 2010, http://www.bjreview.com.cn/books/txt/2007-03/12/content_93846.htm, accessed 30 January 2010.

Biswas S. and Varma A. (2007), 'Psychological climate and individual performance in India: Test of a mediated model', *Employee Relations*, 29, 6: 664–76.

Bita N. and Sainsbury M. (2010), 'Price of Chinese exports set to soar', *The Weekend Australian*, 18 November: 4.

Bjórkman I., Budhwar P., Smale A. and Sumelius J. (2008), 'Human resource management in foreign-owned subsidiaries: China versus India', *International Journal of Human Resource Management*, 19, 5: 964–78.

Bjórkman I., Budhwar P., Smale A. and Sumelius J. (2009), 'HRM in foreign-owned subsidiaries: China versus India', in M. Warner (ed.), *HRM with "Chinese characteristics"*, London: Routledge, 194–208.

Boisot M. and Child J. (1996), 'The institutional nature of China's emerging economic order', in D. Brown and R. Porter (eds), *Management issues in China* Vol. 1, New York: Routledge, 251–367.

Boxall P. and Macky K. (2009), 'Research and strategy on high-performance work systems: Progressing the high involvement steam', *Human Resource Management Journal*, 19, 1: 3–23.

Brown K. (2009), *The rise of the dragon: Inward investment and outward investment in China 1978–2007*, Oxford: Chandos.

Brown R. (2006), 'China's collective contract provisions: Can collective negotiations embody collective bargaining?', *Duke Journal of Comparative and International Law*, 16, 1: 35–77.

Brown R. (2008), 'The "Chindia" globalisation shock: How global mobility trends predict tougher challenges for global companies', *Expatriate Advisor*, Autumn: 1–4.

Browning J. (2011), 'Huawei to enter UK phone market', www.chinadaily.com.cn/business/2011-08/13/content_131056, accessed 29 August 2011.

Bu N. (1994), 'Red cadres and specialists as modern managers: An empirical assessment of managerial competencies in China', *International Journal of Human Resource Management*, 5, 2: 357–83.

Bu N. L., McKeen C. A. and Shen W. G. (2011), 'Behavioural indicators of turnover intention: The case of young professionals in China', *International Journal of Human Resource Management*, 22, 16: 3338–56.

Budhwar P. (2009), 'Managing human resources in India', in J. Storey, P. Wright and D. Ulrich (eds), *The Routledge companion to strategic human resource management*, London: Routledge, 435–46.

Budhwar P. and Bhatnagar J. (2009), *The changing face of people management in India*, London: Routledge.

Budhwar P. and Boyne G. (2004), 'Human resource management in the Indian public and private sectors: An empirical comparison', *International Journal of Human Resource Management*, 15, 2: 346–70.

Budhwar P. and Debrah Y. (eds) (2001), *HRM in developing countries*, London: Routledge.

Budhwar P. and Khatri N. (2001), 'A comparative study of HR practices in Britain and India', *International Journal of Human Resource Management*, 12, 5: 800–26.

Buncombe A. (2010), 'Oldest university on earth is reborn after 800 years', *The Independent (Asia)*, August 4 (Asia Section).

Buzan B. (2010), 'China in international society: Is "peaceful rise" possible?', *The Chinese Journal of International Politics*, 3: 5–36.

Cai F. and Chan K. W. (2009), 'The global economic crisis and unemployment in China', *Eurasian Geography and Economics*, 50, 5: 513–31.

Cai W. and Klyushina U. (2009), 'Talent retention and development within multinational companies in China', Masters thesis, Baltic Business School.

Cai Z. M., Morris J. L. and Chen J. (2011), 'Explaining the human resource management preferences of employees: A study of Chinese workers', *International Journal of Human Resource Management*, 22, 16: 3245–69.

Callahan W. A. (2010), 'China's strategy for a post Western world', *Oilprice*, 7 July: 1–5.
Candland C. (2007), *Labour, democratization and development in India and Pakistan*, London: Routledge.
Cappelli P. (2008), 'Talent management for the twenty first century', *Harvard Business Review*, 86, 3: 74–81.
Cappelli P., Singh H., Singh J. and Useem M. (2010), *The India way: How India's top business leaders are revolutionizing management*, Boston: Harvard Business Press.
Carron A. M. (2008), 'Higher education in Chindia. They try harder, but …', *Chronicles*, Secor Asia Group: 2.
Chan A. (2001), *China's workers under assault: The exploitation of labour in a globalising economy*, New York: M. E. Sharpe.
Chand M. (2010), 'The impact of HRM practices on service quality, customer satisfaction and performance in the Indian hotel industry', *International Journal of Human Resource Management*, 21: 4, 551–66.
Chandrashekar B. K. (1970), 'Labour relations in India: Report of the national commission on labour 1969', *British Journal of Industrial Relations*, 8, 3: 369–88.
Chang I. (2007), 'The NHS performance assessment framework: Limitations and implications', *International Journal of Public Sector Management*, 20, 2: 101–17.
Chang L. (2008), *Factory girls*, London: Picador.
Chatterjee S. (2001), 'Relevance of traditional value frameworks in contemporary Chinese work organizations: Implications for managerial transition', *Journal of Human Values*, 7, 1: 21–32.
Chatterjee S. (2009a), 'Managerial ethos of the Indian tradition: Relevance of a wisdom model', *Journal of Indian Business Research*, 1, 2/3: 136–62.
Chatterjee S. (2009b), 'From Sreni Dharma to global cross-vergence: Journey of human resource practices in India', *International Journal of Indian Culture and Business Management*, 2, 3: 268–80.
Chatterjee S. and Pearson C. (2006), 'Changing work goals of Asian manager: A comparative empirical study in ten Asian countries', *Journal of Asia Pacific Business*, 7, 4: 5–33.
Chatterjee S. R. (2007), 'Human resource management in India: "Where from and where to?",' *Research and Practice in Human Resource Management*, 15, 2: 92–103.
Chatterjee S. R. (2009), 'Trust and learning as moderators in achieving global supply-chain competitiveness: Evidence from the Chinese and Indian auto component sectors', *Global Business Review*, 10, 1: 87–102.
Chatterjee S. R. (2010), presentation at RMIT University, Melbourne, 12 September.
Chatterjee S. R. and Nankervis A. R. (2003), *Understanding Asian management: Transition and transformation*, Perth: Vineyard Press.
Chatterjee S. R. and Nankervis A. R. (2007), *Asian management in transition: Emerging themes*, Palgrave Macmillan: Basingstoke.
Chen C. and Lee Y. (eds) (2008), *Leadership and management in China: Philosophies, theories and practices*, Cambridge: Cambridge University Press.
Chen G. Q., Tjosvold D., Li N., Fu Y. and Liu D. W. (2011), 'Knowledge management in Chinese organizations: Collectivist values for open-minded discussions', *International Journal of Human Resource Management*, 22, 16: 3393–412.
Chen H. (2006), *Recruitment and selection in China: An application to the case of Lenovo*, MA (Management) dissertation, Nottingham University.
Chen M-J. and Miller D. (2010), 'West meets East: Toward an ambi-cultural approach to management', *Academy of Management Perspective*, November: 17–24.

Chen Z. and Francesco A. (2000), 'Employee, demography, organizational commitment and turnover intensions in China: Do cultural differences matter?', *Human Relations*, 53: 69–87.

Cheng M., Dainty A. and Moore D. (2006), 'Implementing a new performance management system within a project-based organization', *International Journal of Productivity and Performance Management*, 56, 1: 60–75.

Child, J. (1994), *Management in China during the age of reform*, Cambridge: Cambridge University Press.

Child J. (2009), 'Context, comparison, and methodology in Chinese management research', *Management and Organization Review*, 5, 1: 57–73.

Child J. and Rodrigues S. (2005), 'The internationalization of Chinese firms: A case for theoretical extension?', *Management and Organization Review*, 1, 3: 381–410.

Child J. and Warner M. (2003), 'Culture and management in China', in M. Warner (ed.), *Culture and myth in Asia*, London: Routledge, 24–47.

China Daily (2011), www.chinadaily.com.cn/bizchina/2009-01/19/content_7408277.htm, accessed 27 April 2011.

Choi K. (2011), 'An economic/social mismatch: Northeast Asia in 2011', *Sustainable Europe Research Institute Quarterly*, 4, 2: 43–51.

Choo J. (2009), 'Ideas matter: China's peaceful rise', *Asia European Journal*, 7: 389–404.

Chow I. H., Huang J. C. and Liu S. (2008), 'Strategic HRM in China: Configurations and competitive advantage', *Human Resource Management*, 47, 4: 687–706.

Cianti R. and Grambel P. (2003), 'Maslow's hierarchy of needs: Does it apply in a collectivist culture?', *Journal of Applied Management and Entrepreneurship*, 8, 2: 143–61.

CIPD (2001), *Performance through people: The new people management – The change agenda*, Wimbledon: CIPD.

CIPD (2005), *Survey Report September 2005*, Wimbledon: CIPD.

Clarke S. (2005), 'Post-socialist trade unions: China and Russia', *Industrial Relations Journal*, 36, 1: 2–18.

Collings D. and Mellahi K. (2009), 'Strategic talent management: A review and research agenda', *Human Resource Management Review*, doi. 10.1016/j.hrmr.2009.04.001.

Collins N., Zhu Y. and Warner M. (2012), 'HRM and Asian socialist economies in transition: China, Vietnam and North Korea', in C. Brewster and W. Mayrhofer (eds), *Handbook of research in comparative human resource management*, Cheltenham, UK: Edward Elgar Publishing, 1–25.

Cooke F. (2005), *HRM, work and employment in China*, London: Routledge.

Cooke F. L. (2008a), 'Enterprise culture management in China: An "insiders"' perspective', *Management and Organization Review*, 4, 2: 291–314.

Cooke F. L. (2008b), *Competition, strategy and management in China*, London: Routledge.

Cooke F. (2009), 'A decade of transformation of HRM in China: A review of literature and suggestions for future studies', *Asia Pacific Journal of Human Resources*, 47, 1: 6–40.

Cooke, F. L. (2010a), 'Women's participation in employment in Asia: A comparative analysis of China, India, Japan and South Korea', *International Journal of Human Resource Management*, 21, 10–12: 2249–70.

Cooke F. L. (2010b), 'Case-study: Managing diversity in a Chinese-owned multinational IT firm', in A. Harzing and A. Pinnington (eds), *International human resource management*, 3rd edition, London: Sage.

Cooke F. L. (2011a), 'Employment relations in China', in G. Bamber, R. Lansbury and N. Wailes (eds), *International and comparative employment relations*, 5th edition, London: Sage and New South Wales, Australia: Allen & Unwin Pty Ltd, 307–29.

Cooke F. L. (2011b), 'Talent management in China', in H. Scullion and D. Collings (eds), *Global talent management*, London: Routledge, 132–54.

Cooke F. L. (2011c), 'The globalization of Chinese telecom corporations: Strategies, challenges and HR implications for the MNCs and host countries', *International Journal of Human Resource Management*, 001.10.1080/09585192.2011.579920.

Cooke F. L. (2011d), 'The role of the state and human resource management in China', *International Journal of Human Resource Management*, 22, 18: 3830–48.

Cooke F. L. (2012a), *Human resource management in China: New trends and practices*, London: Routledge.

Cooke F. L. (2012b), 'Employment relations in China and India', in M. Barry and A.Wilkinson (eds), *Edward Elgar handbook of comparative employment relations*, Cheltenham: Edward Elgar, 184–213.

Cooke F. L. and Huang K. (2011), 'Post-acquisition evolution of the appraisal and reward systems: A study of Chinese IT firms acquired by US firms', *Human Resource Management*, 50, 6: 839–58.

Cooke F. L. and Saini D. (2010a), 'Diversity management in India: A study of organisations in different ownership forms and industrial sectors', *Human Resource Management*, 49, 3: 475–98.

Cooke F. L. and Saini D. (2010b), '(How) does the HR strategy support an innovation-oriented business strategy? An investigation of institutional context and organisational practices in Indian firms', *Human Resource Management*, 49, 3: 375–98.

Cooke F. L. and Wood G. (2011), 'New actors and employment relations in emerging economies', *Relations Industrielles/Industrial Relations*, 66, 1: 7–10.

Cooney S. (2007), 'China's labour law, compliance and flaws in implementing institutions', *Journal of Industrial Relations*, 49, 5: 673–86.

Cunningham L. and Rowley C. (2010), 'SMEs in China: A literature review, HRM and suggestions for further research', *Asia Pacific Business Review*, 16, 3: 319–37.

Dalrymple W. (2007), 'Why India's rise is business as usual', *Time Magazine*, 2 August: 1–2.

Dance with Shadows (2011), www.dancewithshadows.com/mukesh-anil-ambani-split.asp, accessed 25 May 2011.

Davis H. J., Chatterjee S. R. and Heuer M. (2006), *Management in India: Trends and transition*, New Delhi: Response Books.

de Bettignies H. and Tan C. (2007), 'Values and management education in China', *International Management Review*, 3, 1: 17–36.

De Carlo S. (2010), 'Special report: The world's leading companies', *Forbes.com*, 21 April, www.forbes.com/2010/global-2000-leading-world-business-global, accessed 27 April 2010.

De Cieri H., Zhu C. J. and Dowling P. (1998), 'The reform of employee compensation in China's industrial enterprises', *Centre for Advanced Human Resource Studies Working Paper Series*, Paper 118, http://digitalcommons.ilr.cornell.edu/cahrswp/118, accessed 30 November 2010.

De Haan A. (2010), 'The financial crisis and China's "harmonious society"', *Journal of Current Chinese Affairs*, 39, 2: 69–99.

Delaney J. and Godard J. (2001), 'An IR perspective on the high performance paradigm', *Human Resource Management Review*, 11, 2: 395–429.

Delaney J. T. and Huselid M. A. (1996), 'The impact of human resource management practices on perceptions of organizational performance', *Academy of Management Journal*, 39, 4: 949–69.

Delbridge R. and Keenoy T. (2011), 'Beyond managerialism', *International Journal of Human Resource Management*, 21, 5: 799–817.

Deming H. (2010), *A better life? The wants and worries of China's consumers: A report from the Economist Intelligence Unit*, EIU: Bayer.

Dhir A. (2011), 'Growth of the textile industry in China & India: Learning for India', paper presented at the World Textile Conference, 'Vision: Textiles', Mumbai: The Textile Association of India, 6–7 May.

Ding D. Z. and Akhtar, S. (2001), 'The organizational choice of human resource management practices: A study of Chinese enterprises in three cities in the PRC', *International Journal of Human Resource Management*, 12, 6: 946–64.

Ding, D. Z. and Warner, M. (2001), 'China's labour-management system reforms: Breaking the "Three Old Irons" (1978–1999)', *Asia Pacific Journal of Management*, 18: 315–34.

Ding D. Z., Ge, L. and Warner, M. (2001), 'A new form of Chinese human resource management? Personnel and labour–management relations in Chinese township and village enterprises: A case-study approach', *Industrial Relations Journal*, 32, 4: 328–43.

Di Rollo C. 2010, 'The evolution of China's MBA', in M. Warner and K. Goodall (eds), *Management training and development in China*, London: Routledge, 155–74.

Dixit R. (2008), 'Reliance Group sacks 5,000 employees in India across group companies', *Now Public*, 11 December.

Dixon H. (2011), 'The China files, Part 1: How fast can China grow?', *Reuters*, May 9: 1–4.

D'Mello M. and Eriksen T. (2005), 'Software, sportsday and Shecra: Culture and identity process within a global software organization in India', *Information and Organization*, 20, 2: 81–110.

Doh J., Stumpf S., Tymon W. and Haid M. (2008), 'How to retain talent in India', *MIT Sloan Management Review*, Fall, 50, 1: 6–7.

Downing J., Rouleau W. and Stuber S. (2008), *The war for talent in China*, US: Kellogg SOM.

D'Souza E. (2010), 'The employment effects of labour legislation in India: A critical essay', *Industrial Relations Journal*, 41, 2: 122–35.

Dufty N. F. (1965), 'The evolution of the India industrial relations system', *Journal of Industrial Relations*, 7, 1: 40–9.

Economist, The (2004), 'The World in 2004', 17 November: 49.

Economist, The (2010), 'The world turned upside down: A special report on innovation in emerging markets', 17 April: 3–16.

Einhorn B., Deprez E., Srivastava M. and Brigorri M. (2009), 'At Alibaba, investors come last', *Business Week*, Issue 4143: 49–50.

Eliade M. (1992), 'Neo-Confucianism', in M. Eliade (ed.), *Encyclopedia of religion*, NY: McMillan Reference Books.

Engardio P. (ed.) (2007), *Chindia: How China and India are revolutionizing global business*, New York: McGraw-Hill.

Evans-Pritchard A. (2011), 'Will "Chindia" rule the world in 2050, or America after all?', *The Telegraph*, 28 February, www.telegraph.co.uk/finance/comment/ambroseevans_pritchard, accessed 1 June 2011.

Farh J. L. and Cheng B. S. (2000), 'A cultural analysis of paternalistic leadership in Chinese organizations', in J. T. Li, A. S. Tsui and E. Weldon (eds), *Management and organizations in the Chinese context*, London: Macmillan, 94–127.

Farrell D. and Grant A. (2005), 'China's looming talent shortage', *The McKinsey Quarterly*, No. 4, www.mckinseyquarterly.com/article_page.aspx?ar=1685, accessed 12 December 2010.

Felfe J. and Yan W. H. (2009), 'The impact of workgroup commitment on organizational citizenship behaviour, absenteeism and turnover intention: The case of Germany and China', *Asia Pacific Business Review*, 15, 3: 433–50.

Felfe J., Yan W. and Six B. (2008), 'The impact of individual collectivism on commitment and its influence on organizational citizenship behaviour and turnover in three countries', *International Journal of Cross Cultural Management*, 8, 2: 211–37.

Feng J. (2005), 'Into the unknown: Lenovo's precarious leap forward', www.bjreview.cn/EN/05-01-e/1/05-bus-4.htm, accessed 2 May 2011.

Ferguson N. (2010), 'Middle Kingdom re-emerges to claim its place on global stage', *The Weekend Australian*, 18–19 December: 21.

Fletcher O. and Feng S. (2011), 'China passes US as world's biggest PC market', www.chinadaily.com.cn/bizchina/2011-08/24/content_131811, accessed 9 September 2011.

Forster N. (2000), 'Expatriates and the impact of cross cultural training', *Human Resource Management Journal*, 10, 3: 63–78.

Fortune (2011a), 'Global 500 Companies', No. 10: 1–19.

Fortune (2011b), 'The world's largest corporations', No. 10, 25 July: 101–35.

Frenkel S. and Peetz D. (1998), 'Globalization and industrial relations in East Asia: A three-country comparison', *Industrial Relations*, 37, 3: 282–310.

Frenkel S., Li M. and Restubog S. (2011), 'Management, organizational justice and emotional exhaustion among Chinese migrant workers: Evidence from two manufacturing firms', *British Journal of Industrial Relations*, doi: 10.1111/j.1467-8543.2011.00858.x.

Frohn J. (2010), 'The foundation of the China Europe IBS (CEIBS): The spirit of the early years', in K. Goodall and M. Warner (eds), *Management education and development in China*, London: Routledge, 50–68.

Fu Y. and Kamenou N. (2011), 'The impact of Chinese cultural values on human resource policies and practices within transnational corporations in China', *International Journal of Human Resource Management*, 22, 16: 3270–89.

Gaba A. K. (2008), *The role of distance education in the HRD of India*, Indira Gandhi National Open University: New Delhi.

Gamble J. and Huang Q. (2008), 'Organizational commitment of Chinese employees in foreign-invested firms', *International Journal of Human Resource Management*, 19, 5: 896–915.

Ganapathy N. (2011), 'India: Education is a key challenge', *The Straits Times*, 15 January: C1.

Gao J., Arnulf J. and Henning K. (2011), 'Western leadership development and Chinese managers: Exploring the need for contextualization', *Scandinavian Journal of Management*, 27, 1: 55–65.

Gerhaeusser K., Iwasaki Y. and Tulasidhar V. B. (eds) (2010), *Resurging Asian giants: Lessons from The People's Republic of China*, Manila: Asian Development Bank.

Ghooi P. (2010), '*Making sense of Chindia: Jairam Ramesh* – A book review', *Chillibreeze*, April: 1–4.

Ghosh J. (2010), 'Poverty reduction in China and India: Policy implications of recent trends', *Department of Economic and Social Affairs Working Paper No. 92*, NY: UN.

Giacalone R. and Jurkiewicz C. L. (eds) (2003), *Handbook of workplace spirituality and organizational performance*, New York: M.I. Sharpe.

Godard J. (2004), 'A critical assessment of the high performance paradigm', *British Journal of Industrial Relations*, 42, 2: 349–78.

Goldstein A. (2008), *The internationalisation of Indian companies: The case of Tata*, Philadelphia: Center for the Advanced Study of India.

Gong Y. and Chang S. (2008), 'Institutional antecedents and performance consequences of employment security and career advancement practices: Evidence from the people's republic of China', *Human Resource Management*, 47, 1: 33–48.

Goodall K. and Warner M. (eds) (2010), *Management education and development in China*, London: Routledge.

Goodall K., Li N. and Warner M. (2006), 'Expatriate managers in China: The influence of Chinese culture on cross-cultural management', *Journal of General Management*, 32: 67–79.

Gopalakrishnan R. and Tortell L. (2006), 'Access to justice, trade union rights, and the Indian Industrial Disputes Act, 1947', *International Journal of Comparative Labour Law and Industrial Relations*, 22, 4: 529–62.

Grainger R. and Chatterjee S. R. (2008), 'Understanding Asian corporate management: A global comparative framework', *Journal of Asia Pacific Business*, 9, 3: 225–36.

Grant E. A. (2008), 'How to retain talent in India', *MIT Sloan Management Review*: 1–3.

Green M. J. and Kliman D. M. (2011), 'China's hard power and the potential for conflict in Asia', *Sustainable Europe Research Institute Quarterly*, 4, 2: 33–41.

Guest D., Michie J., Sheehan M. and Conway N. (2000), *Employment relations, human resource management and business performance: An analysis of the 1998 Workplace Employment Relations Survey*, London: IPD.

Gupta A. K. and Wang H. (2009a), *Getting China and India right: Leveraging the world's fastest growing economies for global advantage*, New Jersey: John Wiley & Sons.

Gupta A. K. and Wang H. (2009b), 'Five myths about Chindia', *Business Week*, 24 December: 7.

Gupta A. K., Govindarajan V. and Wang H. (2008), *The quest for global dominance*, San Francisco: Jossey-Bass.

Guruswamy M. and Singh Z. D. (2010), *Chasing the dragon: Will India catch up with China?*, New Delhi: Pearson.

Hage A. (2002), 'The Aston Group', in M. Warner (ed.), *The international emergence of business and management*, London: Thomson.

Haier (2009), 'On Haier's corporate culture', www.eng.hi138.com/?i8010196, accessed 18 April 2011.

Hammer A. (2007), 'HRM in China and India', in T. Claydon and X. Beardwell (eds), *HRM: A contemporary approach*, London: Wiley.

Hammer A. (2010), 'Trade unions in a constrained environment: Workers' voices from a new industrial zone in India', *Industrial Relations Journal,* 41, 2: 168–84.

Harcourt T. (2008), *Chindia keeps on keeping on*, Canberra: Austrade.

Harriss-White B. (2010), 'Globalization, the financial crisis and petty production in India's socially regulated informal economy', *Global Labour Journal*, 1, 1: 151–77.

Harzing A. and Pinnington A. (eds) (2011), *International human resource management*, 3rd edition, London: Sage.

Hayter S., Fashoyin T. and Kochan T. (2011), 'Review essay: Collective bargaining for the 21st Century', *Journal of Industrial Relations*, 53, 2: 225–47.

Hechet J. F. and Ruet J. (2009), 'Chinese and India multinationals out to conquer the world', in C. Jaffrelot (ed.), *Emerging states: The wellspring of a new world order*, London: C. Hurst & Company.

Heery E. and Frege C. (2006), 'New actors in industrial relations', *British Journal of Industrial Relations*, 44, 4: 601–4.

Hensman R. (2010), 'Labour and globalization: Union responses in India', *Global Labour Journal*, 1, 1: 111–31.

Hicks R. (2010), 'India's government performance guru delivers key speech', *India futuregov*, 17 March, www.futuregov.in/articles/2010/mar/17, accessed 31 January 2011.

Hill E. (2008), 'India: The self-employed women's association and autonomous organizing', in K. Broadbent and M. Ford (eds), *Woman organising: Women and union activism in Asia*, London: Routledge, 115–35.

Hill E. (2009), 'The Indian industrial relations system: Struggling to address the dynamics of a globalizing economy, *Journal of Industrial Relations*, 51, 3: 395–410.

Hill E. (2011), 'Women, work and care in India', presentation in the Australian Work + Family Policy Roundtable Workshop 'Where are we at, where are we going in the Asia-Pacific on women, work and care?', University of Sydney, 18 November 2011.

Hille K. and Anderlini J. (2011), 'China: Mao and the next generation', www.ft.com/intl/cms, accessed 20 June 2011.

Hiscock G. (2011), 'Aditya Birla Group continues global asset pursuit', *The Australian*, 4 February: 14.

Ho A. L. (2011), 'China: Shrinking pool of rural workers in the cities', *The Straits Times*, 15 January: 2.

Hodge A. (2011), 'India's male bias still growing', *The Weekend Australian*, 2–3 April: 21.

Hofstede G. (1991), *Culture's consequences*, Wimbledon: Sage.

Holslag J. (2008), 'The myth of Chindia: Assessing interdependence between China and India', *Asia Paper*, 3, 2: 1–13.

Holtbrügge D., Friedmann C. and Puck J. (2010), 'Recruitment and retention in foreign firms in India: A resource-based view', *Human Resource Management*, 49, 3: 439–55.

Holz C. (2005), *China's economic growth 1978–2025: What we know today about China's economic growth tomorrow*, Social Science Division, HKUST: 1–52.

Hong C. (2011), 'Maneuver on labor law faces block', *China Daily USA*, 26 July: 1.

Hong J. F. L. and Snell R. S. (2008), 'Power inequality in cross-cultural learning: The case of Japanese transplants in China', *Asia Pacific Business Review*, 14, 2: 253–73.

hrSpectrum (2009), 'Update: global economic crisis hits China HR', *hrSpectrum*, Cornell University, ILR, May 2009, http://www.ilr.cornell.edu/cahrs/hrSpectrum/May09-globalEconomicCrisis.html, accessed 30 November 2010.

Huang R. (2008), 'A study of Chinese style management in the twenty-first century', *The Chinese Economy*, 41, 3: 7–16.

Huang Y. (2008), *Capitalism with Chinese characteristics: Entrepreneurship and the State during the reform era*, New York: Cambridge University Press.

Huang Y. (2010), 'Debating China's economic growth: The Beijing consensus or the Washington consensus', *Academy of Management Perspectives*, May: 31–47.

Huawei (2011), *Huawei's culture*, internal documents.

Hui C., Lee C. and Rousseau D. (2004), 'Employment relationships in China: Do workers relate to the organization or to people?' *Organization Science*, 15, 2: 232–40.

Hui M. K., Au K. and Fock H. (2004), 'Empowerment effects across cultures', *Journal of International Business Studies*, 35, 1: 46–61.

Huselid M. A. (1995), 'The impact of HRM practices on turnover, productivity and corporate financial performance', *Academy of Management Journal*, 38: 635–70.

I love India (2011), www.iloveindia.com/economy-of-india/top-50-companies/reliance-group.html, accessed 25 May 2011.

IMD (2003), *Managing performance at Haier*, Switzerland: IMD.

Jaussaud J. and Liu X. (2011), 'The HRM practices of Chinese and foreign owned enterprises during a global crisis', *Asia Pacific Business Review*, 17, 4: 473–92.

Jenster P. V. (2010), 'The future of management education and business schools in China', in M. Warner and K. Goodall (eds), *Management training and development in China*, London: Routledge, 175–84.

Jobsearch China (2011), www.jobsearchChina.org/news/hrm-news/good-hrm-is-key-to-lenovo's-success, accessed 15 April 2011.

Johnson C. (1987), 'Political institutions and economic performance: The government–business relationship in Japan, South Korea, and Taiwan', in Frederic C. Deyo (ed.), *The political economy of East Asian industrialism*, Ithaca: Cornell University Press, 136–64.

Kase K., Slocum A. and Zhang Y. (2011), *Asian versus Western management thinking: Its culture-bound nature*, Basingstoke: Palgrave Macmillan.

Kazmi A. (2008), 'A proposed framework for strategy implementation in the Indian context', *Management Decision*, 46, 10: 1564–81.

Kedia B. L., Mukherjee D. and Lahiri S.(2006), 'Indian business groups: Evolution and transformation', *Asia Pacific Journal of Management*, 23: 559–77.

Kelly D. A., Rajan R. S. and Goh G. H. L. (2006), 'Managing globalization – Lessons from China and India', Inaugural Conference of the Lee Kuan Yew School of Public Policy, Singapore: World Scientific Publishing Co. Pte. Ltd.

Khanna T. (2007), *Billions of entrepreneurs: How China and India are reshaping their future – and yours*, Boston: Harvard Business School Press.

Khanna T. and Rivkin J. (2001), 'Estimating the performance effects of business groups in emerging markets', *Strategic Management Journal*, 22: 45–74.

Khanna V. (2005), *The economic history of organizational entities in ancient India*, Ann Arbor: Michigan Law and Economics.

Kiesow I. and Norling N. (2007), *The rise of India: Problems and opportunities*, Washington DC: Central Asia-Caucasus Institute and Silk Road Studies Program, Johns Hopkins University SAIS.

Kim D. O. and Bae J. (2005), 'Workplace innovation, employment relations and HRM: Two electronics companies in South Korea', *International Journal of Human Resource Management*, 16, 7: 1277–302.

Kim S, Wright P. and Su Z. (2010), 'Human resource management and firm performance, in China: A critical review', *Asia Pacific Journal of Human Resources*, 48, 1: 58–85.

Kim S. H. and Wright P. (2010), 'Putting strategic human resource management in context: A contextualized model of high commitment work systems and its implications in China', *Management and Organization Review*, 7, 1: 153–74.

Knippenberg D., Knippenberg B., Cremer D. and Hogg M. (2004), 'Leadership, self and identity', *Leadership Quarterly*, 15, 6: 825–56.

Kripalani M. (2005), 'How to divvy up a $22.5 billion empire', *Business Week*, 7 April, Issue 3941: 48.

Krishnan R. T. (2005), 'Linking corporate strategy and HR strategy: Implications for human resource professionals', in R. Padaki., N. M. Agrawal, C. Balaji and G. Mahapatra (eds), *Emerging Asia: An HR agenda*, New Delhi: Tata McGraw-Hill, 215–23.

Krishnan S. and Singh M. (2010), 'Outcomes of intention to quit of Indian IT professionals', *Human Resource Management*, 49, 3: 421–37.

Krug J. and Hegarty W. (2001), 'Predicting who stays and leaves after an acquisition: A study of top managers in multinational firms', *Strategic Management Journal*, 22, 2: 185–96.

Kucukakin S. and Thant S. (2006), *Chindia: A tale of two giants*, May, US: ABN-AMRO.

Kuczera M. and Field S. (2010), *Learning for jobs: OECD review of vocational education and training: Options for China*, Geneva: OECD.

Kulkarni S. (2010), 'Chindia – A story of contrasts: A perspective from India', *Global Economic Intersection*, 2 October: 1–6.

Kumar N. (2009), *India's global powerhouses: How they are taking in the world*, Boston: Harvard Business Press.

Kumar S. (2005), 'A comparative study of role clarity and work locus of control in banks', *Bombay Psychologist*, 20: 14–9.

Kuruvilla S. (1996), 'Linkages between industrialization strategies and industrial relations/human resource policies: Singapore, Malaysia, The Philippines, and India', *Industrial and Labor Relations Review*, 49, 4: 635–57.

Kuruvilla S. and Erickson C. (2002), 'Change and transformation in Asian industrial relations', *Industrial Relations*, 41, 2: 171–227.

Kuruvilla S. and Ranganathan A. (2008), 'Economic development strategies and macro and micro-level human resource policies: The case of India's "outsourcing" industry', *Industrial and Labor Relations Review*, 62, 1: 39–72.

Kuruvilla S. and Ranganathan A. (2010), 'Globalization and outsourcing: Confronting new human resource challenges in India's business process outsourcing industry', *Industrial Relations Journal*, 41, 2: 136–53.

Lam W., Chen Z. and Takeuchi N. (2009), 'Perceived human resource management practices and intention to leave of employees: The mediating role of organizational citizenship behaviour in a Sino-Japanese joint venture', *International Journal of Human Resource Management*, 20, 11: 2250–70.

Lange T., Pacheco G. and Shrotryia V. K. (2010), 'Culture, industrialization and multiple domains of employees' job satisfaction: A case for HR strategy redesign in India', *International Journal of Human Resource Management*, 21, 13: 2438–51.

Law K., Tse D. K. and Zhou N. (2003), 'Does human resource management matter in a transitional economy? China as an example', *Journal of International Business Studies*, 34, 3: 255–65.

Lawler E. (2005), 'Creating high performance organizations', *Asia Pacific Journal of Human Resources*, 43, 1: 10–17.

Lawler J., Chen S. and Bae J. (2000), 'Scale of operations, human resource systems and firm performance in East and Southeast Asia', *Research and Practice in Human Resource Management*, 8, 1: 3–20.

Lee C. H. (2009), 'Industrial relations and collective bargaining in China', *Dialogue Working Paper No. 7*, Geneva: ILO.

Lee C. K. (2007), *Against the law: Labor protests in China's rustbelt and sunbelt*, Berkeley: University of California.

Lee C. K. and Shen Y. (2008), 'The anti-solidarity machine: Labor NGOs in China', paper presented the International Conference 'Breaking down Chinese Walls: The Changing Faces of Labor and Employment in China', Cornell University, 26–28 September 2008, Ithaca, New York.

Lee S. and Eyraud F. (2008), *Globalization, flexibilization and working conditions in Asia and the Pacific*, Oxford: Chandos.

Lee S.-L. and Kim J. W. (2011), 'Intensifying competition for technology in Northeast Asia', *Sustainable Europe Research Institute Quarterly*, 4, 2: 53–63.

Legge K. (1994), 'Managing culture: Fact or fiction?', in K. Sisson (ed.), 2nd edition, *Personnel management: A comprehensive guide to theory and practice in Britain*, London: Blackwell, 397–433.

Legge K. (1995, 2005), *Human resource management: Rhetorics and realities*, Basingstoke: Palgrave Macmillan.

Leininger J. (2007), 'Recent compensation and benefits trends in China', *The China Business Review*, 34, 4: 28–30.

Lenovo (2010a), *2009/10 Annual Report Lenovo: The future is ours*, US: Lenovo.

Lenovo (2010b), *Sustainability for the next generation 2009–2010: CSR Report*, US: Lenovo.

Lepak D. and Snell S. (1999), 'The HR architecture: Toward a theory of human capital allocation and development', *Academy of Management Review*, 24, 1: 31–48.

Leonard M. (2010), 'Social performance management in India: Seeking a market-led approach', MicroSave India *focus note 3*: 1–2.

Lewis R. and Heckman R. (2006), 'Talent management: A critical review', *Human Resource Management Review*, 16: 139–54.

Li J., Tsui A. and Weldon E. (eds) (2000), *Management and organizations in the Chinese context*, Basingstoke: Palgrave Macmillan.

Li J., Qian G., Liao S. and Chu C. (2009), 'HRM and the global-ness of firms: An empirical study in China', in M. Warner (ed.), *Human resource management 'with Chinese characteristics'*, London: Routledge, 58–69.

Li W., Liu X. and Wan W. (2008), 'Demographic effects of work values and their management implications', *Journal of Business Ethics*, 81, 4: 875–85.

Li Y. and Sheldon P. (2010), 'Skill shortages: Where labour supply problems meet employee poaching', in P. Sheldon, S. Kim, Y. Li and M. Warner (eds), *China's changing workplace*, London: Routledge, 129–43.

Lin T. W. (2005), 'OEC management-control system helps China Haier Group achieve competitive advantage: The combination of a new corporate culture that emphasizes excellence, a changed business strategy, and a management control system of work rules and discipline turned a nearly bankrupt company into a success', *Management Accounting Quarterly*, Spring: 2–7.

Lin Z., Tremberth L. and Kelly J. (2010), 'The development and implications of China's employee benefits systems', *Asia Pacific Journal of Human Resources*, 48, 3: 287–301.

Lindholm N. (1999), 'Performance management in MNC subsidiaries in China: A study of host-country managers and professionals', *Asia Pacific Journal of Human Resources*, 37, 3: 18–35.

Liu H. (2010), 'The development strategies of human resource management of Chinese enterprises in the context of financial crisis – Based on enlightenment of Alibaba group', paper presented at the International Conference on E-Business and E-Government, 7–9 May, Guangzhou.

Liu J. (2007), 'Huawei's HR revolution', *ChinaFiberOptics Online*, www.chinafiberoptics.blogspot.com/2007/10/huawei-s-hr-revolution.htm, accessed 15 April 2011.

Liu Y. (2010), 'Reward strategy in Chinese IT industry', *International Journal of Business and Management*, 5, 2: 119–27.

Live India (2011), www.liveindia.com/khajuraho/reliance.html, accessed 25 May 2011.

London Business School (2011), www.london.edu/facultyandresearch/researchactivities/birlaindiacentre.html, accessed 14 June 2011.

Luyckx K., Vansteenkiste M., Gossens L. and Duriez B. (2009), 'Basic need satisfaction and identity formation: Bridging self-determination: Theory and process oriented identity research', *Journal of Counseling Psychology*, 56, 2: 276–88.

McKenna B., Rooney D. and Boal K. (2009), 'Wisdom principles as a meta-theoretical basis for evaluating leadership', *Leadership Quarterly*, 20, 2: 177–90.

Maddison A. (2005), *The world economy: Historical studies*, Paris: OECD.

Mahbubani K. (2008), *The new Asian hemisphere: The irresistible shift of global power to the East*, New York: Public Affairs.

Mak A. (2003), *Performance management practices survey in China 2003*, Hong Kong: DDIWorld, http://www.ddiworld.com/ pdf/ performancemanagementpractices survey-inchina-fullreport_ddi.pdf, accessed 25 November 2010.

Malik M. (2009), *War talk: Perceptual gaps in 'Chindia' relations*, AFAR (Association of Asia Research), The Jamestown Foundation, 11 March, www.asiaresearch.org/articles/3224.html, accessed 20 April 2010.

Mankidy J. (1995), 'Changing perspectives of worker participation in India with particular reference to the banking industry', *British Journal of Industrial Relations*, 33, 3: 443–58.

Mann J. (1997), *Beijing Jeep: A case study of Western business in China*, Boulder, CO: Westview Press.

Maps of India (2011), www.mapsofindia.com/who-is-who/business-economics/aditya-birla.html, accessed 14 June 2011.

Marginson S. (2011), 'Scholars rise in the east', *The Australian Literary Review*, April 6: 12.

Maslow A. (1968), *Towards a psychology of being*, 2nd edition, Princeton, New Jersey: Van Nostrand.

Mathew J. and Ogbonna E. (2009), 'Organisational culture and commitment: A study of an Indian software organisation', *International Journal of Human Resource Management*, 20, 3: 654–75.

Mathur A. (1993), 'The experience of consultation during structural adjustment in India (1990–1992)', *International Labour Review*, 132, 3: 331–45.

Mathur J. S. (1966), 'India's labour policy', *Journal of Industrial Relations*, 8, 3: 283–97.

Meng X., Manning C., Shi L. and Effendi T. N. (2010), *The great migration: Rural–urban migration in China and Indonesia*, Cheltenham, UK: Edward Elgar.

Meng X. H. J. and Jianmin P. W. (2009), 'Based on social responsibility of human resource management', www.eng.hi138.com/?i159707, accessed 15 April 2011.

Meredith R. (2007), *The elephant and the dragon: The rise of India and China and what it means for all of us*, New York: W. W. Norton & Co.

Milelli C., Hay F. and Shi Y. (2010), 'Chinese and Indian firms in Europe: Characteristics, impacts and policy implications', *International Journal of Emerging Markets* 5, 3/4: 377–97.

Mirchandani V. (2006), '*Business Week* on Chindia', *Business Week*, 16 August: 4.

Morris M. W., Podolny J. and Sullivan B. N. (2008), 'Culture and coworker relations: Interpersonal patterns in American, Chinese, German, and Spanish divisions of a global retail bank', *Organization Science*, 19, 4: 517–32.

Morris J., Wilkinson B. and Gamble J. (2009), 'Strategic international human resource management or the "bottom line"? The cases of electronics and garments commodity chains in China', *International Journal of Human Resource Management*, 20, 2: 348–70.

Murthy N. R. N. (2009), *A better India, a better world*, New Delhi: Allen Lane (Penguin Books).

Nacsa (2011), 'ICT Top 100 in Mainland China and the #1 Huawei', www.lazure2.wordpress.com/2011/06/04/ict-top-100-in-mainland-china, accessed 18 October 2011.

Nankervis A. and Chatterjee S. (2011), 'The resurgence of China and India: Collaboration or competition?', *Human Systems Management*, 30, 1: 97–113.

Nankervis A. and Compton R. (2006), 'Performance management: Theory in practice?', *Asia Pacific Journal of Human Resources*, 44, 1: 83–101.

Nankervis A. and Leece P. (1997), 'Performance management: Two steps forward, one step back?', *Asia Pacific HRM*, 35, 2: 88–92.

Nankervis A. and Penrose J. (1990), 'Performance appraisal: Where are we now?', *Asia Pacific HRM*, 28, 3: 74–81.

Nankervis A., Chatterjee S. R. and Coffey J. (2006), *Perspectives of human resource management in the Asia Pacific*, Sydney: Pearson Education Australia.

Naquiri F. (2009), 'Competitive mapping and managing talent', *IUP Journal of Management Research*, viii, 1: 85–94.

National Bureau of Statistics of China (2008), *China Statistical Yearbook 2008*, Beijing: China Statistics Press.

National Bureau of Statistics of China (2010a), *China Statistical Yearbook 2010*, Beijing: China Statistics Press.

National Bureau of Statistics of China (2010b), *China Labour Statistical Yearbook 2010*, Beijing: China Statistics Press.

Nayar V. (2010), *Employees first, customers second*, Boston: Harvard Business Press.

Needham J. (1956), *Science and civilization in China*, Cambridge: Cambridge University Press.

Nelson S. and Choudaha R. (2006), *Optimizing recruitment marketing for attracting quality students*, Denver: Graduate School of International Studies, University of Denver.

Ng S.-H. and Warner M. (1998), *China's trade unions and management*, Basingstoke: Macmillan.

Ngo H. Y., Lau, C. M. and Foley, S. (2008), 'Strategic human resource management, firm performance, and employee relations climate in China', *Human Resource Management*, 47, 1: 73–90.

Nguyen T., Truong Q. and Buyens D. (2011), 'Training and firm performance in economies in transition: A comparison between Vietnam and China', *Asia Pacific Business Review*, 17, 1: 103–19.

Nilekani N. (2008), *Imagining India*, New Delhi: Allen Lane (Penguin Books).

Nilekani N. (2009), *Imagining India: The idea of a nation renewed*, New York: Penguin Press.

Niosi J. and Tschang F. (2009), 'The strategies of Chinese and Indian multinationals: Implications for internationalization theory', *Industrial and Corporate Change*, 18, 2: 269–94.

Nisbett R., Peng K., Choi I. and Norenzayan A. (2001), 'Culture and systems of thought holistic versus analytic cognition', *Psychology Review*, 108, 2: 291–310.

Nishii L., Lepak D. and Schneider B. (2008), 'Employee attributions of the "why" of HR practices: Their effects on employee attitudes and behaviors, and customer satisfaction', *Personnel Psychology*, 61, 3: 503–45.

Nolan P. (2001), *China and the global economy*, Basingstoke: Palgrave.

Noronha E. and D'Cruz P. (2009), 'Engaging the professional: Organising call centre agents in India', *Industrial Relations Journal*, 40, 3: 215–34.

O'Leary G. (ed.) (1998), *Adjusting to capitalism: Chinese workers and the state*. New York: M. E. Sharpe.

Öniş Z. (1991), 'The logic of the development state', *Comparative Politics*, 24, 1: 109–26.

Ou-Yang T. (2003), 'The market economy of Haier', www.nib.kobe-u.ac.ip/academic/ra/dp/English/dp131, accessed 8 August 2011.

Pan C. G. and Lou W. (2004), 'Study on situation and development environment for Chinese talents', in C. G. Pan and L. Wang (eds), *The report on the development of Chinese talents*, No.1, Beijing: Social Sciences Academic Press, 1–46.

Pandey S. M. (1967), 'Inter-union rivalry in India an analysis', *Journal of Industrial Relations*, 9, 2: 140–54.

Parashar S. P. and Salwan P. (2005), *Aditya Birla Group (A): Going global – strategic beginning of a global empire*, asiacase.com, Singapore: Nanyang Technological University, accessed 8 August 2011.

Park A. and Cai F. (2009), 'The informalization of the Chinese labour market', paper presented at the Twenty-First Century Urbanization: Social Science Perspectives on China's Urban Transformation Conference, Ann Arbor, MI, 3 October.

Park B.-S. (2011), 'Northeast Asia's economic integration with China', *Sustainable Europe Research Institute Quarterly*, 4, 2: 13–21.

Parry J. (1999), 'Introduction', in J. Parry, J. Breman and K. Kapadia, *The worlds of Indian industrial labour*, New Delhi: Sage, ix–xxxv.

Paul A. K. and Anantharaman R. N. (2003), 'Impact of people management practices on organizational performance: Analysis of a causal model', *International Journal of Human Resource Management*, 14, 7: 1246–66.

Pauluzzo R. (2010), 'How cultural determinants may affect HRM: The case of Italian companies in China', *Research and Practice in Human Resource Management*, 18, 1: 80–97.

Peng K. Z., Ngo H. Y., Shi J. and Wong C. H. (2009), 'Gender differences in the work commitment of Chinese workers: An investigation of two alternative explanations', *Journal of World Business*, 44, 3: 323–35.

Peng M. and Meyer K. (2011), *International business*, London: Cengage.

Poon I. and Rowley C. (2010), 'Change in Asia: A review of management theory and research related to human resources', *Asia Pacific Business Review*, 16, 4: 591–607.

Porter M. (1985), *Competitive strategy*, New York: Free Press.

Powell B. (2009), 'Five things the US can learn from China', *Time*, 23 November: 21–7.

Power C. (2011), 'India's leading exports: CEOs', *Time*, 1–8 August: 91–4.

Prayag A. (2010), 'HR shifts gear to talent management', *Business Line*, 9 December, www.thehindubusinessline.com/2010/12/10/stories, accessed 22 December 2010.

Pun N. and Smith C. (2007), 'Putting transnational labour process in its place: The dormitory labour regime in post-socialist China', *Work, Employment and Society*, 21, 1: 47–65.

Pye L. (2000), 'Asian values: From dynamos to dominoes?', in L. Harrison and S. Huntington (eds), *Culture matters: How values shape human progress*, NY: Basic Books, 244–55.

Qiao J. (2008), 'Labor contract law in China: Changes and implications', paper presented at the Breaking down Chinese Walls: The Changing Faces of Labor and Employment in China International Conference, Cornell University, 26–28 September, Ithaca, New York.

Qiao K., Khilji S. and Wang X. (2009), 'High performance work systems, organizational commitment, and the role of demographic features in the People's Republic of China', *International Journal of Human Resource Management*, 20, 11: 2311–30.

Raghuram S. (2011), 'Organizational identification among young software professionals in India', *International Journal of Human Resource Management*, first published on 1 June 2011 (iFirst).

Rai S. (2005), 'Outsourcers in India fight for skilled labor', *International Herald Tribune*, 2 November: 11.

Rai S. (2009), 'CEO pay in India: Vulgar and indecent', *globalpost*, 21 October, www.globalpost.com/dispatch/india/091009, accessed 31 January 2011.

Ralston D., Holt D. Terpstra R. and Yu K. (1997), 'The impact of national culture and economic ideology on managerial work values: A study of United States, Russia, Japan and China', *Journal of International Business Studies*, 28, 5: 177–208.

Ramamurti R. and Singh J. V. (2009), *Emerging multinationals in emerging markets*, Cambridge: Cambridge University Press.

Raman S., Budhwar P. and Balasubramanian D. (2007), 'People management issues in Indian KPOs', *Employee Relations*, 29, 6: 696–710.

Ramaswamy E. A. (1988), *Worker consciousness and trade union response*, Delhi: Oxford University Press.

Ramaswamy R., Damani R., Das D., Shah P. A., Chaitanya P., Solanki R., Verma N. and Shori V. (2010), 'Journey towards PSM excellence', *Proceedings of the 25th International Conference of the Center for Chemical Process Safety 2010*: 268–87.

Ramesh J. (2005), *Making sense of Chindia: Reflections on China and India*, New York: India Research Press.

Ramsay H., Scholarios D. and Harley B. (2000), 'Employees and high performance work systems: Testing inside the black box', *British Journal of Industrial Relations*, 38, 4: 501–31.

Rangarajan L. (1992), *The Arthashastra*, New Delhi: Penguin Books.

Rao N. (2011), 'Rabindranath Tagore's vision of India and China: A twenty first century perspective', lecture delivered at the Singapore Consortium for China–India Dialogue, 13 January: 3.

Ratnam V. and Jain H. C. (2002), 'Women in trade unions in India', *International Journal of Manpower*, 23, 3: 272–92.

Redding S. G. (2002), 'The capitalist business system of China and its rationale', *Asian Development Journal of Management*, 19: 221–49.

Redding S. G. and Witt M. A. (2007), *The future of Chinese capitalism*, Oxford: Oxford University Press.

Rekhy R. (2009), 'Checks on CEO compensation', *mydigitalfc.com*, 12 October, www.mydigitalfc.com/op-ed/checks-ceo-compensation-981, accessed 31 January 2011.

Reliance Group (2011), www.reliance.com.tw/aboutReliance.html, accessed 25 May 2011; www.RelianceGroupIndia-RelianceIndustries-RelianceIndustryProfile, accessed 15 June 2011; www.squidoo.com/reliance-group, accessed 25 May 2011.

Rieger V. (2008), *The challenge of management-staff shortage on the Chinese labor market: The development of HRM in China*, BA Thesis, Julius-Maximilians Universitat, Wurzburg.

Robins J. (2010), 'China: A *new* kind of "mixed" economy?', *Asian Business and Management*, 9, 1: 23–46.

Roberts D. (2005), 'Waking up to their rights', *Business Week*, 22 August, www.china-labour.org.hk/en/node/16905, accessed 2 May 2011: 1–4.

Rowley C. and Benson J. (2002), 'Convergence and divergence in Asian human resource management', *California Management Review*, winter, 44, 2: 90–109.

Rowley C. and Cooke F. L. (eds) (2010), *The changing face of Chinese management*, London: Routledge.

Rowley C. and Warner M. (2010a), 'Managers, markets and the globalised economy in China', *Asia Pacific Business Review*, 16, 3: 483–91.

Rowley C. and Warner M. (eds) (2010b), *Chinese management in the harmonious society: Managers, markets and the globalized economy*, London: Routledge.

Rowley C. and Wei J. (2010), 'Rewards system developments: Pay for performance in knowledge-intensive industries in China', *Journal for Global Business Advancement*, 3, 2: 95–111.

Rubery J. and Grimshaw D. (2003), *The organization of employment: An international perspective*, Basingstoke: Palgrave Macmillan.

Rudman S. (2006), *The multinational corporation in China*, Malden, MA and Oxford: Blackwell.

Sabharwal M. (2011), 'Mismatches vitiate employability challenge', *Business Today*, 3 April: 62.

Sahang A. (ed.) (1971), *Max Weber and modern sociology*, London: Routledge.

Saini D. and Budhwar, P. (2008), 'Managing the human resource in Indian SMEs: The role of indigenous realities', *Journal of World Business*, 43, 3: 417–34.

Saini D. S. (2009), 'Labour law in India: Structure and working', in P. Budhwar and J. Bhatnagar (eds), *The changing face of people management in India*, London: Routledge, 60–94.

Sainsbury M. (2010), 'Foxconn cuts off suicide compo', *The Weekend Australian*, 12–13 June: 17.

Sainsbury M. (2011a), 'Social management has no room for dissents', *The Weekend Australian*, June 25–26: 12.

Sainsbury M. (2011b), 'Labour shortages a headache for China', *The Weekend Australian*, 5–6 January: 34.

Schuman M. (2010), 'Lenovo's legend returns', *Time*, 10 May, www.time.com/time/magazine/article/0,91711986004.html, accessed 2 May 2011.

Scribd (2011), www.scribd.com/doc/8495341, accessed 25 May 2011.

Scullion H. and Collings D. G. (2011), *Global talent management*, New York and London: Routledge.

Selmer J. (2006), 'Cultural novelty and adjustment: Western business expatriates in China', *International Journal of Human Resource Management*, 17, 7: 1209–22.

Selvaretnam S. (2011), 'Lenovo: Eye on talent', *HRM Asia*, 14 April.

Sen A. (2005), *The argumentative Indian: Writings on Indian culture, history and identity*, London: Penguin.

Sen Gupta A. and Sett P. (2000), 'Industrial relations law, employment security and collective bargaining in India: Myths, realities and hopes', *Industrial Relations Journal*, 31, 2: 144–53.

Sen S. (2009), 'Transforming the sleeping elephant', *IUP Journal of Business Strategy*, 6, 1: 31–45.

Sengupta S. and Gupta A. (2011), 'Exploring the dimensions of attrition in Indian BPOs', *International Journal of Human Resource Management*, first published on 1 June 2011 (iFirst), DOI: 10.1080/09585192.2011.561211.

Sharma S. (1996), *Management in the new age: Western windows, Eastern doors*, New Delhi: New Age International Publishers.

Sharma S. (2007), *New mantras in corporate corridors: From ancient roots to global routes*, New Delhi: New Age International Publishers.

Sheehan J. (1999), *Chinese workers: A new history*, London: Routledge.

Shen J. (2010), 'Employees' satisfaction with HRM in Chinese privately-owned enterprises', *Asia Pacific Business Review*, 9, 3: 339–54.

Shen J. (2011), 'Huawei moves into the cloud', www.chinadaily.com.cn/business/2011-08/04/content_130516, accessed 29 August 2011.

Shen J. and Zhu C. (2011), 'Effects of socially responsible human resource management on employee organizational commitment', *The International Journal of Human Resource Management*, 22, 15: 3020–35.

Shengiun L. (2011), 'Corporate China's succession struggles', *Business Week*, www.businessweek.com/managing/content/jan2011/ca201101, accessed 18 October 2011.

Sheridan G. (2010), 'Scales tip to a group embracing everyone from the US to India', *The Weekend Australian*, 19–20 June: 23.

Shrivastava A. and Purang P. (2011), 'Employee perceptions of performance appraisals: A comparative study on Indian banks', *International Journal of Human Resource Management*, 22, 3: 632–47.

Shyam Sundar K. R. (2008), 'Trade unions in India: From politics of fragmentation to politics of expansion and integration?', in J. Benson and Y. Zhu (eds), *Trade unions in Asia: An economic and sociological analysis*, London: Routledge, 157–76.

Singh K. (2003), 'Strategic HR orientation and firm performance in India', *International Journal of Human Resource Management*, 14, 4: 530–43.

Singh N. and Krishnan V. (2007), 'Transformational leadership in India: Developing and validation a new scale using grounded theory approach', *International Journal of Cross-Cultural Management*, 7, 2: 219–36.

Singh S. and Chaudhuri A. (2009), 'The reality of India: Folding constraints into business strategy', *Journal of Business Strategy*, 30, 4: 5–16.

Sinha J. (1980), *The nurturant task leader*, New Delhi: Concept Publishers.

Sinopec (2010), 'Sinopec: Employee development', *Sinopec Website*, http://www.sinopecgroup.com/english/Pages/EmployeeDevelopment.aspx, accessed 30 November 2010.

Som A. (2007), 'What drives adoption of innovative SHRM practices in Indian organizations?', *International Journal of Human Resource Management*, 18, 5: 808–28.

Som A. (2010), 'Emerging human resource practices at Aditya Birla Group', *Human Resource Management*, May–June, 49, 3: 547–64.

Sparrow P. and Budhwar P. (1997), 'Competition and change: Mapping the Indian HRM recipe against world-wide patterns', *Journal of World Business*, 32: 224–42.

Sparrow P., Brewster C. and Harris H. (2004), *Globalizing human resource management*, London: Routledge.

Srivastava P. and Bhatnagar J. (2008), 'Talent acquisition due diligence leading to high employee engagement: Case of Motorola India MDB', *Industrial and Commercial Training*, 40, 5: 253–60.

Srivastava P. and Bhatnagar J. (2010), 'Employer brand for talent acquisition: An exploration towards its measurement', *Journal of Business Perspectives*, 14, 1/2: 25–34.

Srivastava S. (2011), 'Tata Manchurian: The Tata Group prepares to go to China', *Business*, 30 April, www.business.in.com/article/special/tata-manchurian-the-tata-group-prepares-to-go-to-china, accessed 25 May 2011.

Stahl G. K., Bjorkman I., Farndale E., Morris S., Stiles P. and Trevor J. (2007), *Global talent management: How leading multinationals build and sustain their talent pipeline*, Faculty & Research Working Papers, INSEAD: Fontainebleau, France.

Stumpf S., Doh J. and Tymon W. (2010), 'The strength of HR practices in India and their effects on employee career success, performance, and potential', *Human Resource Management*, 49, 3: 353–75.

Subramaniam R., Misra R., Jayachandra C. and Singh T. (2008), 'Infosys Technologies Limited: The global talent program', *Asian Case Research Journal*, 12, 2: 249–73.

Subramanian S. (1973), 'The right to strike for public employees – a point of view', *Industrial Relations Journal*, 15, 2: 218–20.

Takahara A. (1992), *The politics of wage policy in post-revolutionary China*, London: Macmillan.

Tam F. (2010), 'Overworked, underpaid – far from selfish', *South China Morning Post*, 16 July: A4.

Taormina R. J. and Gao J. H. (2009), 'Identifying acceptable performance appraisal criteria: An international perspective', *Asia Pacific Journal of Human Resources*, 47, 1: 102–25.

Tata Group internal materials (2010).

Tatlow D. K. (2011), 'Mao's legacy still divides China', *The New York Times*, 5 May: 3.

Taylor B. and Li Q. (2007), 'Is the ACFTU a union and does it matter?', *Journal of Industrial Relations*, 49, 5: 701–15.

Taylor B., Chang K. and Li Q. (2003), *Industrial relations in China*, Cheltenham: Edward Elgar.

Taylor P. and Bain P. (2005), ' "India calling to the far away towns": The call centre labour process and globalization', *Work, Employment and Society*, 19, 2: 261–82.

Taylor P., D'Cruz P., Noronha E. and Scholarios D. (2011), 'The experience of work in India's domestic call centre industry', *The International Journal of Human Resource Management*, first published on 1 June 2011 (iFirst), DOI: 10.1080/09585192.2011.561216.

Teagarden M. B. and Cai D. H. (2009), 'Learning from dragons who are learning from us: Developmental lessons from China's global companies', *Organizational Dynamics*, 38, 1: 73–81.

Thapar R. (1990), *A history of India. Vol. 1*, London: Penguin.

Thapar R. (1996), *Ancient Indian social history: Some interpretations*, India: Orient Longman.

Thite M. and Russell B. (2010), 'Work organisation, HR practices and employee retention in Indian call centres', *Asia Pacific Journal of Human Resources*, 48, 3: 356–74.

Thompson P. (2011), 'The trouble with HRM', *Human Resource Management Journal*, 21, 4: 355–67.

Times of India, The (2011) 'Cyrus Mistry: How he won the race to succeed Ratan Tata?', 24 November, www.timesofindia.indiatimes.com/business/india-business/Cyrus-Mistry-how-he-won-the-race, accessed 20 December 2011.

TMI (2009), *Innovations in talent acquisition: A white paper on TATA Second Career Internship Programme for Women*, Singapore: TMI.

Tsang D. (2010), 'Corruption threatens safety in toy factories', *South China Morning Post*, 10 July: 1, 3.

Tymon W., Stumpf S. and Doh J. (2010a), 'Exploring talent management in India: The neglected role of intrinsic rewards', *Journal of World Business*, 45, 1: 109–21.

Tymon W. G., Stumpf S. A. and Doh J. P. (2010b), 'Exploring talent management in India: The neglected role of intrinsic rewards', *Journal of World Business*, April, 45, 2: 1–56, www.thehindu.com/the hindu/jobs/0407/200472800100.htm, accessed 22 December 2010.

Varkkey B. and Joy R. (2010), 'Case study: Direct sales force at Aviva Life Insurance Company, India', *South Asia Journal of Management*, 17, 1: 99–120.

Varma A., Pichler S. and Srinivas E. (2005), 'The role of interpersonal affect in performance appraisal: Evidence from two samples – the US and India', *International Journal of Human Resource Management*, 16, 11: 2029–44.

Varma A., Pichler S., Budhwar P. and Biswas S. (2009), 'Chinese host country nationals' willingness to support expatriates', *International Journal of Cross Cultural Management*, 9, 2: 199–216.

Vega T. (2011), 'Lenovo aims a campaign at the Apple Crowd', *The New York Times*, 28 www.hrmasia.com/news/feature/lenovo-on-talent/83154, accessed 15 May 2011.

Venkata Ratnam C. S. (1993), 'Impact of new economic policies on the role of trade unions', *Indian Journal of Industrial Relations*, 29, 1: 56–77.

Venkata Ratnam C. S. (2006), *Industrial relations*, Oxford: Oxford University Press.

Venkata Ratnam C. S. (2009), 'Employment relations in India', in P. Budhwar and J. Bhatnagar (eds), *The changing face of people management in India*, London: Routledge, 23–59.

Venkata Ratnam C. S. and Jain H. (2002), 'Women in trade union in India', *International Journal of Manpower*, 23, 3: 277–92.

Venkata Ratnam C. S. and Verma A. (2011), 'Employment relations in India', in G. Bamber, R. Lansbury and N. Wailes (eds), *International and comparative employment relations*, 5th edition, London: Sage and New South Wales, Australia: Allen & Unwin Pty Ltd, 330–52.

Verma A. and Yan Z. M. (1995), 'The changing face of human resource management in China: Opportunities, problems and strategies', in A. Verma, T. Kochan and R. Lansbury (eds), *Employment relations in the growing Asian economies*, London: Routledge, 315–35.

Virmani B. (2007), *The challenge of Indian management*, New Delhi: Response Books.

Wabba A. and Bridgewell L. (1976), 'A review of research on the Need Hierarchy Theory', *Organization, Behaviour and Human Performance*, 15: 212–40.

Wang J. (2009), *Strategic challenges and strategic responses: The transformation of state-owned enterprises*, Oxford: Chandos.

Wang J., Yan R., Hollister K. and Zhu D. (2008), 'A holistic review of management science research in China', *The International Journal of Management Science* 36: 919–32.

Wang L., Nicholson J. and Zhu J. (2009), 'Pay systems in Chinese state-owned enterprises: A review', *Chinese Management Studies*, 3, 4: 328–55.

Wang S., Yi X., Lawler J. and Zhang M. (2011), 'Efficiency of high-performance work practices in Chinese companies', *The International Journal of Human Resource Management*, 22, 11: 2419–41.

Wang X. (2009), 'Lenovo reboots again for 2010', *China Daily*, 19 January, www.chinadaily.com.cn/bizchina/2009-01/19/content_7408277.htm, accessed 27 April 2011.

Wang X. (2010), 'Degree-for-fee expose, just the tip of rampant academic fraud', *South China Morning Post*, 12 July: 3.

Wang X., Bruning N. and Peng S. Q. (2007), 'Western high performance HR practices in China: A comparison among public-owned, private and foreign-invested enterprises', *International Journal of Human Resource Management*, 18, 4: 684–701.

Wang Y. (2008), 'Emotional bonds with supervisor and co-workers: Relationship to organizational commitment in China's foreign-invested companies', *International Journal of Human Resource Management*, 19, 5: 916–31.

Warner M. (1992), *How Chinese managers learn: Management and industrial training in China*, Basingstoke: Macmillan and New York, NY: St Martin's Press.

Warner M. (1993), 'Human resource management "with Chinese Characteristics"', *International Journal of Human Resource Management*, 4, 4: 45–65.

Warner M. (1995), *The management of human resources in Chinese industry*, Basingstoke: Macmillan and New York: St Martin's Press.

Warner M. (1997), 'China's HRM in transition: Towards relative convergence?', *Asia Pacific Business Review*, 3, 4: 19–33.

Warner M. (1999), 'Human resources and management in China's "hi-tech" revolution: A study of selected computer hardware, software and related firms in the PRC', *International Journal of Human Resource Management*, 10, 1: 1–20. April, www.nytimes.com/2011/04/29/business/media/29adco.html, accessed 2 May 2011.

Warner M. (2002), 'Globalization, labour markets and human resources in Asia Pacific economies: An overview', *International Journal of Human Resource Management*, 13, 3: 384–98.

Warner M. (2005), *Human resource management in China revisited*, London and New York: Routledge.

Warner M. (2008a), 'Trade unions in China: Towards the harmonious society', in J. Benson and Y. Zhu (eds), *Trade unions in Asia*, London and New York: Routledge, 140–56.

Warner, M. (2008b), 'Reassessing human resource management with "Chinese Characteristics": An overview', *The International Journal of Human Resource Management*, 9, 5: 771–801.

Warner M. (ed.) (2009), *Human resource management with 'Chinese Characteristics'*, London: Routledge.

Warner M. (2010a), 'In search of Confucian HRM: Theory and practice in Greater China and beyond', *International Journal of Human Resource Management*, 21, 12: 2053–78.

Warner M. (ed.) (2010b), *'Making Sense' of HRM in China: Economy, enterprises and workers*, London and New York, NY: Routledge.

Warner M. (2011a), 'Society and HRM in China', *International Journal of Human Resource Management*, 22, 16: 3223–44.

Warner M. (2011b), 'Commentary: Management training and development in China revisited', *Asia Pacific Business Review*, 17, 4: 397–402.

Warner M. (2011c), *In search of Confucian HRM in Greater China: Theory and practice*, London: Routledge.

Warner M. and Goodall K. (eds) (2010), *Management training and development in China*, London: Routledge.

Warner M. and Ng S. H. (1999), 'Collective contracts in Chinese enterprises: A new brand of collective bargaining under "Market Socialism" ', *British Journal of Industrial Relations*, 37, 2: 295–314.

Warner M. and Rowley C. (2010), 'Chinese management at the crossroads: Setting the scene', *Asia Pacific Business Review*, 16, 3: 273–84.

Warner M. and Zhu Y. (2010), 'Labour and management in the People's Republic of China: Seeking the "harmonious society",' *Asia Pacific Business Review*, 16, 3: 285–98.

Warner M., Edwards V., Polansky G., Pucko D. and Zhu Y. (2005), *Management in transitional economies: From the Berlin Wall to the Great Wall*, London and New York: Routledge.

Warner M., Zhu Y. and Feng T. (2011), 'People-management and organised labour in China's harmonious society: "Top-down" versus "Bottom-up" strategies', paper presented at the 7th International Symposium on 'Multinational business management', Nanjing University, June.

Wasserstrom J. (18 June 2010), 'Strike out: What the foreign media misses in covering China's labor unrest', www.foreignpolicy.com/articles/2010/06/18/strike_out, accessed on 28 August 2010.

Watts J. (2010), 'Chinese workers strike at Honda Lock parts supplier', *guardian.co.uk*, Friday 11 June 2010, Internet source: www.guardian.co.uk/business/2010/jun/11/honda-china, accessed on 28 August 2010.

Wei L. and Lau C. M. (2005), 'Market orientation, HRM importance and competency: Determinants of strategic HRM in Chinese firms', *International Journal of Human Resource Management*, 16, 10: 1901–18.

Wei Q. and Rowley C. (2009), 'Changing patterns of rewards in Asia: A literature review', *Asia Pacific Business Review*, 15, 4: 489–506.

Wei W. (2005), 'China and India: Any difference in their FDI performances?', *Journal of Asian Economics*, 16: 719–36.

Wellins R. S., Brandt J. R. Taninecza R. and Tong, R. T. L. (2005), 'Super human resource management in China: Practices, performances, and opportunities among China's manufacturers', *Development Dimensions International, Working Paper*, http://64.233.183.104/search?q=cache:9K49HR7iwEJ:www.ddiworld.com/pdf/superhrchina, accessed 12 June 2007.

Westwood R., Chan A. and Linstead S. (2004), 'Theorizing Chinese employment relations comparatively: Exchange, reciprocity and the moral economy', *Asia Pacific Journal of Management*, 21, 3: 365–89.

Williamson P. and Zheng M. (2009), 'Value for money: Strategies for recessionary times', *Harvard Business Review*, March: 66–74.

Wise D. (2010), '10 executive compensation issues for aligning pay strategies', *Society for Human Resource Management India*, 29 July, www.shrmindia.org/10-exec-comp-issues-aligning-pay-strategies, accessed 31 January 2011: 1–4.

Wood S. and Albanese M. (1995), 'Can you speak of a high commitment management on the shop floor?', *Journal of Management Studies*, 32, 2: 215–47.

Wood S. and de Menezes L. (1998), 'High commitment management in the UK: Evidence from the workplace industrial relations survey, and employers' manpower and skills practices survey', *Human Relations*, 51, 4: 485–515.

World Bank, The (2006a), *Gender Stats Database of Gender Statistics*, http://genderstats.worldbank.org/home.asp, accessed 20 March 2007.

World Bank, The (2006b), *India country overview 2006*, http://worldbank.org, accessed 16 March 2007.

Xin K. and Pucik V. (2006), *Competing through people: Learning from China*, Switzerland: IMD.

Xu F. (2009), 'The emergence of temporary staffing agencies in China', *Comparative Labor Law and Policy Journal*, 30, 2: 431–62.

Yaghi B., Neely A., Wang Z. and Youell N. (2008), *Enterprise performance management: The Chinese state of the art*, Working Paper, Cranfield: Cranfield University.

Ye Q., Hiu Q. and Li Y. (2008), 'How organizational culture shapes competitive strategies: A comparative case study of two e-commerce firms in China', Paper No. 102, *Proceedings of the Conference on Information Systems*, www.llaisael.aisnet.org/pacis2008/102, accessed 21 September 2011.

Yeates C. (2010), 'Asia in the box seat: IMF', *The Age (BusinessDay)*, 17 June: 3.

Yeung A., Warner M. and Rowley C. (eds) (2008), 'Introduction: Growth and globalization, evolution of human resource management practices in Asia', *Human Resource Management*, 47, 1: 1–13.

Yeung H. (2009), *Chinese capitalism in a global era: Towards hybrid capitalism*, London: Routledge.

Yidan L. (2009), *Strategic plan for Haier's global brand-building*, Bachelor's dissertation, Mikkeli University of Applied Sciences.

Youndt M., Snell S. A., Dean J. W. and Lepak D. P. (1996), 'HRM, manufacturing strategy and firm performance', *Academy of Management Journal*, 39, 4: 836–66.

Yue B. (2011), 'Executives enjoy salary bonanza', www.europe.chinadaily.com.cn/business/2011-09/06/content_13627, accessed 9 September 2011.

Zhan J. (2010), *World investment report 2010: Investing in a low-carbon economy*, Geneva: Division on Investment and Enterprise, United Nations Conference on Trade and Development.

Zhang Y. (2011), 'China's new growth strategy', *Sustainable Europe Research Institute Quarterly*, 4, 2: 23–31.

Zhang Y. C. and Li S. L. (2009), 'High performance work practices and firm performance: Evidence from the pharmaceutical industry in China', *International Journal of Human Resource Management*, 20, 11: 2331–48.

Zhao S. M. and Chen W. (2010), 'Human resource development and management training in China: A Nanjing case study', in M. Warner and K. Goodall (eds), *Management education and development in China*, London: Routledge.

Zhao Z. (2009), 'The rise of Chindia and its impact on the world system', in R. Huisken (ed.), *Rising China: Power and reassurance*, Canberra: ANU E Press, www.epress.anu.edu.au/sdrc/rc/ch06.html, accessed 20 April 2010.

Zhen Y. (2009), *Globalization and the Chinese retailing revolution: Competing in the world's largest market*, Oxford: Chandos.

Zhu C. and Dowling P. (2002), 'Staffing practices in transition: Some empirical evidence from China', *International Journal of Human Resource Management*, 13, 4: 569–97.

Zhu C., Cooper, B., De Cieri, H. and Dowling, P. (2005), 'A problematic transition to a strategic role: Human resource management in industrial enterprises in China', *International Journal of Human Resource Management*, 16, 4: 513–31.

Zhu C. J. (2005), *Human resource management in China: Past, current and future HR practices in the industrial sector*, London: Routledge.

Zhu J. M. (2004), 'Local developmental state and order in China's urban development during transition', *International Journal of Urban and Regional Research*, 28, 2: 424–47.

Zhu Y., Warner M. and Rowley C. (2007), 'HRM with "Asian" characteristics: A hybrid people management system in East Asia', *Working Paper*, 02/2007, Cambridge: Judge Institute.

Zhu Y., Webber M. and Benson J. (2010), 'Intangible management and enterprise success in the Chinese transitional economy', *Asia Pacific Business Review*, 16, 3: 437–60.

Zhu Y., Warner M. and Feng T. Q. (2011), 'Employment relations "with Chinese Characteristics": The role of trade unions in China', *International Labour Review*, 150, 1–2: 127–43.

Internet references

www.cia.gov/library/publications/the-world-factbook, accessed 18 September 2010.

www.forbes.com/2010/global-2000-leading-world-business, accessed 27 April 2010.

www.economist.com, accessed 18 September 2010.

www.eiu.com/PublicDefault.aspx, accessed 18 September 2010.

www.iloveindia.com/economy-of-india/top-50-companies/reliance-group.html, accessed 25 May 2011.

www.iloveindia.com/khajuraho/reliance.html, accessed 25 May 2011.

www.london.edu/facultyandresearch/researchactivities/birlaindiacentre.html, accessed 14 June 2011.

www.mapsofindia.com/who-is-who/business-economy/aditya-birla.html, accessed 14 June 2011.

www.philip-sen.com/othermeans/2006/11/the-myth-of-chindia.html, accessed 20 April 2010.

www.RelianceGroupataglance/Reliance-Industries-Limited.html, accessed 15 June 2011.

www.reliance.com.tw/aboutReliance.html, accessed 25 May 2011.

www.RelianceGroupIndia-RelianceIndustries-RelianceIndustryProfile.html, accessed 15 June 2011.

www.scribd.com/doc/8495341/Ppt-for-Tata-Motors-for-HRM, accessed 25 May 2011.

www.squidoo.com/reliance-group, accessed 25 May 2011.

Index